Rights vs. Responsibilities

Recent Titles in
Contributions to the Study of Mass Media and Communications

RIGHTS VS. RESPONSIBILITIES

The Supreme Court and the Media

Elizabeth Blanks Hindman

Contributions to the Study of Mass Media and Communications,
Number 50
Bernard K. Johnpoll, Series Adviser

GREENWOOD PRESS
Westport, Connecticut • London

Library of Congress Cataloging-in-Publication Data

Hindman, Elizabeth Blanks, 1962–
    Rights vs. responsibilities : the Supreme Court and the media /
Elizabeth Blanks Hindman.
        p.   cm.—(Contributions to the study of mass media and
communications, ISSN 0732–4456 ; no. 50)
    Includes bibliographical references and index.
    ISBN 0–313–29922–6 (alk. paper)
    1. Freedom of the press—United States.   2. Mass media—Law and
legislation—United States.   3. Journalistic ethics—United States.
4. Journalism—United States—Objectivity.   5. United States.
Supreme Court.   I. Title.   II. Title: Rights versus
responsibilities.   III. Series.
KF4774.H56   1997
342.73′0853
[347.302853]—DC20   96–38794

British Library Cataloguing in Publication Data is available.

Library of Congress Catalog Card Number: 96–38794
ISBN: 0–313–29922–6
ISSN: 0732–4456

First published in 1997

Greenwood Press, 88 Post Road West, Westport, CT 06881
An imprint of Greenwood Publishing Group, Inc.

Printed in the United States of America

The paper used in this book complies with the
Permanent Paper Standard issued by the National
Information Standards Organization (Z39.48–1984).

10 9 8 7 6 5 4 3 2

For Doug, Katie, and Will

(

Contents

Acknowledgments

While many people contributed in some way to this work, a few deserve special thanks:

Professor Donald Gillmor of the University of Minnesota's School of Journalism and Mass Communication asked the right questions at the right times and introduced me to the first amendment and the pleasure of studying it. Professor Phillip Tichenor, also from the School of Journalism and Mass Communication at the University of Minnesota, taught me about quality research and how to formulate research questions and find appropriate ways to answer those questions. Professor Vernon Jensen of the University of Minnesota's Department of Speech introduced me to the field of communication ethics, and University of Minnesota historian and Regents' Professor Paul Murphy taught me to be concerned not just with historical events but with the political and social issues surrounding them.

I also would like to acknowledge the Silha Center for the Study of Media Ethics and Law at the University of Minnesota, which provided three years of fellowship support and a wonderful, collegial atmosphere; The Graduate School of the University of Minnesota, which granted me a doctoral dissertation fellowship for the 1992–1993 school year, allowing me to concentrate on my research; and the Department of Communication at North Dakota State University, which provided the chance to update the work and prepare it for publication.

My greatest thanks go to Professor Hazel Dicken-Garcia of the University of Minnesota's School of Journalism and Mass Communication, whose tireless work, support, and friendship have made this a delightful experience, and to Professor Douglas Blanks Hindman of the Department of Communication at North Dakota State University, whose patience, enthusiasm, and love kept me going throughout the project.

Introduction

Rights and Responsibilities, Politics and Philosophies

"The great rights guaranteed by the First Amendment carry with them great responsibilities as well." [1]

"From the earliest days of our history, this free society, dependent as it is for its survival upon a vigorous free press, has tolerated some abuse." [2]

Despite countless discussions, numerous conferences and articles, and a number of fine books on the subject, there is no consensus on the meaning of press responsibility, in classroom, courtroom or newsroom. Additionally, little research has explored the role of the United States Supreme Court in shaping media responsibility as understood and practiced. In particular, scholars have seldom looked to legal philosophy or the intersection of legal and ethical theories in their efforts to understand media responsibility. Certainly, through its decisions the Supreme Court affects media responsibility. By setting limits on media behavior and expounding on the media's role in society, the Court influences notions of media responsibility held by the public and by media practitioners. But the Court does not act in a vacuum nor, if we believe in the purposes for which American institutions were established, does it act outside some philosophical framework.

This work, therefore, examines the Supreme Court's conceptions of media responsibility as demonstrated through Court opinions and dicta from *Near v. Minnesota*, decided in 1931 and its first major media case, through the 1995–1996 term. An underlying assumption of this examination of the Supreme Court's conceptions of media responsibility in its decisions was that those decisions over time reflected various conceptions of media responsibility going beyond traditional libertarian theory. While for the most part the Court has protected media freedom, the justices' decisions over time exhibited identifiable conceptions of the purpose of the media's freedom and how the media should behave. Further, these views varied by time period, individual justice, and topic. For example, press responsibility was seen very differently by the Stone and Rehnquist courts, by Justices Black and Frankfurter, and by the collective cases on libel and those on questions of free press and fair trial.

The Court's conceptions of media responsibility clustered into coherent theories or philosophical positions, differing among justices and topics, and over time. More importantly, Supreme Court decisions articulated, if sometimes indirectly, connections between legal and moral responsibility. Even though articulation of responsibility of the media changed over time and among justices, various understandings of the media's responsibility—to society and to themselves—became apparent through the study of Court decisions. While the majority decisions primarily emphasized the traditional conception of media being free to do as they wish, opposing viewpoints were apparent within the Court.

Specifically, this work explores the Court's conceptions of media responsibility from 1931 to 1996, identifies the legal and ethical traditions inherent in those conceptions, examines how the judicial philosophies of selected justices influenced their decisions, and determines the connection between rights and responsibilities as demonstrated in Court opinions. Analysis focused on both rulings and underlying rationales and philosophies, which included official Court opinions and concurring and dissenting opinions.[3] It should be noted that this was far more than a search for the Court's uses of the word "responsibility"; in fact, the justices seldom used the term in relation to the media.

Dimensions of the meaning of responsibility were determined in several ways. First, the actual ruling of the Court—that is, whether or not the Court voted to hold the media accountable for their actions—often provided clues about the majority's definitions of media responsibility. For example, in 1989 the entire Court voted against a newspaper that had knowingly avoided a crucial source of information.[4] Second, overt discussions by individual justices of the media's roles and responsibilities also were illuminating, as when Justice Felix Frankfurter wrote, "The business of the press . . . is the promotion of truth."[5] Third, implied and indirect requirements of certain behavior of the media furnished further examples of the Court's definitions. For example, Justice Potter Stewart required very little of the media in certain situations. In an obscenity case he wrote: "[T]he Constitution protects coarse expression as well as refined, and vulgarity no less than elegance. . . . In the free society to which our Constitution has committed us, it is for each to choose for himself."[6] In situations such as this, the justices' conceptions of the responsibilities of the press were necessarily inferred, either from the holding or from comments from individual justices.

The intent was neither to find *the* definition or *one* definition that might serve the role of an ideal type by which to measure or judge conceptions of responsibility found in case opinions, nor to go to the cases with a definition to be *imposed* on the Court's language. Rather, the intent was to ascertain what definitions might *emerge* from the case opinions. The method, therefore, was to analyze the case opinions for what could be identified as conceptions of responsibility with the ultimate goal of ascertaining whether those cohered around some dominant "theory" or definition of media responsibility used by the Court.

All Supreme Court press cases from 1931 to the end of the 1995–1996 Court term were analyzed. The year 1931 was chosen as the starting point because it marks the beginning of the Court's substantial efforts to define a coherent theory of the first amendment's press clause, in *Near v. Minnesota*,[7] when for the first time it applied the first amendment's press clause to the states through the fourteenth amendment. Only after *Near* in 1931 could the Court rule on state statutes abridging press freedom and, of course, it is from the states that most of the laws inhibiting press freedom come.

From a first reading of 380 cases focusing on the media,[8] 195 dealing with some aspect of media responsibility were chosen for detailed analysis. These 195 cases formed the basis from which evidence was gathered, though perhaps only one quarter of those contained detailed discussion of the roles and responsibilities of the press.

DIMENSIONS OF MEDIA RESPONSIBILITY

Though cases were read to ascertain the justices' definitions of media responsibility, a general understanding of that concept was needed at the outset to provide a starting point for analyzing the Court's and justices' opinions. An examination of the literature about media responsibility yielded important analytical and definitional concepts useful in analyzing opinions in the cases studied. Particularly, frameworks for one form of analysis of the opinions were drawn from two sources, whereas distinctions drawn from other sources regarding rights, responsibility, and accountability helped refine the precision of analysis. These frameworks are considered in detail below, with attention first to the functions and canons of journalism used for analyzing the court cases followed by discussion of several scholars' treatment of media responsibility, with special emphasis on recent work of three scholars.

Functions of the Media

While the press serves innumerable functions in U.S. society, according to Louis Hodges, they can be reduced to four primary categories: political, educational, mirroring, and bulletin board. The first two tend to encompass discussion of the media's role in society, particularly when the first amendment is involved. The political function or role of the media, which includes implied responsibilities of the media, involves the media's role in the U.S. political system, specifically their watchdog role. Here the media are seen as the eyes and ears of the people, passing along information about government and the work of the people's representatives and watching to keep those representatives acting in the best interests of all. The Court often gives this "fourth estate" role as a primary reason for the protection granted the media in the Constitution, as when, for example, the Court protects many defamatory statements about public officials.

Equally important in arguments favoring a free media is the second role, that of education. By education Hodges does not mean the simple provision of information, but the media's function of providing a place to test ideas and opinions—the classic marketplace model of the media. The media offer the best place to examine "those political, religious, and moral ideas and ideals that we use in shaping our individual and corporate lives," Hodges writes. "For that we need a truly public forum. It is a form of education that occurs best when conflicting opinions can face each other in open debate."[9]

The third and fourth functions are as important in the cultural, if not the political, realm of society. What Hodges calls the "mirroring" role of the media helps people understand one another as human beings. This role is fulfilled in part by human interest stories that "remind us of the fragility of life, evoke in us a deepened sense of compassion. . . . Such stories show what we are as a people, and perhaps influence what we may become."[10] These stories, both positive and negative, allow each individual to participate more fully in the unfolding human story, creating a sense of community among people and nations. Through this function, for example, Americans can better understand both the tragedies and successes of humanity.

Finally, the bulletin board function of the media, while perhaps not as profound as the other three, also fulfills a crucial aspect of U.S. culture. Through the media people learn basic information about daily living—where to vote, who has died, married, and been born, what the weather will be tomorrow, where the road construction is likely to slow traffic, and so on. This very practical role involves "things we need very badly to know," Hodges writes. "They make daily life better, simpler, safer, more comfortable, and often more enjoyable."[11]

Canons of Ethical Behavior

The functions of the media in U.S. society can be somewhat agreed upon, for they are fairly general and commonly accepted. Finding principles of responsible behavior upon which the media should act is more difficult, however, for arguments can be made for many principles as bases for responsible action. Part of the purpose here was to discover what principles (and roles) the Supreme Court demanded of the media in relation to responsibility. As a result, a starting point was needed by which to define principles of responsible behavior. As with the media functions outlined above, the principles were guides for examining media responsibility, and not intended as an all-encompassing list.

Although many have attempted, with more or less success, to define principles used in decision-making by journalists, Edmund Lambeth has developed one of the more comprehensive frameworks, using five primary principles of ethical decision-making. Lambeth's principles, used as the basis of a system of ethics, can also be used as guides for determining whether or not behavior is responsible or irresponsible. Lambeth refers to them as principles, but here they are called "canons" to distinguish them from legal scholar Ronald Dworkin's use of the term "principle," outlined later.

Lambeth's canons of responsible behavior are not universal, he admits, for they come from a Western, Judeo-Christian framework, one that is a product of a certain time and specific philosophical traditions: "Conceived in the Renaissance, born in the Enlightenment, and nurtured to robust life in the modern west, journalism inherits the legacy of the larger society."[12] In other words, although these may be good canons for all of humankind, they are necessarily limited in their applicability to western society in the twentieth century. But because the philosophies discussed here, and the Supreme Court itself, are products of those same historical and philosophical traditions, the following principles are useful as guidelines for defining press responsibility.

Lambeth's five canons are not specific to journalism; however, within journalism they do have specific uses. Further, each can be applied to social life in general, as well as to journalism as an institution. The first canon, that of *telling the truth*, applies to all people, but it applies to journalists in a particular way. Journalists should both strive to be accurate in their reporting, Lambeth suggests, and "seek not only the facts but also the larger truths behind the facts."[13] Thus, truth telling includes the expectations that journalists be fair and unbiased, that they provide appropriate context for events and issues, that they acquire and retain skills of gathering information, and that they become familiar with the language unique to the various social institutions, such as science, business and government. To be successful "truth tellers," and thus act morally, Lambeth explains, journalists must be competent at their work, and to be competent they must effectively and accurately report complicated issues in a way their readers can understand. Examples of truth telling in Supreme Court cases studied included the Court's demand that broadcasters provide fair coverage of controversial public issues and that the press avoid publishing false statements knowingly.[14]

The second journalistic canon is *justice*, which emphasizes both fairness and the general establishment of justice in society. First, journalists must constantly be aware of the impact of their stories on the audience and society at large. They should, Lambeth notes, be fair in their dealings with colleagues, sources, superiors, and the public, and they should be particularly aware when covering sensitive topics. This is not to say those topics—terrorism, criminal trials, and the like—should be avoided. Rather, such topics should be treated with caution and an awareness that they do not necessarily have right and wrong answers. The second aspect of justice is equally important. The media must, according to Lambeth, be aware of whether or not just decisions are made in the seats of power and, to quote philosopher John Rawls, watch the "way in which the major social institutions distribute fundamental rights and duties."[15]

The third canon is *freedom*, by which Lambeth means journalists should guard their own autonomy, both from government and other social forces. On one level, this means the media must guard the first amendment—their protection from government intrusion. Examples include the creation of the First Amendment Congress and the Reporters Committee for Freedom of the Press, Lambeth explains. On another level, however, freedom means freedom not from government interference, but from that of other powerful social institutions. Journalists must remain distant from the influence of advertising, for example, and business in general. They must avoid being "used" by sources, though they also should be fair to sources. Finally, the very practice of journalism—what constitutes news and how it is treated—cannot be taken for granted, for succumbing to rigid definitions of news and its treatment can harm freedom.

The fourth canon journalists should follow is *humaneness*. They should "give assistance to another in need . . . do no direct harm, prevent harm."[16] This canon involves what Lambeth calls a "natural duty," "the very minimum that one human owes another."[17] Obviously, this canon may directly conflict with others, particularly truth telling. In these situations, the canons must be balanced to find the most responsible decision.

The last canon of press responsibility is *stewardship*: "[T]he individual's responsibility to manage his life and property with proper regard to the rights of others."[18] To this end, journalists must guard the rights of free press and speech, for, as Lambeth points out, these rights belong to all, though they are exercised more frequently by the press than by others. In addition to upholding these five individual canons, it is the responsibility of the journalist to understand the larger good these rights protect and to act so that that larger good is itself not harmed.

The functions and canons outlined here provide a framework by which to assess the Supreme Court's conceptions of media responsibility. The reading of Court decisions demonstrated that the Court as a whole, as well as individual justices, made significant use of some of the functions and canons, though, of course, it did not necessarily refer to them by name.

Rights and Responsibilities in Other Literature

The search of literature about media responsibility revealed various views of the concept, both in general terms and as specifically related to the media. These are detailed below, beginning with some of the most significant contributions, for present purposes, by Mary Ann Glendon, Lee Bollinger, and Judith Lichtenberg. Of special relevance here, the distinction between responsibility and accountability emerging from this literature led to an exploration of the various views of these concepts in the literature on media ethics.

The concept of responsibility has received little attention within the U.S. political tradition, argues Harvard Law School Professor Mary Ann Glendon. In fact, she suggests that rights and their consequent responsibilities were divorced long before the drafting of the Constitution and Declaration of Independence, two documents that in fact make no mention of responsibility. Glendon notes that in *The Social Contract*, philosopher Jean Jacques Rousseau focused heavily on the responsibility of government and society to provide for the subsistence needs of the community—ideas he drew from classical and biblical traditions. Rousseau based his argument, she maintains, on the idea of stewardship, in which the right of property entails obligations, including the responsibility to provide for the needy. While this idea has been perpetuated in Christian ethics and in European political discourse, it is not the case within American political philosophy. Instead, the writers of the Declaration of Independence and Constitution chose to follow the work of John Locke and English jurist Sir William Blackstone, who gathered English law into a series of commentaries.[19]

Blackstone, like Locke, focused on property as the fundamental right of human beings. Property ownership was vital to the continuance and stability of society, Blackstone wrote, and property rights are "absolute, individual, and exclusive."[20] Property was a natural right, existing before society; thus, society could impose no obligations upon it. Therefore, the highest form of individual right carried with it no responsibilities, according to the tradition that most influenced the founders of the United States.

This absence of any conception of individual or corporate responsibility permeates what Glendon calls America's "rhetoric of rights," which she argues is simplistic, unrealistic, and harmful to social relations. Americans tend to view nearly every social interaction in terms of rights, to feel entitled to almost everything, and to be unwilling to admit obligations to others, she asserts. This rhetoric of rights has had a significant negative impact:

Our rights talk, in its absoluteness, promotes unrealistic expectations, heightens social conflict, and inhibits dialogue that might lead toward consensus, accommodation, or at least the discovery of common ground. In its silence concerning responsibilities, it seems to condone acceptance of the benefits of living in a democratic social welfare state, without accepting the corresponding personal and civil obligations. In its relentless individualism, it fosters a climate that is inhospitable to society's losers, and that systematically disadvantages caretakers and dependents, young and old. . . . Our simplistic rights talk regularly promotes the short-run over the long-term . . . and particular interests over the common good. It is just not up to the job of dealing with the types of problems that presently confront liberal, pluralistic, modern societies.[21]

Americans, Glendon suggests, have ignored that with rights come responsibilities.

This emphasis on rights to the exclusion of responsibilities has important consequences, writes Glendon. First, Americans tend to phrase all wants in the form of rights, which in turn degrades true rights. Second, and perhaps more importantly, the focus on rights diminishes the concept of community and leads to an "unexpressed premise that we roam at large in a land of strangers, where we presumptively have no obligations toward others except to avoid the active infliction of harm."[22] We cannot function as a society, Glendon maintains—at least as a healthy, progressive society—without a concept of obligations to others. However, in our rights rhetoric we see ourselves as having few or no duties at all.

This lack of emphasis on duty is part of the American legal, as well as political, tradition. In the vision of Rousseau, accepted primarily in the legal and political philosophies of continental Europe, Glendon argues, law is seen as a tool for creating and maintaining a good society and citizens. American legal philosophy, however, follows more closely the idea of law-as-command, rather than law-as-ethical-framework. Thus, in the United States, law and morality are seen as separate.

Supreme Court Justice Oliver Wendell Holmes, Jr., who espoused this separation, strongly influenced twentieth century politics and legal development. In "The Path of the Law,"[23] which Glendon calls the "single most widely quoted legal article ever written by an American,"[24] Holmes contended that law and morality are, and should be, separate. Furthermore, he suggested that legal rights exist only by consent as part of living within society; he argued that law should not even have "moral connotations," such as "rights, and duties, and malice, and intent, and negligence, and so forth."[25] Rather, he wished that "every word of moral significance could be banished from the law altogether, and other words adopted which should convey legal ideas uncolored by anything outside the law."[26] For Holmes, then, rights and responsibilities had no necessary connection.

Glendon analyzes the implications of rights but does not apply her assertions to any specific rights, including freedom of the press. University of Michigan Law School Dean Lee Bollinger, in *Images of a Free Press*, does discuss the implications of press rights and potential responsibilities. He outlines what he calls the costs of the autonomous press, that is, the trade-offs made by society when it insulates the press from government interference and regulation. As he puts it, "there is no guarantee that the press will not abuse the freedom it possesses under the autonomy model," for the autonomous press is free to make choices, which could include presenting only certain points of view through "omission [or] active misrepresentation."[27] In addition, the press could be irresponsible by playing to people's prejudices or avoiding public issues and focusing on "cheap entertainment."

Yet the Court can have a tremendous influence on the press and on society at large, Bollinger maintains. In addition to making judgments on the meaning of the Constitution, the Court also helps define and affect the American community's values, because the cases it takes and the questions it decides are "central to the character of society"; thus the Court is able "to develop a deep vision of society."[28] And to a certain extent, suggests Bollinger, the Court has done this with the press. For example, with its ruling in *New York Times v. Sullivan*,[29] the Court began to construct an image of how the press should function in society, particularly in relation to government. Post-*New York Times* decisions have continued that image, which, Bollinger argues, is of the press as "noble, even heroic" in its quest to watch over government doings. The Court has portrayed the press as crucial to the workings of a successful democracy, the "guardian . . . of the political rights of the people."[30] In addition, by placing the press on this pedestal and giving it immense power, the Court has created the possibility that the media will abuse their role while also presenting an image of what good journalism should be.

Judith Lichtenberg, on the other hand, discusses the responsibility of the media from within a philosophical structure. A senior research scholar with the University of Maryland's Institute for Philosophy and Public Policy, Lichtenberg carefully distinguishes between freedom of speech and freedom of the press, suggesting that the former is nearly unconditional. Freedom of the press, however, should be measured, she argues, by "the degree to which it promotes certain values at the core of our interest in freedom of expression generally." She continues, "Freedom of the press, in other words, is an instrumental good"[31] that can claim constitutional protection only if it promotes those core values, such as diversity of opinion and the watchdog role.

Lichtenberg acknowledges that much first amendment interpretation belies her thesis, but she resolves this dilemma by redefining the crucial right in question with regard to the press. Press freedom is vital, she says, but it means not that the owners or publishers alone have the right. No one, media owners included, has a first amendment right of editorial autonomy or a right to publish where she or he chooses. Instead, the right to publish where one chooses is a property right, Lichtenberg argues; thus, the media, like all other property, can be regulated in society's interest. Owners can claim a property right to publish, but that right is not as strong as the first amendment rights of speech and press, and it carries with it obligations, as do all property rights. For example, owning and operating a public restaurant entail certain responsibilities to society—the obligation to serve all people who are appropriately attired, or are not abusive, and so on—and restaurant owners may not use their property right to do whatever they wish. It should be the same with media owners, Lichtenberg maintains. While everyone has a fundamental right to speak freely, media owners using their property in a public sense have obligations to society to use it justly with regard to other individuals.

Unlike Glendon and Bollinger, Lichtenberg articulates a conception of media responsibility, namely, that the media are in some sense a very public institution and thus have duties to the public. In outlining her conception, Lichtenberg goes beyond merely explaining what the media *should* do and explains what they *must* do. In other words, she goes beyond media responsibility to media accountability. The distinction is significant, for it helps describe the difference between what is acceptable under the first amendment to expect of the media, and what is not. The key difference between the two concepts, as Hodges explains, is that responsibility refers to defining what is proper conduct that may be expected, whereas accountability refers to the power (of government, the people, other institutions, and so on) to demand particular behavior. It is acceptable, then, to expect responsible behavior, but not to demand it. Or, as Hodges puts it,

"Responsibility has to do with defining proper conduct; accountability with compelling it."[32]

Freedom of the media, understood within this interpretation of the first amendment, is based on the distinction between responsibility and accountability. Accountable media cannot be free, for to render them accountable to someone or some institution is to take away their autonomy and to give power over them to another person or institution. Thus, if the Supreme Court or any other government body demands certain behavior from the media, Hodges suggests, that body holds the press accountable and consequently violates the free press guarantee. A discussion of media accountability necessarily focuses on the power of an outside institution to compel the media.

On the other hand, a discussion of media responsibility focuses on the media's performance and their "nature and functions."[33] Here media freedom is not an issue, for the media remain free to behave as they wish, without coercion from an outside source. Responsibility, including that of the press, Hodges argues, concerns "the content of our moral duties and obligations, [and] the substance of what we should do."[34] The distinction, then, is between *should* and *must*. As Hodges notes, the media may be free and responsible—that is, the media can regard their functions and role in society as something they should uphold, but they must choose this course of action. Yet the media cannot be free and accountable, for to hold them accountable is to take away the choice to behave responsibly.

Clearly, there are many ways to categorize concepts of media rights and responsibilities. Regardless of specific expectations of media roles and behavior, it is apparent that views on the general accountability of the U.S. media constitute a continuum, from no expectations of media responsibility on one end to acceptance of limited government intervention to ensure a responsible media on the other. In addition, media freedom as a right may be viewed in several ways. If one agrees with Glendon's assessment of the "rhetoric of rights," media freedom should carry obligations, but it has not been interpreted to do so. Bollinger argues that the U.S. Constitution has been interpreted as demanding a trade-off: the right of press freedom granted under the first amendment diminishes the power of government to require responsibility on the part of the press. Lichtenberg, however, sidesteps that issue by focusing on press freedom as a property right, because property rights currently enjoy less absolute legal protection than other individual rights.

The work of Glendon, Bollinger, and Lichtenberg, along with that of Hodges and Lambeth, lent several useful conceptions of media responsibility, both general and specific. The functions and canons as outlined by Hodges and Lambeth provided a concrete framework for the inquiry, while the discussion of media responsibility, accountability, and rights presented a more general structure within which the Court's conceptions were examined. In addition, each of these approaches to rights and responsibilities attempted to resolve a key question— whether rights include consequent responsibilities. That question also forms part of the basis for the theoretical framework used here and outlined in the next section.

COLLECTIVISM AND INDIVIDUALISM

The theoretical framework relied upon here arises from competing visions of the interplay between rights and responsibilities, as demonstrated in the conflict between two political philosophies—individualism and collectivism.

Individualist philosophy, which stems from the work of John Locke, Thomas Paine, and Ronald Dworkin, to name a few, centers on the individual and her or his rights. Individual rights are supreme and must be protected from both state intervention and diminishment by the democratic majority. Further, individualism requires that collective goals give way to individual rights, though individual rights may be balanced against each other. This comes in part because individualist philosophy relies on the concept of natural rights—the notion that people have certain inalienable rights before and in spite of any form of government. Because rights are natural, no collective—government, society, or democratic majority—may abridge them. In addition,

[t]he individualist tends to believe that rights are natural in the sense that they preexist the state and are supported by moral judgments that are valid objectively and without regard for what the collectivity or the majority may happen to believe or to enact into positive law. . . . Individualism holds that individual rights should have the widest possible scope and that the state should have no authority to limit rights except to protect other rights.[35]

In the previous discussion, Bollinger's view could best be described as individualistic.

Individualism contrasts with collectivism, whose adherents conclude

that the collectivity or the majority is the ultimate value in political society and is superordinate to the individual. More specifically, collectivists argue (1) that the individual has only positive rights, that is, those rights that are granted to him or her (usually through legislation) by the state; and (2) that the interests of the collectivity or the majority should take priority over the rights of the individual whenever there is a conflict between the two.[36]

Collectivism, also known as communitarianism, has its roots in the philosophies of Plato, Rousseau, the utilitarians, and John Dewey, each of whom valued the community over the individual. For collectivists, values and morality are defined by society, often through legislation, and all members of a society must agree on at least the same general values. Glendon and Lichtenberg represent collectivism.

Individualism and collectivism advance drastically different views of the role of the individual within society, of the origin and purposes of rights, values, and morality, and of responsibility. Within Supreme Court opinions on the media, the struggle between the two viewpoints typically appears in discussions of one of four related debates, whose components correspond well with collectivism and individualism. These debates consist of theories of (1) natural law versus legal positivism; (2) social responsibility versus libertarianism; (3) negative versus affirmative interpretations of press freedom; and (4) liberalism versus conservatism.

Each of the four debates is linked with the others through the beliefs about rights, government, and the legal process held by adherents to the various philosophies. For example, political conservatives believe law should reflect the "good," that is, the values they think society should uphold. Liberals, on the other hand, argue that government should not define for individuals what their values should be. In another example, those adopting a natural law viewpoint maintain that the *results* of laws are important (and results must reflect standards of morality), whereas legal positivists argue that the *process* used to arrive at particular laws is crucial. For a legal positivist, then, a law is valid not because it achieves desired results but because appropriate methods were used in creating it. Other similarities between the four components include debates over the appropriateness of government intervention to protect individual rights, the existence of natural rights, and whether a link exists between law and morality.

Legal Positivism and Natural Law

Legal philosophy can be divided into two broad categories: (a) that favoring a revised natural law theory, as represented in the United States by Ronald Dworkin and Lon Fuller;[37] and (b) that following the legal positivism tradition, best outlined by British legal scholar H.L.A. Hart.[38] These branches of legal philosophy affect legal interpretation in a number of ways, primarily through their views of the sources of law and rights. To oversimplify, they split over whether there exists a "higher" law of individual liberties and rights or whether created laws provide the extent of those liberties and rights. In both its classical and modern forms, natural law is individualistic and favors "inalienable" rights—rights that exist before and beyond the law. Legal positivism, on the other hand, is a collectivist theory that recognizes only those rights granted by political and legal institutions. These two philosophies of law provide one of the few discussions of the intersection of law and morality, a discussion crucial to the examination of Supreme Court conceptions of media responsibility.

Classical natural law theory, the older of the two philosophies, has two main propositions: First, there exists a natural morality that is independent of humankind and is discoverable. Second, laws and morality are intertwined; hence, law cannot be separated from morality. The legal positivist tradition originated to counter these claims. Legal positivism is "the simple contention that it is in no sense a necessary truth that laws reproduce or satisfy certain demands of morality."[39] In essence, legal positivism argues for the separation of law and morals. Thus, proponents of this theory agree that law can reflect morality, but the point is that law is not necessarily tied to morality. Laws can be moral, immoral, or amoral.

According to proponents of legal positivism, because laws have no necessary connection to morals, laws and legal systems are simply sets of social rules. What keeps these rules in place is not some mysterious outside, "natural" force, but rather the agreement of members of the society to follow the rules. Legislators are not required to enact moral laws, and judges are not required to base their decisions in some moral principle for a legal system to be valid. Legal positivism, therefore, promotes a process-oriented vision of the law rather than a result-oriented vision; that is, as long as the appropriate process for creating law is followed, the results—no matter what they are—are valid.

Contrasted to both classical natural law, which has been criticized for equating the laws of humans with specific moral systems that they claimed were somehow divine, and legal positivism is a new rendition of natural law. According to its proponents, the new natural law relies on several key ideas, all centering on the concept of moral principles. First, judges do not create law; they use moral principles to guide them in finding new law. Dworkin, an individualist, writes that principles are "standard[s] that are to be observed, not because [they] will advance or secure an economic, political, or social situation deemed desirable, but because [they are] a requirement of justice or fairness or some other dimension of morality."[40] Second, if two principles conflict, one may be used as more appropriate without negating the existence of the other. And third, principles can be used to create new legal rules. According to Dworkin, in difficult legal cases— cases in which there is no previous rule for judges to use, or in which precedent or statutes clearly conflict with a moral principle—principles are used to justify the judgment about particular rights.

Not every legal decision rests on a moral principle, however. Policies, too, play a role, Dworkin maintains. Principles are used to establish individual rights, whereas policies are used to establish collective goals. Both are concerned with rights, but in Dworkin's view policies are weaker, because collective goals can be abandoned for other collective goals. Dworkin explains the difference using free speech as an example: American constitutional lawyers view freedom of speech and press as protecting the audience's right to hear; a collectivist argument. Thus, courts have protected journalists from censorship and liability so that audiences are more likely to have access to information. According to Dworkin, this comes from our concept of the marketplace of ideas, where all opinions are heard and truth will win over falsehood. An individualistic theory of free speech and press, however, places emphasis on the speaker's right. This focus on the individual suggests that the right of free expression should be upheld, not because of some social good but because not to do so would deny the equal concern and respect due all persons.[41]

Justifications for free speech and press that focus on audience are collectivist arguments from policy, Dworkin maintains. He cites, for example, the argument that reporters should have special privileges because those will benefit society as a whole. Therefore, emphasizing the speaker is to view freedom of expression as a principle, for a speaker's "special position as someone wanting to express his convictions on matters of political or social importance entitles him, in fairness, to special consideration, even though the community as a whole may suffer."[42]

In this example, the collectivist, policy-based argument giving reporters special privileges so society can benefit can be overridden if it is shown that society would be better off if those privileges were withheld. And, of course, there are instances where that is likely—in a fair trial situation, for example. Making the argument for free expression from an individualistic perspective, Dworkin suggests, would give much more weight to the rights of speech and press. Free expression as a matter of principle cannot be overridden on the basis of community welfare alone. Unless a "competing interest [exists] that is very great—unless publication threatens some emergency or other grave risk—the individual's right must outweigh the social interest, because that is what it means to suppose that [the individual] has this sort of right."[43] The first amendment protections of speech and press should be seen as principle, not policy, Dworkin maintains, because only principle-based arguments can truly protect the first amendment.

Affirmative and Negative Conceptions of Media Freedom, Liberal and Conservative Political Philosophies

The liberal and conservative political positions have undergone great change during the twentieth century. Liberals of the 1930s and 1950s—epitomized in legal culture by the Warren Court—were easily defined. Liberals were, Ronald Dworkin suggests, "for greater economic equality . . . for freedom of speech and against censorship, for greater equality between the races and against segregation, . . . for greater procedural protection for accused criminals . . . and for an aggressive use of central government to achieve all these goals." Conservatives, on the other hand, held the opposite views.[44]

Despite changes in the traditional definitions during the 1960s and beyond, Dworkin argues, a "core difference" remains between liberal and conservative positions, a distinction that is key to the discussion of media rights and responsibilities. This core difference centers on differing conceptions of "equality" and its promotion by government. As part of individualist theory, the liberal conception calls on government to promote equality of all individuals and requires government to be neutral on, as Dworkin puts it, "the question of the good life." In other words, this conception of equality carries with it no inherent understanding of how society "ought" to function. Political decisions should be made, then, without specific values in mind. This is so, Dworkin suggests, because different individuals have different views on what the "good life" entails, what values are to be cherished, and government should not dictate to all what values will be held in higher esteem. If a government does treat some conceptions of the good life as more appropriate than others, it is not treating people equally. To hold one conception of the good life as somehow better than another denigrates other choices.[45]

The conservative conception, which is collectivist in nature, also requires government to promote equality, but assumes that this cannot be done without an understanding of what is good; what values ought to be encouraged. Followers of this view believe people cannot be treated equally and with dignity unless society has an overall conception of how individuals and society "ought to be."[46]

The differences between liberals and conservatives, and between negative and affirmative interpretations of freedom, including media freedom, share key characteristics. Both disagreements stem in part from different beliefs about the role of government in the area of individual rights. The liberal political viewpoint, according to Dworkin, values opportunity for the individual, sponsored either by government or by other institutions; the conservative viewpoint does not. This coincides directly with affirmative and negative views of rights and freedom found throughout political philosophy. The negative view of rights and freedom, which focuses primarily on what the government may *not* do, is the more traditional within U.S. political philosophy. In this notion, government is the result of an agreement among people; among its primary roles is the protection of individual rights. The government is responsible for maintaining freedom and cannot, without the consent of the governed, interfere with people's rights. Government interference only hinders freedom in this realm, for negative views of freedom place great faith in the market to provide and promote freedom. Negative freedom is, therefore, "freedom from" interference in the individual's pursuit of traditional rights such as liberty, property, and happiness. With regard to economic rights, this concept of rights and freedom has been associated primarily with the conservative wing of the traditional political establishment in the late twentieth century. But when debate concerns individual rights, the concept has more often been adopted by liberals.

In the affirmative view the marketplace does not automatically define the virtuous individual. In the conservative, negative view of rights, characteristics such as talent, drive, ability, gender, or race are irrelevant, for each person theoretically has the freedom to do as she or he wishes; each can choose to succeed or not. The liberal affirmative view, however, sees these aspects of the individual personality as inseparable from rights, at least with regard to the opportunity to succeed. Talent and ability are distributed unequally throughout the population, and American society for centuries has not permitted women and racial and ethnic minorities the freedom to succeed that it has given nonminority men. Thus, the positive view of rights regards opportunity as crucial, and, to be treated equally, people must have equal opportunities to succeed. Therefore, all have a right to equal education, to fair treatment in business dealings, and so on. But even more importantly, government under this individualistic conception has the obligation to protect those rights by providing those opportunities, even if that means stepping in to "interfere." For example, affirmative action laws have been used to provide an equal footing to individuals and groups that have not been treated equally. Similarly, in interpretations of the first amendment, the affirmative conception of rights has been used to argue for access to the media for nonmainstream opinions in order to increase the diversity of views expressed.

Libertarian and Social Responsibility Media Theories

The libertarian model of the media, which is an individualistic theory, is based upon several key premises, including a belief in individuals' inherent rationality and ability to discern truth from falsehood, the natural success of laissez-faire economics, and the existence of certain fundamental, inalienable individual rights. Under this model the press is left alone to function in the marketplace, unimpeded by government regulation so that the best newspapers, magazines, broadcast stations, and other media organizations will survive through efficiency and giving the public what it wants. This model does best job, argue its proponents, of mirroring the diversity of American opinion, of watching government, of serving society. The members of the media themselves decide what appropriate, responsible behavior is, and act accordingly, for if they do not, eventually the public will discard them and they will not survive.

According to the libertarian model, the media have very specific roles and functions. Siebert, Peterson, and Schramm list several: to inform, entertain, act as a basis for the economic system—in other words, to promote business through advertising—promote debate and discussion on public issues, guard individual rights by watching the government, and be self-sufficient.[47] The underlying rationale for these functions is to promote the finding of truth by members of society, particularly truth relating to government. In addition, individual members of society have the right to criticize the government, because it operates only with their consent. The media's role, therefore, is to provide the means by which people can both speak out on, and read about, the activities of leaders entrusted to protect their rights: The media, with the help of the people, are to operate as an extra-legal check on the government, as a watchdog. Logically, then, because of their role as a check on government, the media must be free from government intervention, whether dangerous or benign.

And what of the media's responsibility? In the libertarian model, the media have specified, important roles and functions. But what if the media abuse their freedom or do not fulfill their roles? The libertarian model does not deal with these possibilities. Libertarians admit that the media are sometimes overzealous and may cause harm to individuals, especially public officials, but they see that as an unavoidable consequence of the media's role as watchdog. The government simply has no right to interfere with the media, even to punish for irresponsible behavior. If the government were to draw a line between acceptable and unacceptable media behavior, libertarians argue, the line could too easily be drawn to inhibit legitimate criticism of the government and its officials. Instead of advocating government regulation to stop media irresponsibility, the model relies upon the good will of the media to regulate themselves through the competition of the market and by individual media organizations.

The libertarian model of the media shares many characteristics with natural law, modern conservative economic policies, and the negative conception of freedom. As with natural law theory, a fundamental tenet of libertarian philosophy is the existence of natural human rights, at least the rights of liberty, conscience, and property. Like conservative economic policies and negative freedom, the libertarian model opposes government intervention to ensure opportunity for expression of rights (including the freedom of the press) and concludes that the best way to put opinions into the public arena is through the economic marketplace, in which the various media compete to gain audiences.

Yet the libertarian model also shares characteristics with liberal political philosophy, for it has no conception of the good—no preordained understanding of what society should value and strive for—except what the marketplace of ideas and the economic market bring. Equality of opportunity, so important in liberal politics and the affirmative conception of rights, has little place in the libertarian model, which assumes that all the opportunities people need can be found in the marketplace without assistance from outside (including government) sources.[48]

By the mid-twentieth century the premises of the libertarian model were no longer so clear. Advances in the technology necessary to publish newspapers and to broadcast on the airwaves led to more efficient, more complicated media serving larger audiences. But the expense of these new technologies led American mass media to cluster into larger and larger chains and networks, leaving smaller newspapers and broadcast stations eventually to die. And in Europe the press had not stopped the rise of fascism in Italy or the National Socialist Party in Germany.

In addition, new theories in psychology, theology, and philosophy had long since cast doubt on the concept of the inherent rationality of people and the rightness of the laissez-faire doctrine. The work of Sigmund Freud led to discussion early in the century about the inner workings of the human mind, and even earlier Charles Darwin's thesis of evolution had cast doubt on the uniqueness of humanity, and thus on the notion of special human rights. In American Christianity, the turn-of-the-century Social Gospel movement, epitomized in Walter Rauschenbusch's *Christianity and the Social Crisis*,[49] applied the work of the church to urban problems and suggested that the economic doctrines of laissez faire were at least somewhat incompatible with Christian teachings.[50]

The writings of William James, John Dewey, and other pragmatists had given America its first home-grown philosophy, stressing the collective nature of society over the individualism emphasized by liberal philosophy.[51] Although the United States did not suddenly become a collectivist society, the influence of these thinkers and the Progressive political movement created an emphasis on the interdependent nature of larger human communities.[52] And along with this new emphasis on interdependence, naturally enough, came a focus on obligation, to society at large and to other individuals. A sense of obligation began to appear in American business, suggest Siebert, Peterson, and Schramm. The American press followed suit, developing "a sense of mission requiring it to serve the general welfare. As it did so, it planted the seeds for a coherent theory of social responsibility."[53]

Seeds of the social responsibility model were planted by early twentieth century philosophers, politicians, and theologians, but it remained for a group of scholars in the 1940s to give the model a coherent articulation. The Commission on Freedom of the Press, chaired by University of Chicago Chancellor Robert M. Hutchins, concluded that self-regulation by the media, although the ideal for promoting responsibility of the press, had not worked. The Commission struggled with traditional and newer assumptions about the role of the media in a diverse society. In the words of journalism historian Jerilyn S. McIntyre, "The philosophical conflict underlying the commission's attempts to deal with the choice between self-regulation and external control was between the traditional assumptions that the press should be *free from* external constraints, and the social requirement that there should also be *freedom for* communication and action in a free society."[54] The Commission struggled with whether freedom of the press was a negative or affirmative freedom, concluding finally that both interpretations were on occasion appropriate.

According to the Commission members, the traditional (libertarian) model missed a crucial element of the right of media freedom. Thus, the Commission argued that freedom of the press was not unconditional: To retain it, the press had to uphold certain obligations, certain duties. With this argument, the Commission added a new strain to philosophies surrounding the function of the press. And they placed this new strain within a collectivist context: No longer were the press or individuals free to do as they chose, for they had a responsibility to the larger community: "If a man is burdened with an idea, he not only desires to express it; he ought to express it. He owes it to his conscience and the common good. The indispensable function of expressing ideas is one of obligation—to the community and also to something beyond the community—let us say to truth."[55] That responsibility, argued the Commission, meant that no one had a moral or legal right to own a press or other means of mechanical communication. Owners of the mass media cannot use their ownership as a reason to deny their duty to publish or broadcast a diverse array of opinion. The Commission noted: "The press is not free if those who operate it behave as though their position conferred on them the privilege of being deaf to ideas which the processes of free speech have brought to public attention."[56] And the Commission went further, suggesting that if the media do not follow their duty to the social good, the moral right to their freedom disappears: "In the absence of accepted moral duties there are no moral rights."[57]

Thus the Commission outlined a radically different conception of media freedom. The media are free, in one sense, to publish a variety of opinion. But if they do not do so, if they do not uphold their moral responsibilities, they lose the moral right of freedom. Freedom of the media, then, is a conditional right.

This implied, wrote the Commission, "[T]hat the press must also be accountable. It must be accountable to society for meeting the public needs and for maintaining the rights of citizens and the almost forgotten rights of speakers who have no press."[58]

The social responsibility model of the media reflects a distinct vision of the good and a belief that the media play a role in bringing about that good, like conservative political philosophy. Like legal positivism, it sees no necessity for the concept of natural rights beyond the scope of law.[59] And like the affirmative conception of rights, it suggests that government (and other institutions) can and should actively participate in bringing about the rights granted to people in a political setting.

The social responsibility model shares its foundations with the libertarian model, which it updates, in an attempt to make the latter meaningful in the twentieth century. The social responsibility model does more than call for individual freedom; it calls for provision of the means to attain that freedom. In this conception, then, the media are seen as instrumental—as a means to a larger end. The media's role is to aid in the attainment of individual freedom by providing the opportunity for various viewpoints to be heard, and that role is more important than the media's freedom from government intervention.

Finally, and most central to the differences between them, the social responsibility model, unlike the libertarian, views rights as including responsibilities. This difference demonstrates the connection of libertarianism and social responsibility to individualism and collectivism, respectively. Libertarians maintain that individuals are born with certain rights that cannot be taken away by government or institutions, or given up by the individual. These rights are unconditional. But proponents of social responsibility argue that no rights are unconditional, because for every right there is a reason given for that right. We have the right of free speech, the argument goes, because without it we cannot have freedom of thought. Yet making a case for this right automatically gives a reason for its existence. And if that reason for its existence were no longer valid, there would be no need for the right. Thus, argue proponents of social responsibility, there can be no unconditional, inalienable rights. And if an individual (or the press) does not uphold his or her responsibility under the former model, she or he cannot continue to claim moral rights. Rights come only with responsibility.

CONCLUSION

To summarize, until now no attempt has been made to examine the Court's philosophy of media responsibility. By searching for the connection between media theory and legal philosophy, this work examines the Court's ideas on the issue and contributes to scholarship on both media freedom and the connection between law and morality. An examination of media cases within the context of these theoretical perspectives, searching for patterns and theories of media responsibility put forth in opinions, clarifies the Court's conceptions (or lack of conceptions) of the intersection of law and morality. More importantly, the analysis provides insight about the meaning of media responsibility as interpreted and imposed by the Court. Such analysis should ultimately illuminate both for the media and society how such values as media responsibility are shaped and modified, and what the implications of those values are for the media and society at large.

Of the four components of the collectivist/individualist framework, the social responsibility/libertarian and natural law/legal positivism debates are the two most essential to the discussion of the intersection of law and morality. The natural law/legal positivism debate indirectly augments conceptions of media freedom within the law as well as within morality, whereas the social responsibility and libertarian theories of the media have very clear, if not necessarily specific, definitions of media responsibility. The common thread through these first two debates, which are at a deep level two formations of the same debate, is the relationship of rights to responsibilities, and how moral principles affect decision making—of people in general, of the media, and of legal interpreters. On one hand, the individualistic natural law and libertarian theories both maintain that somehow "larger" moral principles inform discussion and interpretation of law; thus, under these theories media responsibility should be articulated both on a theoretical level and with specific examples and should be grounded in language calling upon "higher" laws. On the other hand, legal positivism and social responsibility theories, both collectivist, deny the existence—or at least the necessity—of moral principles in the interpretation of law; therefore, theories of media freedom under them should tend to be more practical, less universal, and rely only upon interpretation of enacted, not higher, law. Yet there is an irony here, especially as revealed in court cases. Though it is libertarian theory, rather than social responsibility theory, that relies on a larger understanding of human rights—on natural-law-type principles—courts using the libertarian theory of press freedom have vehemently denied the existence of higher moral principles within their interpretation of the law. The Supreme Court in *Miami Herald v. Tornillo*[60] expressly distanced itself from a social responsibility conception of media freedom and made an argument directly from the libertarian perspective. Yet those same justices would likely disagree with the assertion that they rely on higher moral laws in their decisions. Such inconsistency within the Court's legal interpretation has implications for the media and society as a whole, particularly when anticipating future Court interpretations of media cases.

NOTES

1. *Dun and Bradstreet v. Greenmoss Builders,* 105 S.Ct. 2939, 2948 (1985), Chief Justice Warren Burger, concurring.

2. *Rosenbloom v. Metromedia,* 91 S.Ct. 1811, 1823 (1971), Justice William Brennan, plurality opinion.

3. Throughout this work, the term "Court opinion" refers to the official opinion of the majority or plurality in a given case. Concurring and dissenting opinions are always identified as such.

4. *Harte-Hanks Communications, Inc. v. Connaughton*, 109 S.Ct. 2678 (1989).

5. *Associated Press v. United States*, 65 S.Ct. 1416, 1428 (1945), Justice Frankfurter, concurring.

6. *Ginzburg v. United States*, 86 S.Ct. 942, 956 (1966), Justice Stewart, dissenting.

7. *Near v. Minnesota*, 51 S.Ct. 625 (1931).

8. Defined as newspapers, newsletters, magazines, television, radio, cable, motion pictures, and photography.

9. Louis W. Hodges, "Defining Press Responsibility: A Functional Approach," *Responsible Journalism*, ed. Deni Elliott (Beverly Hills: Sage, 1986), 23.

10. Hodges, 27–28.

11. Hodges, 29.

12. Edmund B. Lambeth, *Committed Journalism: An Ethic for the Profession* (Bloomington: Indiana University Press, 1986), 27.

13. Lambeth, 29.

14. *Red Lion Broadcasting Co. v. Federal Communications Commission*, 89 S.Ct. 1794 (1969) and *New York Times v. Sullivan*, 84 S.Ct. 710 (1964).

15. Lambeth, 33, quoting John Rawls, *A Theory of Justice* (Cambridge: Harvard University Press, 1971), 7.

16. Lambeth, 35–36.

17. Lambeth, 31.

18. Lambeth, 37.

19. Glendon notes that the French Declaration of Rights of Man and Citizen (1789) emphasized that individuals had duties as well as rights, whereas the American Declaration of Independence (1776) did not.

20. Quoted in Mary Ann Glendon, *Rights Talk: The Impoverishment of Political Discourse* (New York: The Free Press, 1991), 23.

21. Glendon, 14–15.

22. Glendon, 77.

23. Oliver Wendell Holmes, "The Path of the Law," *Harvard Law Review* 10 (1897): 457–78.

24. Glendon, 86.

25. Holmes, 460.

26. Holmes, quoted in Glendon, 87.

27. Lee Bollinger, *Images of a Free Press* (Chicago: University of Chicago Press, 1991), 26.

28. Bollinger, 41.

29. 84 S.Ct. 710 (1964).

30. Bollinger, 44.

31. Judith Lichtenberg, "Foundations and Limits of Freedom of the Press," *Democracy and the Mass Media*, ed. Judith Lichtenberg (Cambridge: Cambridge University Press, 1990), 104.

32. Hodges, 14.

33. Hodges, 14.

34. Hodges, 14.

35. Donald Elfenbein, "The Myth of Conservatism as a Constitutional Philosophy," *Iowa Law Review* 71 (1986): 421.

36. Elfenbein, 403.

37. See, for example, Ronald Dworkin, *Taking Rights Seriously* (Cambridge: Harvard University Press, 1977); *A Matter of Principle* (Cambridge: Harvard University Press, 1985); "'Natural' Law Revisited," *University of Florida Law Review* 34.2 (1982): 165–88. Also, Lon Fuller, *The Morality of Law* (rev. ed.) (New Haven: Yale University Press, 1969).

38. See H.L.A. Hart, *The Concept of Law* (Oxford: Clarendon Press, 1961).

39. Hart, 181.

40. Dworkin, *Taking Rights Seriously*, 23.

41. For Dworkin, the right of all individuals to "equal concern and respect" is perhaps the most fundamental right with which the law should be concerned, for it provides a foundation for many principles lawmakers (legislators and judges) use to create fair and just laws. In his use of this principle, Dworkin is indebted to the work of philosopher John Rawls, who persuasively argues that given the opportunity, people would choose "equal concern and respect" as a fundamental moral principle upon which to order their lives and their society. In applying this distinctly moral principle to the legal system, Dworkin suggests that the law is inherently and fundamentally connected to moral principles. For Rawls' argument, see Rawls, *A Theory of Justice*.

42. Dworkin, *Matter of Principle*, 386.

43. Dworkin, *Matter of Principle*, 387.

44. Ronald Dworkin, "Liberalism," *Public and Private Morality*, ed. Stuart Hampshire (Cambridge: Cambridge University Press, 1978), 113.

45. Dworkin, "Liberalism," 127.

46. Dworkin, "Liberalism," 127.

47. Fred S. Siebert, Theodore Peterson, and Wilbur Schramm, *Four Theories of the Press* (Urbana: University of Illinois Press, 1956), 74.

48. Siebert, Peterson, and Schramm admit that the libertarian model opposes monopolies, for anyone should have the ability to own a form of mass communication. But rather than inviting government intervention to stop monopolies, the libertarian model assumes that the mass media themselves will see the error of forming monopolies, and thus will refrain from doing so. In this way, then, this model assumes responsible behavior of the press.

49. Walter Rauschenbusch, *Christianity and the Social Crisis* (New York: Macmillan, 1907).

50. Sydney E. Ahlstrom, *A Religious History of the American People*, vol. 2 (Garden City, New York: Image Books, 1975), 250–73.

51. See, for example, John Dewey, *Experience and Nature* (New York: Dover, 1958), and Charles Morris, *The Pragmatic Movement in American Philosophy* (New York: George Braziller, Inc., 1970).

52. For information on the Progressive Era, see Richard Hofstadter, *The Age of Reform* (New York: Knopf, 1955), Paul Murphy, *World War I and the Origin of Civil Liberties in the United States* (New York: Norton, 1979), and William L. O'Neill, *The Progressive Years* (New York: Dodd, Mead, 1975).

53. Siebert, Peterson, and Schramm, 83.

54. Jerilyn S. McIntyre, "The Hutchins Commission's Search for a Moral Framework," *Journalism History* 6.2 (1979): 54–57, 63.

55. Commission on Freedom of the Press, *A Free and Responsible Press*, ed. Robert D. Leigh (Chicago: University of Chicago Press, 1947), 8–9.

56. Commission, 9.

57. Commission, 10.

58. Commission, 18.

59. The Commission arrived at this conclusion through the following reasoning: Rights are typically justified by use of a reason, such as the right to use our property as we wish as long as we do not infringe upon the rights of others. These reasons can be considered obligations. If those obligations are not met, moral (and some legal) rights can be terminated. Since rights can be terminated if certain conditions are not met, rights are not unconditional. Because rights are conditional, they cannot be "inalienable" or natural, existing beyond the law. Society grants rights and may take them away. However, to do so might itself be an immoral act, as well as ultimately detrimental to society.

60. *Miami Herald v. Tornillo*, 94 S.Ct. 2831 (1974).

Chapter One

Functions and Canons: Defining Media Responsibility

In 1931 a divided United States Supreme Court decided that a Minneapolis newspaper had the right to publish anti-Semitic, racist, and unpleasant attacks on newsworthy people, though not without later punishment. Both the five-justice majority and the four dissenters in *Near v. Minnesota*[1] based their arguments on collective ideas: One side concluded that society would be best served by allowing newspapers to publish their views, while the other maintained that society could not stand such attacks on community leaders. Both arguments acknowledged the role community had to play in defining media freedom and responsibility, but they differed in their views of the *purposes* of the media. For the liberal majority, the media's role was to present all ideas, no matter how unattractive, in order to educate the public on civic issues. The conservative dissenters, on the other hand, believed that the media should uphold community standards.

Thus, while both groups agreed at one level, they disagreed on the *definitions* of media roles and consequent responsibilities. This chapter examines those definitions as advanced by the Court and individual justices, using Louis Hodges' media functions and Edmund Lambeth's canons of ethical journalism as a starting point. No attempt is made here to place the justices' opinions in historical context or chronological order; this will be done in later chapters. Instead, the focus here is on collecting and analyzing concrete definitions of media responsibility as outlined by the Court overall. This reading provided evidence of two primary media functions, according to the Court, and two dominant canons of media responsibility.

Briefly, the four functions include the *political*, which describes the role of the press in watching the doings of government; *educational*, which focuses on the provision of a "marketplace of ideas"; *mirroring*, which allows people to more fully understand "what we are as a people . . . and what we may become";[2] and the *bulletin board*, which provides basic information about daily life.

The five canons of ethical journalism Lambeth discussed include: *truth telling*, involving the journalist's responsibility to be accurate, unbiased, familiar with the issues covered, and to provide appropriate context; *justice*, emphasizing fairness and the establishment of justice within government and society at large; *freedom*, involving the journalist's obligations both to guard the first amendment and to remain free of outside influence; *humaneness*, requiring the media to avoid harm whenever possible; and *stewardship*, the general responsibility to "manage . . . life and property with proper regard to the rights of others."[3]

Though the four functions and five canons provided the practical definitions of media responsibility throughout the reading of cases, two functions—the political and the educational—and two canons—truth telling and stewardship—dominated in Court decisions. A number of cases discussed here are also used extensively in later chapters. Though they are analyzed more than once, they are brought up in later chapters for different reasons. Thus, the cases discussed overlap between the chapters, but the purposes for examining them do not.

THE POLITICAL FUNCTION OF THE MEDIA

The political, or democratic, function provided the most common rationale offered both for the protection given to the media under the first amendment and for demands that the media report on issues of public importance, in particular issues of government. This function means the media act as an agent of the citizenry whose task, in the words of Justice William O. Douglas, is "to explore and investigate events, inform the people what is going on, and to expose the harmful as well as the good influences at work." Douglas added, "There is no higher function performed under our constitutional regime."[4] Throughout opinions studied, the justices repeatedly alluded to this function, sometimes in more general terms, as above, and at other times much more specifically, as when Justice Tom Clark, writing for the majority in *Times-Picayune v. United States* in 1953, wrote, "By interpreting to the citizen the policies of his government and vigilantly scrutinizing the official conduct of those who administer the state, an independent press stimulates free discussion and focuses public opinion on issues and officials as a potent check on arbitrary action or abuse."[5]

Using the political function to justify media freedom, however, causes a dilemma. Giving a reason for freedom of the press—in this case the larger purpose of a self-governing society—demonstrates a conception of how the press should act. By rationalizing media freedom, then, the Court sets guidelines for media responsibility. This dilemma arose often in the Court's discussion of the political function and is illustrated by opposing points of view. Some justices argued that the press is free even to act irresponsibly, that irresponsible behavior is a cost society must bear to maintain a representative democracy. Other justices maintained also that the press is free, but suggested that freedom has limits, that the press should be responsible, and that the press has responsibilities originating in its role as guardian for the people. In both situations, however, the justices typically used a collectivist rationale, casting media freedom as a policy, rather than a principle, to use Dworkin's definitions.

Perhaps the most ardent arguments in favor of a press free to be irresponsible came, not surprisingly, in the opinions of two of the most libertarian justices of the twentieth century, Hugo Black and William O. Douglas. Both could be absolutist in their views of the first amendment, arguing that it allows no government interference with the press, regardless of the consequences. For example, Black once wrote simply that "[u]nconditional freedom to criticize the way such public functions are performed is in my judgment necessarily included in the guarantees of the first amendment."[6] And although the 1964 case *New York Times v. Sullivan* is traditionally seen as a victory for the press, protecting it from most libel suits brought by public officials, Black and Douglas often argued in later cases that in *New York Times* the Court had not done enough to protect the media. In their view, the 1964 decision left the media open to the very dangers others thought it prevented. In other words, while *New York Times* did give the media a margin of safety in criticizing public officials (and in publishing some false statements about them), Black and Douglas said the Court had not gone far enough in protecting the media from government officials' harassment through libel suits. *New York Times*, Black wrote in a 1966 concurrence, was a "short and inadequate step" toward guarding press freedom and provided "little protection against high emotions and deep prejudices which frequently pervade local communities where libel suits are tried."[7]

Such libertarian views were not confined to libel cases. The concept that the media may be irresponsible in the exercise of their freedom appeared often. As early as 1941, Justice Black's opinion for the Court in *Bridges v. California*, a contempt of court case, stated, "[I]t is a prized American privilege to speak one's mind, although not with perfect good taste, on all public institutions."[8] It was not just the Court liberals who saw the necessity of the "evil"; later moderates and conservatives occasionally admitted that coarse, unpleasant, even irresponsible, behavior might have to be tolerated to preserve the political function of the press. Writing for the Court in 1988, Chief Justice William Rehnquist argued that satire as a political form must be protected: "Despite their sometimes caustic nature, from the early cartoon portraying George Washington as an ass down to the present day, graphic depictions and satirical cartoons have played a prominent role in public and political debate."[9]

Perhaps the best articulation of why the media must be allowed to be irresponsible in the pursuit of their political function came in Justice Byron White's concurrence in *Miami Herald v. Tornillo* in 1974. In this case, a unanimous Court overturned Florida's right-of-reply statute, which had required a newspaper to offer column space to political candidates claiming that specific coverage had harmed (but not libeled) them. Tornillo, a candidate for the state legislature, had argued that the *Miami Herald* hurt his election effort when it called him a "czar" and said he should not be elected. This was irresponsible behavior, Tornillo insisted. However, the justices, who on one level may have agreed with Tornillo, were not willing to hold the newspaper accountable. This statute, they pointed out, penalized a newspaper for its content, which if allowed would lead to self-censorship by the press in controversial areas and harm the political function of the press. The Court's ruling, therefore, permitted the press to be irresponsible to protect the political function. In concurring, Justice White wrote, "Of course, the press is not always accurate, or even responsible, and may not present full and fair debate on important public issues. But the balance struck by the first amendment with respect to the press is that society must take the risk that occasionally debate on vital matters will not be comprehensive and that all viewpoints may not be expressed."[10] This represents well the dominant view of the Court concerning the political function of the media.

But it was not the only view found. In many cases throughout the sixty-five years studied, members of the Court argued that the media have responsibilities, that they should be responsible, and that there can be limits on acceptable media behavior, even within the political function. Nevertheless, these arguments typically were compatible with the conception of a media free from government intervention. For example, analysis of the responsibilities of the media sometimes flowed directly from discussions of the need for a free media. In *New York Times v. United States/United States v. Washington Post* (the "Pentagon Papers" case of 1971), Justice Black, joined by Justice Douglas, wrote, "Only a free and unrestrained press can effectively expose deception in government." This statement was not surprising, coming from the two Court libertarians. But the next sentence outlined what Black saw as an obligation the press should uphold: "And paramount among the responsibilities of a free press is the duty to prevent any part of the government from deceiving the people and sending them off to distant lands to die of foreign fevers and foreign shot and shell."[11] Thus, even Black and Douglas, ardent supporters of an absolutely free press, had ideas of why the press was free. The press, to Black and Douglas, had an obligation to protect the people from their government. And in another example, Justice White suggested in a 1975 case that the press has tremendous responsibility precisely because of its political function. Individuals, White wrote, have limited time and resources with which to gather information relevant to the political system and their role in it;[12] therefore, the media must do it for them.

As a result, the media's role is to act as an agent for the public, bringing that information in a "convenient form" to the people. White wrote: "Great responsibility is accordingly placed upon the news media to report fully and accurately the proceedings of government."[13] The notion of the media as public agent with consequent obligations to provide information permeated much of the discussion of the media's political function. Though the media typically were seen as protected from government intervention—thus "free"—the rationale underlying this political function was that the media are free in order to perform a vital task whose absence would irreparably harm the U.S. system of governing. Ultimately, the Court could not resolve the conflict between a media free to be irresponsible on one hand and expectations of certain behavior—accountability—on the other.

It seems unlikely that this conflict could be resolved, because the evidence suggests that the Court views the political function as a policy within the libertarian model. The function is libertarian because it requires that the media be left alone to do their work. It is a policy because the political function is based on a social need rather than a moral principle. As a social need, it necessarily has conditions attached to it: Society must benefit from the political function in order for it to be a justification for media freedom. Thus, unless the Court bases its arguments for media freedom upon a principle, this conflict cannot be resolved.

While the Court's admonitions to the media in the examples discussed so far are fairly general, the justices' expectations in certain situations were much more specific. In cases involving trial issues—either contempt charges against the media or concerns about a fair trial of a suspect—the Court expected, and sometimes required, responsible behavior. During the 1940s, when the Court heard several cases in which the media were charged with contempt of court because they criticized the judicial process, the justices articulated specific expectations of responsibility. Though the Court in each case found in favor of the media, the justices debated whether the press should be expected to treat judicial proceedings with deference. In *Pennekamp v. Florida* in 1946, Justice Stanley Reed argued for an unanimous Court that the press should find a middle ground between "free discussion of the problems of society" and "public comment of every character upon pending trials or legal proceedings." "Understanding writers," Reed commented, would comprehend the dangers involved in commenting upon pending legal cases and would refrain whenever possible. A balance should be maintained, either by the media themselves or by the courts: "Freedom of discussion should be given the widest range compatible with the essential requirement of the fair and orderly administration of justice."[14]

The following year, however, the Court divided on the issue. In *Craig v. Harney*, another contempt case involving press criticism of the judicial process, the majority maintained that the newspaper in question had a right to editorialize against a judge. Justice Frank Murphy, concurring, argued that the press could not constitutionally be punished for this sort of criticism, that "unscrupulous and vindictive criticism of the judiciary is regrettable," but perhaps inevitable.[15] Even two of the three dissenters in this case (Justice Felix Frankfurter and Chief Justice Fred Vinson) agreed, commenting that criticism of judges and the judicial system, "no matter how irresponsible or misrepresentative,"[16] is a necessary part of the political function of the press. The third dissenter disagreed, however. Justice Robert Jackson wrote that the press had "passed beyond the legitimate use of press freedom" in criticizing the judge. He accused his colleagues of potentially encouraging future press irresponsibility by overturning this particular contempt citation, calling the Court opinion "ill-advised, or worse."[17]

Contempt citations against the media were not the only instances in which justices commented upon the irresponsible behavior of the media. Fair trial issues also brought discussion of media responsibility. Though the media were never one of the parties in the fair trial cases studied,[18] the issue of unfair or overzealous coverage of sensational trials caused the justices to weigh carefully the contrasting rights of media freedom and the individual right to a fair trial. And in each case the Court was careful always to place responsibility for a fair trial upon the presiding judge. Still, comment about media behavior was inevitable. In the 1965 case *Estes v. Texas* in particular, the Court divided sharply over whether the media's actions were acceptable. The Court held that Billie Sol Estes, a close friend of President Lyndon Johnson, had been deprived of due process and a fair trial in part because of the televising of his trial on swindling charges. Justice Tom Clark, writing for the five-justice majority, argued that the press, though it should be as free as possible to report on trials, "must necessarily be subject to the maintenance of absolute fairness in the judicial process."[19] Clark went further than this general sentiment, however, specifically to attack the use of television cameras in the courtroom. Television, he reasoned, harmed the judicial process and in this instance made a fair trial impossible. Television had a negative impact upon the jurors, witnesses, and defendant, he argued. Its presence was "a form of mental—if not physical—harassment, resembling a police line-up or the third degree" to the defendant. In this case, television harmed Estes' dignity, his privacy, and his concentration on the trial. "Trial by television," Clark concluded, "is foreign to our system."[20]

Still, in the fair trial cases the Court recognized the need for a media free from government intervention and instead focused on trial judges, making them responsible for decorum in their courtrooms. Thus, if the media behaved irresponsibly in subsequent cases (which, of course, on occasion they did), the Court's wrath was felt by lower court judges, not by the media. In this way, in fair trial cases the Court found the balance between allowing the media the freedom needed to perform the political function deemed so crucial to U.S. democracy and the inevitable expectations of media responsibility brought about by that very function.

But achieving that balance is rare. The Court faces a difficult task when it applies the political function of the media, for it must weigh the requirements of the first amendment against the needs of a democracy. Inherent in that balance is a fundamental conflict the Court has not resolved. The first amendment seemingly requires that government place no restrictions whatsoever on the media; thus, the media cannot be required to behave responsibly. This, of course, is the libertarian view. Yet, in acknowledging the necessary role the media play in the political sphere, the Court does limit the media—it expects the media to aid self-governance. This is clearly a policy-based argument, for when the media do not perform their political function, the justices feel compelled to criticize them, because, in their view, society's needs are not being met. At the same time, however, the justices rely on the political function to justify media freedom. The media are free, the Court has argued, and they perform a useful function in American democracy. Unfortunately, the justices cannot have it both ways:

Either the media are free, or they should aid the political process. By making an argument based on policy, rather than on principle, the Court sets up an unworkable conflict.

THE EDUCATIONAL FUNCTION OF THE MEDIA

The educational function of the media shares several characteristics with the political function, including protection of the media as a means to a larger end. That larger end is the "free and open debate" on public issues. The case analysis demonstrated that the two functions also share the conflict between the first amendment and society's needs. While the political function of the media furthers democratic goals by giving individuals a better grasp of the workings of government, the educational function is more general. Here, the media are to provide the "marketplace of ideas," the concept made famous by Justice Oliver Wendell Holmes that encompasses the means through which ideas and opinions on public issues can be put forth, tested, and refined.[21] Ultimately, the goal of the educational function is the attainment of some truth, whether that be defined by the individual or by society. In addition, the justices have viewed the educational function of the media as vital to American society; yet, they have admitted that this function limits media behavior. Thus, in the midst of its many calls for media freedom to provide a marketplace of ideas, the Court also has acknowledged a need for media responsibility.

Throughout the cases analyzed, the justices outlined basic statements of the educational function, often tying it to the attainment of "truth." For example, in 1945 Frankfurter wrote, "The business of the press . . . is the promotion of truth."[22] In 1962 Chief Justice Earl Warren wrote, "Men are entitled to speak as they please on matters vital to them; errors in judgment or unsubstantiated opinions may be exposed, of course, but not through punishment for contempt for the expression." Warren continued: "The First Amendment envisions that persons be given the opportunity to inform the community of both sides of an issue."[23] And the press is given, according to the Court in an opinion written by Justice Lewis Powell, a "special and constitutionally recognized role"[24] so that it may inform and educate people on a range of issues. In addition, various justices, in particular Potter Stewart, have argued for giving the media special protection from newsroom searches and grand jury subpoenas because of the educational function.[25] But, in essence, the educational function of the media remains grounded in a belief in the power of individuals to choose their own truth. Justice Stewart wrote in a 1966 case:

[T]hose who wrote our First Amendment . . . believed a society can be truly strong only when it is truly free. In the realm of expression they put their faith, for better or for worse, in the enlightened choice of the people, free from the interference of a policeman's intrusive thumb or a judge's heavy hand. So it is that the Constitution protects coarse expression as well as refined, and vulgarity no less than elegance. A book worthless to me may convey something of value to my neighbor. In the free society to which our Constitution has committed us, it is for each to choose for himself.[26]

Thus, the media are protected for the educational function, as for the political function, so that they may perform a duty to society and fulfill an obligation to provide information and opinions on all subjects, whether or not those subjects are pleasant or widely accepted.

To promote this educational function, the Court has been at times willing to grant the media almost total freedom. For example, Justice Douglas wanted to ensure the free marketplace of ideas by protecting anything the media (or individual speakers) had to say, no matter how dangerous, vulgar, or inappropriate, until the "speech" became some kind of action.[27] Chief Justice Rehnquist, despite believing that "false statements of fact are valueless," acknowledged in a 1988 case that to impose strict liability on a publisher of false statements would deny the first amendment the "breathing space" it needs.[28] And to give the first amendment—and consequently the marketplace of ideas—that breathing room, the Court has allowed some irresponsible behavior by the press. As Justice William Brennan wrote in 1971: "In an ideal world, the responsibility of the press would match the freedom and public trust given it. But from the earliest days of our history, this free society, dependent as it is for its survival upon a vigorous free press, has tolerated some abuse."[29]

But again, this freedom is based upon a wider obligation—to provide individuals with free choice both in what they say and in what they consume through the media. And the Supreme Court has struggled constantly to find an appropriate balance between media freedom and obligations in the educational function. Despite their protection of media freedom, the justices just as often admitted the existence of limitations on media behavior. Media freedom, even to maintain the marketplace of ideas, is not absolute—occasionally, other social needs outweigh society's need for free debate on public issues. The Court has limited media freedom in the name of responsibility in two general areas: broadcast regulation—to be discussed later—and commercial speech.

In cases involving the "traditional" media—newspapers, magazines, and broadcast—the Court has typically balanced media freedom against social needs for responsibility from the media. However, in the regulation of commercial speech the justices have tended to agree more on the necessity of requiring responsible behavior, but have disagreed on whether advertising has any first amendment rights arising from its role as educator of the public. Three cases illustrate the Court's dilemma over commercial speech, responsibility, and the first amendment.

In its first commercial speech case, *Valentine v. Chrestensen*, the Court ruled that purely commercial speech had no protection under the first amendment. On occasion during the next few decades, the Court again confronted issues of commercial speech, most notably in *New York Times v. Sullivan*, which involved an advertisement raising funds for the Martin Luther King, Jr., defense fund. In that case the Court ruled that the advertisement did in fact have first amendment protection. But it was not until the 1970s that the Supreme Court began facing commercial speech cases challenging the ruling in *Valentine v. Chrestensen*. In *Bigelow v. Virginia* in 1975, the Court ruled that an advertisement in a Virginia newspaper for abortions available in New York had some measure of constitutional protection. At the time of the ad, 1971, abortion was legal in New York but not in Virginia, though by the time of the Court's ruling in 1975 abortion was legal across the country. The Court, with Justice Harry Blackmun writing for the seven-justice majority, suggested that the advertisement in *Bigelow* was protected because it "did more than simply propose a commercial transaction. It contained factual material of clear 'public interest.'"[30] The commercial speech in question, although it dealt with an economic transaction, also played a role in debate over a current political issue. The advertisement was protected, then, because it aided the educational function and promoted a key responsibility of the media.

The following year the Court heard a case involving purely commercial speech with no political undertones. In *Virginia State Board of Pharmacy v. Virginia Citizens Consumer Council* in 1976, the Court held that a ban on advertising the prices of prescription drugs violated the first amendment rights of consumers to receive information, even though that information was strictly economic. Justice Blackmun, again writing for the Court, reasoned that in many cases people would be far more interested in information such as the competitive prices of prescription drugs than in political issues. In addition, even strictly commercial expression is dissemination of information valuable to the economy and society at large: "So long as we preserve a predominantly free enterprise economy, the allocation of our resources in large measure will be made through numerous private economic decisions. It is a matter of public interest that those decisions, in the aggregate, be intelligent and well informed."[31] Despite protecting commercial expression for the sake of the educational function of the media, the Court did place some restrictions upon that expression. Not all commercial speech is completely protected from government intrusion, the Court suggested; for example, regulations are acceptable in the area of untruthful advertising. The dissemination of purely commercial information, then, has at least some part to play in the educational function, as long as it is done responsibly.

In *Central Hudson Gas and Electric Corporation v. Public Service Commission of New York* in 1980, the Court expanded its explanation of what is and is not acceptable commercial expression. The Court held that the Public Service Commission of New York could not ban promotional advertising by the utility company, arguing that presentation of even one side of an issue aided public discussion: "[S]ome accurate information is better than no information at all."[32] Nevertheless, eight justices agreed that commercial speech has less protection than "other constitutionally guaranteed expression," for it is protected only because of its informational, or educational, value. If it is not informational or educational, or if it somehow detracts from that purpose, it can be regulated or banned. The first amendment is not compromised, wrote Justice Powell, in the case of "suppression of commercial messages that do not accurately inform the public about lawful activity."[33] If the expression is not misleading and concerns lawful activity, the government may restrict the expression only to achieve collective goals—and then only if the restriction is narrow and directly serves the government's purpose.

Not all the justices agreed with even this limited protection of commercial expression for the purpose of public education. Justice Rehnquist dissented in *Central Hudson*, as he had in *Virginia Board of Pharmacy*. In Rehnquist's view commercial expression did not have anything to do with the educational function of the media, and it should not be accorded protection under the first amendment. To Rehnquist, granting protection to commercial expression opened a "Pandora's Box," creating many problems and issues for which the first amendment had not been designed. While he believed strongly in the protection of political expression, Rehnquist was not willing to extend that protection to nonpolitical ideas. Political expression is protected only because of its role in self-government—the political function—Rehnquist maintained, and the educational function has little importance as far as the Constitution is concerned: "The free flow of information is important in this context not because it will lead to the discovery of any objective truth, but because it is essential to our system of self-government."[34]

The educational function, based upon the marketplace of ideas concept in which some "truth" is found through the competition of all ideas and opinions, provides a strong rationale both for protecting media freedom *and* for expecting certain behavior from the media. The educational function of the media, like the political function, operates both as a reason for media freedom and a larger rationale for expectations of media responsibility. The conflict between these two is inherent in the way the Court has viewed the functions of the media. Although the justices have argued that the first amendment protection of the media is nearly absolute (thus, very little responsibility can be expected), they have used the political and educational functions as the foundation of that protection—the first amendment provides protection *so that* the media can serve society.

In structuring their rationale for the first amendment this way, the justices use collectivist arguments and set up a policy, as Dworkin defines that term, rather than a principle. Policies establish collective goals, whereas principles guard individual rights. If the collective goals are not served, however, the protection resting on a policy can be revoked. In other words, if the media do not serve society's political and educational needs, they can be held responsible to do so. If the justices relied on a principle to justify the first amendment, however, protection for the media could be more absolute and expectations of responsibility lessened.

THE CANON OF TRUTH TELLING

Truth telling is key to both the Supreme Court's view of media responsibility and the media's view of their own role in U.S. society. Telling the truth—that is, representing various views as fairly and accurately as possible—about society is seen as a primary responsibility of the media, one about which the Court has thought carefully. Throughout the sixty-five years covered by this analysis, the Court commented many times on the value of accurate information and the special role the media play in presenting that information to the public. Over time, the justices articulated a conception of the role of truth telling as a part of the larger responsibility of the media. Journalists, according to the Court, should tell the truth, for that is part of their responsibility of enlightening the public. To ensure both self-government and the free marketplace of ideas, the Court usually was willing to protect some inaccurate information as inevitable and unavoidable in the search for truth. Thus, although the Court did require a minimum level of responsible behavior in the area of truth telling, unintentional mistakes, even harmful ones, were generally forgiven. Purposeful lying, however, was not. The Court has never condoned intentional misrepresentation, and has sometimes punished the media for this. According to the Court, journalists have a responsibility to tell the truth, to avoid mistakes whenever possible, and to avoid conscious lies.

Though the value here is the telling of truth, the justices admitted often that protecting truth also involves protecting mistakes of fact. The Court has protected inaccuracies, however, only because of their potential relation to the truth—some mistakes must be accepted to allow the press the fullest freedom to pursue truth. Genuine mistakes, while valueless themselves, are necessary to promote the larger good. As Justice White explained in one libel case, "The first amendment is not so construed, however, to award merit badges for intrepid but mistaken or careless reporting. Misinformation has no merit in itself; standing alone it is as antithetical to the purposes of the first amendment as the calculated lie. . . . The sole basis for protecting publishers who spread false information is that otherwise the truth would too often be suppressed."[35] Despite this limited protection for mistakes, some justices maintained that the media have responsibilities in the area of truth telling. Justice John Marshall Harlan, for example, in a 1967 case, wanted to hold the media to a standard of "reasonableness"; that is, he believed courts should require the media to make a reasonable attempt at truth telling, rather than simply forgive journalists for careless reporting leading to unintentional mistakes.[36] In another example, in the "Pentagon Papers case" of 1971, a dissenting Justice Blackmun scolded the *New York Times* and the *Washington Post* for forgetting their "duty" to the country:

I strongly urge, and sincerely hope, that these two newspapers will be fully aware of their ultimate responsibilities to the United States of America. . . . If, however, damage has been done [by the publication of documents concerning the Vietnam War] . . . and if, with the Court's action today, these newspapers proceed to publish the critical documents and there results therefrom . . . a prolongation of the war and of further delay in the freeing of U.S. prisoners, then the Nation's people will know where the responsibility for these sad consequences rests.[37]

And on occasion the majority of the Court has required responsible truth telling: In *Cantrell v. Forest City Publishing Co.* in 1974 eight justices voted against a newspaper that had, through known inaccuracies, created a false impression of a family surviving the tragic death of the husband and father. The reporter implied he had interviewed the mother, when in fact he had not, and he inaccurately described the family's living conditions. The Court concluded that these misrepresentations were undeserving of first amendment protection;[38] thus, in this case, the Court's minimum standard of responsibility was truth.

Telling the truth can mean more than just reciting accurate factual information. It can also mean presenting various perspectives, which taken together represent a "larger" truth about, or picture of, society. In cases examined, the Court used both definitions. For the most part, the media have been protected in their dissemination of truthful factual information, particularly concerning judicial[39] and other government proceedings.[40] But factual information has not received absolute protection. If a "substantial" state interest is involved, the Court has maintained, dissemination of truthful information might not be protected.[41] For example, the press is not guaranteed the right to publish information gathered through pretrial discovery, for that might violate the right to a fair trial.[42] In addition, the Court explicitly said in a 1989 case that all truthful information is not necessarily protected: "We do not hold that truthful publication is automatically constitutionally protected, or that there is no zone of personal privacy within which the State may protect the individual from intrusion by the press. . . . We hold only that where a newspaper publishes truthful information which it has lawfully obtained, punishment may lawfully be imposed, if at all, only when narrowly tailored to a state interest of the highest order."[43] Information not lawfully obtained, however, apparently is another question.

The second definition of truth telling, the presentation of various perspectives, also found proponents among the justices studied, though they typically articulated this definition in the call to protect newsgathering from unorthodox sources. In *Saxbe v. Washington Post* in 1974, a dissenting Justice Powell argued that the press needed face-to-face access to federal prison inmates in order to better report on conditions inside prisons. Only through in-person interviews, Powell contended, could journalists determine the credibility of their sources and thus pass along truthful information to the public.[44]

The journalist's relationship with sources arose in other cases as well. In a trio of 1972 cases involving requiring journalists to testify before grand juries about dissident groups or illegal activity (the Black Panthers in two cases, the making of illegal drugs in the third),[45] the majority ruled that journalists could be required to testify about their sources of information. However, three justices dissented angrily (a fourth dissented separately), arguing that the right to a confidential relationship with news sources was vital to the truth-telling canon. Wrote Justice Stewart, with the agreement of Justices Brennan and Marshall: "Familiarity with the people and circumstances involved in the myriad background activities that result in the final product called 'news' is vital to complete and responsible journalism, unless the press is to be a captive mouthpiece of 'newsmakers.'"[46] In other words, to be responsible, to uphold its truth-telling imperative, the press must be allowed to gather news from many perspectives and voices, for only in this way will a fuller "truth" be revealed.

While the Court defined the media's responsibility in this area as presenting both accurate factual information and diverse perspectives, over time it also developed a third definition of truth telling, illustrated best through the evolution of libel law after 1964. Libel cases by nature deal with the line between truth and falsehood. Both how and where the Court has drawn that line gives further insight into the justices' conceptions of media responsibility.

Federal constitutional libel law began with the Court's 1964 decision in *New York Times v. Sullivan*. The Court ruled that Montgomery, Alabama, Commissioner Louis Sullivan could not win a libel suit against the *Times* unless he could prove the newspaper published statements about him with what Justice Brennan called "actual malice"—"knowledge that [the statements were] false or with reckless disregard of whether [they were] false or not."[47] With one vote, the Court gave tremendous protection to the media in coverage of public officials. The media were safe from libel suits if they published true but unflattering statements, and also if they published false statements, if these were genuine mistakes.[48] But viewed from another perspective, *New York Times v. Sullivan* solidified aspects of prior libel law and the Court's own definition of media responsibility. The media would not be permitted to lie knowingly, nor would the Court allow them to be extremely careless with the reputations of public officials. Limited though these expectations of media behavior were, they did put the Court on a new path of defining responsibility.

Over time the justices dealt frequently with whether to protect the media when they disseminated false information. In 1967 the Court extended protection by requiring public figures involved in libel suits also to prove the press acted with actual malice—that it knowingly lied or was extraordinarily careless. Writing for the Court, Justice Harlan suggested that a responsible journalist was one acting reasonably: A public figure could recover damages from the press "on a showing of highly unreasonable conduct constituting an extreme departure from the standards of investigation and reporting ordinarily adhered to by responsible publishers."[49] Harlan defined responsibility as what other "responsible" publishers would do. Though an expression of the desirability of press responsibility, this was not a very helpful definition, noted Chief Justice Warren, who concurred in the case. By defining media irresponsibility in terms of "highly unreasonable conduct" and "extreme departure from the standards of . . . responsible publishers," the chief justice wrote, the Court had made the complicated definition of libel even more confusing, both for juries and the media.

Later cases came closer to a definition of media responsibility in the area of truth telling. In *Monitor Patriot v. Roy* in 1971, for example, the Court overturned a libel decision against a New Hampshire newspaper because the judge had instructed the jury to find against the newspaper if it found the "publication false and not made in good faith for justifiable purpose and with a belief founded on reasonable grounds of the truth of the matter published."[50] The press, therefore, did not have to exhibit good faith and justifiable reasons for publishing. And on the same day in 1971, the justices ruled in favor of *Time* magazine, which had in the course of interpreting a Civil Rights Commission report neglected to include the word "alleged" in reference to charges of brutality by a Chicago police detective. Though this was an unusual situation, the justices admitted, to require the media to accurately interpret what "somebody said" would hold it to too high a standard. As Justice Stewart explained, "The question of 'truth' of such an indirect newspaper report represents rather complicated problems. A press report of what someone has said about an underlying event of news value can contain an almost infinite variety of shadings. . . . Any departure from full direct quotation of the words of the source, with all its qualifying language, inevitably confronts the publisher with a set of choices."[51] And publishers, according to the Court, should be given leeway in making those choices; they should be defining their own responsibility.

Later in 1971 the justices extended media freedom even further by expanding the *New York Times* rule to include matters of general public interest.[52] Thus, even private individuals, those who were neither public officials nor public figures of any sort, had to prove knowledge of falsity or reckless disregard for the truth to win libel suits. Though the minimum definition of media responsibility held, the media did gain more freedom to be irresponsible as a result of this decision. But this standard of responsibility did not last long: Just three years later the Court reversed itself. In *Gertz v. Welch*, the justices held 5–4 that private individuals did not have to meet the difficult *New York Times* actual malice standard, after all. Private individuals would still have to prove the media acted negligently, though, with negligence to be defined by the various states. In creating the "negligence" standard and leaving the definition to the individual states, the Supreme Court in effect raised the level of expected responsibility.

This ruling provoked angry dissents from both sides of the responsibility issue. Chief Justice Warren Burger, arguing for lesser standards of media responsibility, contended that "negligence" was too vague a standard and that private individuals should still have to prove actual malice according to the *New York Times* standard. Justices Douglas and Brennan agreed and maintained in separate dissents that allowing states to define negligent behavior would harm freedom by requiring not only too much media responsibility, but too many varied definitions of it. However, Justice White argued for an even stricter standard of media responsibility, suggesting that the burden of proving negligent behavior would be too much for many private plaintiffs. When truly private individuals have been libeled, White wrote, the media should be responsible for their actions:

"The Court rejects the judgment of experience that some publications are so inherently capable of injury, and actual injury is so difficult to prove, that the risk of falsehood should be borne by the publisher, not the victim. . . . Under the new rule the plaintiff can lose, not because the statement is true, but because it was not negligently made."[53] To White, the media should tell the truth, and if they do not, they should be held accountable.

Throughout the 1970s and 1980s the Court continued to define further media's responsibility in the area of libel and truth telling. In *Time v. Firestone* in 1976, the justices refused to extend the *New York Times* actual malice test to all reports on judicial proceedings, choosing instead to retain the stricter standard of responsibility in cases involving private individuals. In this case involving a bitter divorce proceeding in a prominent industrial family, Justice Rehnquist wrote for the majority that *Time* magazine had not interpreted the divorce decree correctly. *Time*, Rehnquist noted, "must be able to establish not merely that the item reported was a conceivable or plausible interpretation of the decree, but that the item was factually correct."[54] Here the Court held *Time* to a strict standard of accountability: Rather than allowing the magazine to choose among interpretations of a confusing judicial decree, the justices insisted that *Time* choose the "correct" interpretation.

At other times, however, the Court was more lenient with the media. In another case involving a private figure, Justice Blackmun, concurring, wanted to give the media some breathing space. While accuracy is very important, he acknowledged, the necessities of gathering and checking information under a time constraint may mean journalists cannot be as careful as might be desired. "A reporter trying to meet his deadline," Blackmun wrote, "may find it totally impossible to check thoroughly the accuracy of his sources."[55] And in a suit concerning a consumer review of stereo speakers, the Court allowed inaccurate, but not reckless, statements, commenting that "the statement in this case represents the sort of inaccuracy that is commonplace in the forum of robust debate to which the *New York Times* rule applies."[56]

Thus the Court vacillated, with its expectations of media responsibility in the area of truth telling and libel depending in part upon the identity of the person defamed or the issue involved. In the mid-1980s these two came together in a suit involving a credit reporting firm's mistaken report that a building company had declared bankruptcy. The question in *Dun & Bradstreet v. Greenmoss Builders* was whether a libelous statement of no public interest should invoke the *New York Times* test or the stricter negligence standard. The justices ruled 5–4 that the negligence standard applied; thus, Greenmoss Builders had to prove only that the credit report was prepared carelessly, rather than recklessly or with knowledge of its falsity.

Important in this case are concurring opinions by Chief Justice Burger and Justice White, both of whom wanted to overturn the *Gertz* decision, which they argued did not demand enough press responsibility. Burger wanted to return to Justice Harlan's "reasonable care" standard outlined in 1967 in *Curtis v. Butts*, which had been expressly repudiated by the majority in *Rosenbloom v. Metromedia* in 1971. Actual malice under the *New York Times* standard could be defined adequately as a lack of reasonable care, Burger wrote, and the Court should reexamine its understanding and definition of this rule. Clearly, for Burger the Court had moved too far; its articulation of libel law did not require sufficient media accountability. As he explained: "The great rights guaranteed by the first amendment carry with them certain responsibilities as well."[57]

Justice White, too, wanted a return to stricter requirements of media responsibility, and suggested that in its ruling the Court had harmed media freedom by permitting irresponsible behavior. In his concurring opinion, White argued for a return to pre-*New York Times* state libel laws, which in his view had given the necessary protection to defamed individuals. Prior to the Court's decision in *New York Times* (which White had joined), individuals typically had to prove that "a false written publication" had exposed them to "hatred, contempt, or ridicule."[58] Plaintiffs had to prove falsity and defamation, White pointed out, but not actual malice, and injury to the individual's reputation was presumed. *New York Times* and later cases, White argued, had placed too much burden on defamed individuals and not enough responsibility on the media. This in turn harmed the media's function of examining the performance of government officials, because it allowed the media to win too many cases in which the statements were false. Circulation of false statements about public officials, he suggested, lessened the people's confidence in government. Thus the *New York Times* rule brought about "two evils: first, the stream of information about public officials and public affairs is polluted and often remains polluted by false information; second, the reputation and professional life of the defeated plaintiff [who could not prove actual malice despite the existence of false statements] may be destroyed by falsehoods that could have been avoided with a reasonable effort to investigate the facts."[59] The Court had gone too far, White thought, and in its determination to protect the political function of the media had greatly harmed that function by allowing too much media irresponsibility.

Though the Court did not take Justice White's advice about the *New York Times* standard, the discussion was not over. In 1986 White joined three colleagues dissenting in another private-person libel case. The five-justice majority in *Philadelphia Newspapers v. Hepps*, with Justice Sandra Day O'Connor writing the opinion, held that a private individual alleging defamation had to prove falsity if the issue was of public concern. This protected media whose statements could not be proved false. Justice John Paul Stevens, joined by White, Rehnquist, and Burger, dissented, arguing that the media should be responsible for their false and irresponsible statements. The majority's "pernicious result," wrote Stevens, would benefit only those media acting "negligently or maliciously." Placing such a heavy burden on the individual, and none on the media, allowed the press to "vilify private personages" and "contribute little to the marketplace of ideas." While the first amendment, wrote Stevens, requires libel plaintiffs to prove the media's fault and protects true statements, it does not, or should not, allow a "character assassin" to defame with statements that cannot be proved true or false.[60]

Finally, in the last two significant libel cases of this sixty-five-year period, the Court dealt again with the issue of media responsibility, and once again provided mixed messages. In *Milkovich v. Lorain Journal* in 1990, the Court held that all statements the media claimed to be "opinion" were not necessarily protected from libel suits. Instead, only "real" opinion enjoyed guaranteed constitutional protection.[61] Relying on earlier cases, Chief Justice Rehnquist, writing for the Court, noted that only provably false statements lost their constitutional protection. Thus, a "real" opinion would be protected, because a real opinion could not be proved false. Despite its strong protection of opinion, *Milkovich* considerably limited what statements could be considered opinion; thus, the decision required more accountability on the part of the media.

In the final libel case, *Masson v. New Yorker*, however, the Court returned to more protection, and consequently fewer expectations of responsibility, of the media. Here a writer for the *New Yorker* had apparently made up statements and attributed them to the subject of her story. Though some of what the subject had said was similar to the "quoted" material, the writer could not prove that the quoted material was in fact verbatim. The Court held that the quoted statements were not by themselves evidence of actual malice. It is unrealistic, explained Justice Anthony Kennedy for the Court, to expect print journalists to quote exactly what sources say: "The existence of both a speaker and a reporter; the translation between two media, speech and the printed word; the addition of punctuation; and the practical necessity to edit and make intelligible a speaker's perhaps rambling comments, all make it misleading to suggest that a quotation will be reconstructed with complete accuracy."[62] Though the Supreme Court returned the case to a lower court for further consideration, the justices made it very clear that in this situation the media were allowed some freedom of interpretation. Misquotes were evidence of actual malice, the Court ruled, only if they made a "material change" in the meaning of the actual words spoken. In this final libel case, then, the Court relieved the print media of the responsibility to quote sources exactly.

The libel cases demonstrate well the struggles the Supreme Court has had to define media responsibility in the area of truth telling. True statements are protected, for by definition they cannot be libelous. But false statements have no value in themselves; when they are protected, it is only to serve the greater good of the marketplace of ideas. The media do have some responsibility, but the only definition the entire Court agreed to over time was the responsibility not to lie knowingly. Beyond this simple requirement, the justices have articulated various conceptions of responsibility: Act with reasonable care, provide discussion on public issues, and present information fairly and from a variety of perspectives. But they never agreed on an overall theory of media responsibility with regard to truth telling.

THE CANON OF STEWARDSHIP

Though the Court primarily emphasized the canon of truth telling in the cases examined, stewardship also proved an important part of its discussions of media responsibility. As Lambeth explained, stewardship implies guardianship of rights—in this case, the first amendment and other rights, as well. In addition, stewardship as a more general term means accountability to others. Thus, stewardship as conceived by the Supreme Court involves two primary definitions: First, a general accountability required or expected of the media, and second, an expectation that the media will guard rights, both their own and those of others. More specifically, discussion of the concept of stewardship generally took one of three avenues in the cases studied: First, the Court expected the media, like any person or institution, to uphold minimum standards of acceptable behavior in order for society to function adequately. Second, the media are supposed to act as responsible guardian for the rights of individuals in society. This occasionally included Court demands of responsible behavior to protect even the first amendment. And third, the Court expected broadcasters to guard the airwaves, public resources with which they have been entrusted.

On the most basic level, the Court required generally responsible actions by the media. Though the justices recognized the value of protecting the media from strict requirements of behavior they, as individuals and sometimes as a group, also maintained that the media should uphold a basic level of responsibility. Justice Harlan, for example, argued for this basic level. However, his conception of minimum responsibility differed vastly from that of other justices. For Harlan the minimum standard involved the media acting with reasonable care not to harm others. Accidental harm was acceptable to him; but harm caused by carelessness was not. Lawyers and doctors, he suggested, operate under requirements not to harm people. Why should the media, just because they are protected by the first amendment, be any different? The first amendment, he wrote in 1976, "cannot be thought to insulate all press conduct from review and responsibility for harm inflicted. . . . [The press should be sanctioned when] it creates a severe risk of irremediable harm to individuals involuntarily exposed to it and powerless to protect themselves against it."[63]

While Harlan could find majority acceptance for his "reasonable care" standard in only one case,[64] other justices throughout the sixty-five years agreed with him in principle. For example, Justice Reed, writing for the Court in *Pennekamp v. Florida* in 1946, suggested that the media ought to be aware of the harm they could do and act to avoid it: "[T]here are areas of discussion which an understanding writer will appraise in the light of the effect on himself and on the public of creating a clear and present danger. . . . "[65] Justice Jackson, dissenting in 1952 in *Beauharnais v. Illinois*, noted that "more than forty" state constitutions protected media freedom but held the media responsible for abuse of that freedom.[66] Even Justice Douglas, normally a libertarian arguing for press freedom at all costs, at one point in 1961 quoted a "noted Jesuit" to argue that while prior restraint was simply unacceptable, anyone acting irresponsibly in the course of his or her freedom of expression could be "summoned after the fact to responsibility before the judgment of the law."[67]

Rarely, however, did the entire Court agree that media conduct had been so irresponsible that it should be sanctioned. One case in which the justices were unanimous about the media's reprehensible behavior involved the apparently deliberate avoidance of a source. In *Harte-Hanks Communications v. Connaughton* in 1989, all nine justices found evidence of actual malice on the part of the Hamilton, Ohio, *Journal News*. The *Journal News* supported an incumbent in a local judicial race. One month before the election, the incumbent's Director of Court Services resigned and was arrested on charges of bribery. During a grand jury investigation of those charges, a grand jury witness accused the incumbent's challenger, Connaughton, of offering her and her sister incentives for their help in the investigation. One week before the election, the *Journal News* published the witness' allegations, even though editors had reason to suspect her charges were untrue. In addition, according to the Court, the newspaper's editors deliberately failed to interview the witness' sister, apparently fearing that the sister would not corroborate the story. This was, wrote Justice Stevens for the entire Court, "an extreme departure from professional standards."[68]

Despite this condemnation, Stevens and the other justices were careful to note that "departure from professional standards," the equivalent of Justice Harlan's "reasonable care" standard, was not enough evidence of irresponsibility to tilt the case to the public official. Connaughton still had to prove actual malice, as the Court had outlined it in *New York Times v. Sullivan*. But in this case the *Journal News*' behavior qualified as actual malice. Six other grand jury witnesses had denied the charges against Connaughton. The only reason the *Journal News* could have had for not interviewing the sister, wrote Stevens, was that editors "had serious doubts concerning the truth of [the witness'] remarks" and suspected that the sister would confirm those doubts.[69] In addition to refusing to interview the sister personally, the newspaper staff also refused to listen to tape recordings of a conversation she had with Connaughton, tapes that could have confirmed or denied the charges. Further, the day before the *Journal News* published the accusations, the paper published an editorial intimating that "further information concerning the integrity of the candidates might surface in the last few days of the campaign."[70] This suggested, wrote Stevens, that the paper had already decided to publish the accusations, no matter what the grand jury decided. The newspaper, the Court concluded, had not met the minimum level of acceptable behavior required of it. While its "failure to investigate" was above the minimum standard and not evidence of actual malice, its "purposeful avoidance of the truth"[71] was unacceptable. In this case, at least, the entire Court agreed on a standard of responsibility.

The second aspect of the canon of stewardship involves the protection of rights, those found in the first amendment and others, as well. Specific admonitions by the Court to the media concerning the rights of others were relatively rare in the cases studied. Most of the free press/fair trial cases included some discussion of media rights versus those of a defendant, but often those discussions focused not on the media's responsibility in protecting the rights of others but on the right of the media to carry out their constitutional functions. Most of the Court's statements concerning the media's responsibility to guard the rights of others were part of larger discussions of the role of the media in performing the educational and political functions. For example, in *Estes v. Texas* in 1965, concerning whether or not television cameras should be allowed in courtrooms, Chief Justice Warren, concurring, noted that television, "like other institutions . . . must respect the rights of others and cannot demand that we alter fundamental constitutional conceptions for its benefit."[72] In *Harper and Row v. Nation Enterprises* in 1985, Justice O'Connor, writing for the majority, maintained that *The Nation* magazine, through its unauthorized publication of sections of former President Ford's memoirs, had intentionally violated "the copyright holder's commercially valuable right of first publication."[73] In *Bridges v. California* in 1941, Justice Frankfurter offered a similar opinion in a contempt of court case. The press did have a privilege to discuss public issues, he agreed, but it also had a responsibility to use that privilege wisely: "For the recognition of a privilege does not mean that it is without conditions or exceptions."[74] And in 1962 Justice Harlan argued that a sheriff's press release questioning a grand jury investigation into block voting by African-Americans was a dangerous use of press freedom. The sheriff, Harlan maintained, had "accused . . . Superior Court judges of fomenting race hatred; of misusing the criminal law to persecute and to intimidate political and racial minorities. . . . He compared the calling of the grand jury to the activities of the Ku Klux Klan. Speech creating a sufficient danger of an evil which the State may prevent may certainly be punished regardless of whether that evil materializes."[75] The rights of the people to conduct their criminal justice system, as well as the media's political function, were being harmed by the sheriff's activities, Harlan suggested.

Perhaps the best articulation of this conception of responsibility, however, was demonstrated in a 1945 case, *Associated Press v. United States*. The Court ruled that the Associated Press had violated the Sherman Anti-Trust Act by allowing its members to block membership of their local competitors. This effectively allowed member news organizations to keep their competition from receiving the Associated Press' news services. Lack of membership in the Associated Press could harm the ability of news organizations to compete in some markets. The Court, with Justice Black writing, held that the Associated Press' status as part of the press did not allow it to create monopolies in local markets, for this harmed the freedom of expression of nonmember news organizations. The first amendment, wrote Black, could not allow private organizations, any more than government, to harm constitutional rights:

It would be strange indeed however if the grave concern for freedom of the press which prompted adoption of the First Amendment should be read as a command that the government was without power to protect that freedom. The First Amendment, far from providing an argument against application of the Sherman Act, here provides powerful reasons to the contrary. That Amendment rests on the assumption that the widest possible dissemination of information from diverse and antagonistic sources is essential to the welfare of the public, that a free press is a condition of a free society. Surely a command that the government itself shall not impede the free flow of ideas does not afford non-governmental combinations a refuge if they impose restraints upon that constitutionally guaranteed freedom. Freedom to publish means freedom for all and not for some. Freedom to publish is guaranteed by the Constitution, but freedom to combine to keep others from publishing is not. Freedom of the press from government interference under the First Amendment does not sanction repression of that freedom by private interests.[76]

For Black and the rest of the five-justice majority, the political and educational functions required the media to guard the rights of others. To them media freedom carried a significant responsibility to the rest of society.

Though most of the Court's statements on this type of stewardship concerned protecting others' rights, on occasion individual justices argued that the first amendment itself could only be protected by requiring responsible behavior on the part of the media. While this may seem illogical, these justices believed that media behavior could irreparably harm the first amendment. Hence, the protection of freedom of expression as a principle became more important than protection of the freedom of any individual or news organization. One example of this can be found in Justice White's dissent in *Gertz v. Welch*, the libel case requiring private individuals to prove negligence—defined by the individual states—on the part of the media. Though this required more media responsibility than did public-plaintiff libel cases, it nevertheless took away from the states some power to define that responsibility. The new "negligence" standard, White maintained, gave too much protection to the media. "Under the new rule," he wrote, "the plaintiff can lose, not because the statement is true, but because it was not negligently made."[77] This "emasculation" of the state libel laws, he continued, would eventually harm the first amendment itself, by "provok[ing] a new and radical imbalance in the communications process" and by allowing the press to be irresponsible, which could result in caution by private individuals in "speaking out and concerning themselves with social problems. This would turn the first amendment on its head."[78]

In another example of the Court protecting the first amendment by requiring media responsibility, the majority agreed that allowing the media to "make up" statements and attribute them to sources would harm the first amendment. As already discussed, in *Masson v. New Yorker* a writer was accused of fabricating a source's statements. By doing so, argued Justice Kennedy for the Court, the writer implied that the words were the source's, not hers. The Court could have allowed journalists the freedom to place words in their sources' mouths, admitted Kennedy, but to do so would "diminish to a great degree the trustworthiness of the printed word. . . . Not only public figures but the press doubtless would suffer under such a rule. . . . We would ill serve the values of the First Amendment if we were to grant near absolute, constitutional protection for such a practice."[79] In other words, to allow the media to be irresponsible in this case would ultimately undermine the public trust in the media and thus the media's ability to perform their first amendment functions. The first amendment, according to the Court, depended upon media responsibility.

The third requirement of the media under the concept of stewardship is the protection of public resources, specifically the airwaves. This aspect of stewardship applies only to the broadcast media, which have been set apart under the first amendment. Because they use part of the electromagnetic spectrum, which theoretically belongs to all people, broadcast media have been required since their early days to act as public trustees or fiduciaries. Consequently, the courts and government have expected more responsible behavior from them. Nevertheless, the Supreme Court has also recognized that broadcast media, like print media, are protected from government intervention under the first amendment. The justices must continually balance this freedom with their concept of broadcasters as public trustees. Although the Court has heard many cases involving broadcasters and this conflict, an examination of several cases demonstrates the Court's various conceptions of the responsibility of the broadcast media.

In *Red Lion Broadcasting v. Federal Communications Commission* in 1969,[80] a classic example of the Warren Court's emphases on equal opportunity and affirmative interpretations of the first amendment, the Court ruled unanimously that radio stations could be required to provide free response time to individuals attacked on the air. Specifically, the Court upheld an F.C.C. order to that effect, arguing that F.C.C. regulations allowing replies to personal attacks enhanced first amendment values by providing both sides of a conflict. Though the radio station maintained that the F.C.C. requirement to provide free air time to an attacked individual harmed its constitutional freedom, the Court saw a larger good involved and limited the freedom of the station in order to enhance the overall marketplace of ideas and equality of opportunity. The Court, then, joined with the F.C.C. to require responsible behavior from the broadcast media.

Justice White, writing for his colleagues, argued that the F.C.C.'s policy was not only legal, but that it actually aided in the constitutional functions of the media. Broadcasters were obligated, he noted, to present issues of public controversy and to present them fairly. The essence of the policy, he pointed out, was an affirmative obligation on the part of broadcasters to make sure "both" sides of a controversy were presented.

Clearly the Court felt that the unique position of broadcasters as recipients of a public resource required them to act responsibly. A government-granted license did not give the broadcaster the right to impose her or his views on the listening audience. "A license permits broadcasting," wrote White,

but the licensee has no constitutional right to be the one who holds the license or to monopolize a radio frequency to the exclusion of his fellow citizens. There is nothing in the first amendment which prevents the Government from requiring a licensee to share his frequency with others and to conduct himself as a proxy or fiduciary with obligations to present those views and voices which are representative of his community.[81]

Broadcasters were obligated, therefore, to act in the best interests of the community, no matter what their own best interests might be.

The Court rested this requirement of responsibility squarely on the foundation of the two main functions of the press: political education and education about general social issues. The requirement that broadcasters uphold these two functions, because of broadcast media's nature as a public trustee, overrode even the first amendment's demands about government interference with the press. Justice White wrote:

It is the right of the viewers and listeners, not the right of the broadcasters, which is paramount. . . . It is the purpose of the first amendment to preserve an uninhibited marketplace of ideas in which truth will ultimately prevail, rather than to countenance monopolization of that market, whether it be by the Government itself or by a private licensee. . . . It is the right of the public to receive suitable access to social, political, esthetic, moral, and other ideas and experiences which is crucial here.[82]

Though over the next two decades the Court did not use *Red Lion* as a precedent for requiring even greater responsibility on the part of broadcasters, the case shows that at one point, at least, every justice agreed that broadcasters had a responsibility to their communities, based on their stewardship of public resources.

Four years later the Court again faced the question of broadcasters' obligation to provide an adequate marketplace of ideas. This time, however, the majority concluded that first amendment protection outweighed any fiduciary responsibility, and refused to require broadcasters to accept editorial advertisements. In *Columbia Broadcasting System v. Democratic National Committee*, the majority held that the F.C.C. could not interfere with the free speech of broadcasters, except when "the interests of the public are found to outweigh the private journalistic interests of the broadcasters."[83] This did not conflict with the holding in *Red Lion*, Chief Justice Burger reasoned, for the Court in that case had ruled that denial of a broadcasting license was not a denial of free speech. No one has a right to a license, he suggested; thus, to deny the license cannot be considered a denial of a right. Only after the license was granted, apparently, did the first amendment protect broadcasters.

Once Burger had dispensed with the issue of *Red Lion*'s applicability, he outlined his argument against requiring editorial advertisements. The broadcaster's responsibility is indeed to present issues fairly, he admitted, but it is also the broadcaster's right to decide how to do so. Broadcasters are allowed editorial discretion, explained Burger, for they know how best to cover social issues. "The initial and primary responsibility for fairness, balance, and objectivity," wrote

Burger, "rests with the licensee."[84] The F.C.C. is only to act as "overseer," ensuring that overall coverage is fair and balanced. To demand that broadcasters sell editorial time to various groups, in Burger's words, would "be antithetical to the very ideal of vigorous, challenging debate on issues of public interest."[85] Thus, broadcasters have the right to decide how to treat individual issues—and whether to sell editorial advertisements concerning those issues—coupled with the responsibility to provide balance in their overall coverage of all issues. The responsibility, therefore, is broad, affecting general coverage but not individual stories.

Justices Brennan and Marshall, usually strong proponents of allowing the media freedom to the exclusion of requirements of responsibility, in this case argued for "the people's right to engage in and hear vigorous public debate on the broadcast media."[86] By deciding that broadcasters could refuse to sell editorial advertisements, they argued, the majority was in fact harming public debate. While F.C.C. policy did require some responsibility of broadcasters, it did not go far enough, Brennan and Marshall maintained. F.C.C. policy obligated broadcasters to represent their community's views on issues. That, however, "tend[ed] to perpetuate coverage of those 'views and voices' that are already established, while failing to provide for exposure of the public to those 'views and voices' that are novel, unorthodox, or unrepresentative of prevailing opinion."[87] Requiring broadcasters to sell air time for editorial advertisements, Brennan and Marshall argued, would enhance public debate and uphold the fundamental responsibility of the media.

It is worth noting that in both *Red Lion* and *CBS v. DNC* Brennan and Marshall required broadcasters to provide an arena for public debate. Only in broadcast cases, however, did these two justices favor government intervention to promote media responsibility and an affirmative interpretation of the first amendment, for in their views only broadcasters carried a special responsibility. At first, their positions in these cases might seem to contradict their philosophies, particularly when compared to their ardent support of most other expression. But their stances make sense when the principles of late-twentieth-century liberalism are applied. Late-twentieth-century liberals value "equal concern and respect" of individuals. Applied to broadcast cases, this principle requires a concern for minority voices and a commitment to their protection. If broadcasters do not provide opportunity for minority views, reasoned the liberals, they need to be held accountable.

A later case vindicated Brennan and Marshall somewhat. In *Columbia Broadcasting System v. F.C.C.* the Court allowed the F.C.C. to revoke licenses of broadcasters who repeatedly refused to sell advertising time to "legally qualified candidates" for political office. The Federal Election Campaign Act of 1971 had required broadcasters to sell time to federal candidates, and in October 1979 the Carter-Mondale Presidential Committee requested thirty minutes on each of the three major networks, all of which refused. The F.C.C. ruled that all three networks had violated the Act, and the Supreme Court agreed.

Chief Justice Burger again wrote the majority opinion, but this time he leaned toward requiring more responsibility of the broadcast media. In passing the Election Campaign Act, Congress had outlined specific obligations broadcasters had to uphold to retain their licenses, obligations that included selling time to candidates during the campaign. Nevertheless, Burger argued, broadcasters still had some journalistic discretion. As long as they abided by their general obligation to sell time, they could refuse to sell ads if other factors were involved:

In responding to access factors, however, broadcasters may also give weight to such factors as the amount of time previously sold to the candidate, the disruptive impact on regular programming. . . . [But, to] justify a negative response, broadcasters must cite a realistic danger of substantial program disruption . . . or of an excessive number of equal time requests. . . . If broadcasters take the appropriate factors into account and act reasonably and in good faith, their decisions will be entitled to deference even if the Commission's analysis would have differed in the first instance.[88]

So, despite its ruling that the networks had violated their obligation, once again the Court required only general responsibility of broadcasters and refused to demand specific action. The Court expected broadcasters to present issues fairly, but left implementation of that requirement to their discretion. Broadcasters were still obliged to protect public resources, but the meaning of that protection had changed and the level of responsibility expected had diminished since the unanimous ruling in *Red Lion* twelve years before.

Stewardship, therefore, had three general meanings in cases analyzed: the media were expected to first, uphold a minimum standard of behavior; second, to protect the rights of others by acting as guardian for the public, including acting responsibly to protect the first amendment both for themselves and for society in general; and third, to act as trustee of the airwaves. This latter conception of stewardship reached its height in *Red Lion* and diminished slightly in succeeding cases. Nevertheless, the cases studied revealed a conception of stewardship as a general accountability of the media to the rest of society, and to the first amendment itself.

CONCLUSION

Examining how the Supreme Court has defined media responsibility over a sixty-five-year period by focusing on media functions and on significant canons of ethical journalism appearing in case decisions showed that the Court has valued the political and educational functions and defined press responsibility primarily in terms of truth telling and stewardship.

The canon of truth telling provided some of the clearest examples of the Court's expectations of media responsibility. The Court did not permit the media willfully to misrepresent factual information if that misrepresentation harmed an individual. In other words, the media cannot knowingly lie. In addition, the justices frowned upon inaccurate information of any kind, though they grudgingly accepted its inevitability in the performance of the media's educational and political functions. Expectations that the media must tell the truth were most obvious in libel cases.

The Court decisions also emphasized stewardship, which encompassed much of what the justices saw as appropriate behavior by the media. "Stewardship" to the Court meant both that the media will exhibit a general responsibility and that they will guard their rights and the rights of others. Like other institutions and individuals, the media must maintain a minimum level of responsibility to others in order for society to function.

Whereas the canons of truth telling and stewardship provided concrete examples of how the United States Supreme Court has defined media responsibility in its decisions, the two functions of the media provided both concrete and abstract illustrations of the Court's conceptions of media responsibility. Further, the Court's use of the political and educational functions to justify media freedom, rather than enhancing that freedom, led to certain conceptions of media responsibility and a seemingly unresolvable conflict.

The educational function of the media embodies the "marketplace of ideas" conception of media freedom: The media are protected so that they can present diverse perspectives on issues of public importance. If all perspectives are heard, people will be able to discern the "truth" and choose to follow it, thus benefiting society. According to the Court, this conception of the media's role means the media should be as free as possible to perform their educational function. In decisions studied, the Court protected nearly all true statements from the media and many false ones as well. Nevertheless, the Court occasionally limited the media's freedom in this area. Fabricating information—whether "direct quotes" or general description—is punishable. And the Court expected the broadcast media to uphold the affirmative conception of the first amendment by requiring them to present varying viewpoints on public issues. In every case involving the marketplace of ideas, the justices relied on the educational function as a rationale for the media's first amendment protection.

Justices used the same reasoning with the political function. The media are protected so they may serve the political system, through watching over government to keep it honest and explaining its workings. However, this function contains a contradiction: To represent the people and keep government honest, the media must be free from interference by government, including the court system. Yet the media are expected to perform their political function responsibly. Though for the print media this is only an expectation, broadcasters have been required to uphold the political function. Thus, the government, in the form of the F.C.C. and the courts, requires the broadcast media to watch the government. The media are "free" from government intervention, yet they are expected to uphold certain obligations. This conflict, present in the Supreme Court's articulations of both the political and educational functions, appears unresolvable.

The conflict arises because of the way the Court views media freedom. The cases studied show that, in their descriptions of media freedom, the justices almost always rationalized that freedom. The media are free to educate the public, to be a steward, to tell the truth, to serve the political system. Media freedom is never seen as an unconditional, or natural, right. As Hutchins Commission member William Hocking[89] explained, when reasons are given for the existence of rights, those "rights" become conditional. When they are conditional, they can be taken away if the conditions for their existence disappear. In Dworkin's view, they are not rights at all, but merely requirements of social policies.

The key to this conflict between the rights and responsibilities of the media, then, is the Court's reliance on policy rather than principle, or on a collectivist rather than an individualist rationale—in its articulation of media freedom. Following individualist theory, principles form the basis for rights and are moral requirements not grounded in any social need. Policies, on the other hand, are used to establish and enact collective goals. As such they are weaker than principles, for if the collective goal disappears or changes, so does the policy. To apply this to the current discussion, if the need for public education or the political function changed, the rationale for media freedom would disappear. Or, if the media did not uphold their function, if the collective goal of public education were not met, again theoretically, media freedom could be taken away. By relying on policy rather than principle, collectivist over individual, the Supreme Court leaves open the possibility that if the media are not responsible, their rights would be unnecessary.

This situation may be inevitable, however, because of the uniqueness of the constitutional requirement of press freedom. The rights granted the press are the only rights in the Constitution given to an institution.[90] All other rights belong to individuals. Dworkin's principle/policy distinction is based on the existence of individual, not institutional, rights. It is possible, certainly, that there can be no such thing as institutional rights, and that institutional freedoms must be based on collective goals or policies. If that is the case, then the conflict between media "rights" and responsibilities can be resolved in one of two ways. First, it could be acknowledged that there are no institutional rights and that the media's freedoms are indeed conditioned on satisfactory, responsible performance of their functions. Second, media rights could be seen as belonging only to individuals—not the institution—and thus be based on principles, in which case, little or no responsibility could be required. Either of these solutions would involve new conceptions of media freedom and responsibility.

NOTES

1. *Near v. Minnesota*, 283 U.S. 697 (1931).
2. Louis W. Hodges, "Defining Press Responsibility: A Functional Approach," *Responsible Journalism*, ed. Deni Elliott (Beverly Hills: Sage Publications, 1986), 28.

3. Edmund B. Lambeth, *Committed Journalism: An Ethic for the Profession* (Bloomington: Indiana University Press, 1992), 37.

4. *United States v. Caldwell*, 92 S.Ct. 2646, 2692 (1972), Justice Douglas, dissenting.

5. *Times-Picayune v. United States*, 73 S.Ct. 872, 877 (1953), Justice Clark, Court opinion.

6. *Rosenblatt v. Baer*, 383 U.S. 75, 94 (1966), Justice Black, concurring.

7. *Rosenblatt v. Baer*, 383 U.S. 75, 95 (1966), Justice Black, concurring.

8. *Bridges v. California*, 62 S.Ct. 190, 197 (1941), Justice Black, opinion.

9. *Hustler Magazine v. Falwell*, 108 S.Ct. 876, 881 (1988), Chief Justice Rehnquist, opinion.

10. *Miami Herald v. Tornillo*, 94 S.Ct. 2831, 2841 (1974), Justice White concurring.

11. *New York Times v. United States*, 91 S.Ct. 2140, 2143 (1971), Justice Black, concurring.

12. *Cox Broadcasting Corp. v. Cohn*, 95 S.Ct. 1029, 1044 (1975), Justice White, Court opinion.

13. *Cox Broadcasting Corp. v. Cohn*, 95 S.Ct. 1029, 1044 (1975), Justice White, Court opinion.

14. *Pennekamp v. Florida*, 66 S.Ct. 1029, 1037 (1946), Justice Reed, opinion.

15. *Craig v. Harney*, 67 S.Ct. 1249, 1258 (1947), Justice Murphy, concurring.

16. *Craig v. Harney*, 67 S.Ct. 1249, 1261 (1947), Justice Frankfurter, dissenting.

17. *Craig v. Harney*, 67 S.Ct. 1249, 1264 (1947), Justice Jackson, dissenting.

18. *Stroble v. California*, 72 S.Ct. 599 (1952); *Marshall v. United States*, 79 S.Ct. 1171 (1959); *Irvin v. Dowd*, 81 S.Ct. 1639 (1961); *Estes v. Texas*, 85 S.Ct. 1628 (1965); *Sheppard v. Maxwell*, 86 S.Ct. 1507 (1966); *Murphy v. Florida*, 95 S.Ct. 2031 (1975); *Mu'Min v. Virginia*, 500 U.S. 415 (1991).

19. *Estes v. Texas*, 85 S.Ct. 1628, 1631 (1965), Justice Clark, Court opinion.

20. *Estes v. Texas*, 85 S.Ct. 1628, 1636 (1965), Justice Clark, Court opinion.

21 *Abrams v. United States*, 250 U.S. 616 (1919), Justice Holmes, dissenting.

22. *Associated Press v. United States*, 65 S.Ct. 1416, 1428 (1945), Justice Frankfurter, concurring.

23. *Wood v. Georgia*, 82 S.Ct. 1364, 1372, 1373 (1962), Chief Justice Warren, Court opinion.

24. *First National Bank of Boston v. Bellotti*, 98 S.Ct. 1407, 1418 (1978), Justice Powell, Court opinion. Though the Court recognizes this "special role," it also admits that the media are not the only social institution protected to promote the marketplace of ideas.

25. On special protection from newsroom searches, see Justice Stewart's dissent (joined by Justice Marshall) in *Zurcher v. Stanford Daily* [98 S.Ct. 1970 (1978)]; on protection from grand jury testimony, see Stewart's dissent (joined by Justices Brennan and Marshall) in *Branzburg v. Hayes* [92 S.Ct. 2646 (1972)].

26. *Ginzburg v. United States*, 86 S.Ct. 942, 956 (1966), Justice Stewart, dissenting.

27. See *Pittsburgh Press Co. v. Pittsburgh Commission on Human Relations*, 93 S.Ct. 2553, 2565 (1973), Justice Douglas, dissenting.

28. *Hustler Magazine v. Falwell*, 108 S.Ct. 876, 880 (1988), Chief Justice Rehnquist, Court opinion.

29. *Rosenbloom v. Metromedia*, 91 S.Ct. 1811, 1823 (1971), Justice Brennan, plurality opinion.

30. *Bigelow v. Virginia*, 95 S.Ct. 2222, 2232 (1975), Justice Blackmun, Court opinion.

31. *Virginia State Board of Pharmacy v. Virginia Citizens Consumer Council*, 96 S.Ct. 1817, 1827 (1975), Justice Blackmun, Court opinion.

32. *Central Hudson Gas and Electric Corp. v.. Public Service Commission of New York*, 100 S.Ct. 2343, 2349 (1980), Justice Powell, Court opinion.

33. *Central Hudson Gas and Electric Corp. v.. Public Service Commission of New York*, 100 S.Ct. 2343, 2350 (1980), Justice Powell, Court opinion.

34. *Central Hudson Gas and Electric Corp. v. Public Service Commission of New York*, 100 S.Ct. 2343, 2368 (1980), Justice Rehnquist, dissenting.

35. *Ocala Star-Banner v. Damron*, 91 S.Ct. 628, 632-33 (1971), Justice White, concurring.

36. *Time v. Hill*, 87 S.Ct. 534, 553 (1967), Justice Harlan, dissenting. See also *Curtis Publishing Co. v. Butts*, 87 S.Ct. 1975 (1967), Justice Harlan, Court opinion.

37. *New York Times v. United States*, 91 S.Ct. 2140, 2165–66 (1971), Justice Blackmun, dissenting.

38. *Cantrell v. Forest City Publishing Co.*, 95 S.Ct. 465 (1974).

39. "The special protected nature of accurate reports of judicial proceedings has repeatedly been recognized," *Cox Broadcasting Corp. v. Cohn*, 95 S.Ct. 1029, 1045 (1975), Justice White, Court opinion; "Truthful reports of public judicial proceedings have been afforded special protection against subsequent punishment," *Nebraska Press Association v. Stuart*, 96 S.Ct. 2791, 2803 (1976), Chief Justice Burger, Court opinion.

40. "The article published by Landmark provided accurate factual information about a legislatively authorized inquiry . . . and in so doing clearly served those interests in public scrutiny and discussion of governmental affairs which the first amendment was adopted to protect," *Landmark Communications v. Virginia*, 98 S.Ct. 1535, 1542 (1978), Chief Justice Burger, Court opinion.

41. See *Smith v. Daily Mail Publishing Co.*, 99 S.Ct. 2667 (1979), Chief Justice Burger, Court opinion. Though the Court did rule in favor of dissemination of truthful information here, Burger noted that the Court did not hold that truthful information would always be protected.

42. *Seattle Times v. Rhinehart*, 104 S.Ct. 2199 (1984).

43. *Florida Star v. B.J.F.*, 109 S.Ct. 2603 (1989), Justice Marshall, Court opinion.

44. *Saxbe v. Washington Post*, 94 S.Ct. 2811 (1974).

45. The Black Panther cases were *In re Pappas* and *United States v. Caldwell*; the illegal drug case was *Branzburg v. Hayes*, 92 S.Ct. 2646 (1972).

46. *Branzburg v. Hayes*, 92 S.Ct. 2646, 2673 (1972), Justice Stewart dissenting.

47. *New York Times v. Sullivan*, 84 S.Ct. 710, 726 (1964), Justice Brennan, Court opinion.

48. Prior to this case, libel was defined by the states through their statutory, constitutional, and common law. Protection for libel varied tremendously across the United States, as did conceptions of the press' responsibility in the area of libel. See Norman L. Rosenberg, *Protecting the Best Men: An Interpretive History of the Law of Libel* (Chapel Hill: University of North Carolina Press, 1986).

49. *Curtis Publishing Co. v. Butts*, 87 S.Ct. 1975, 1991 (1967), Justice Harlan, Court opinion.

50. *Monitor Patriot v. Roy*, 91 S.Ct. 621, 625 (1971), Justice Stewart, Court opinion.

51. *Time v. Pape*, 91 S.Ct. 633, 637 (1971), Justice Stewart, Court opinion.

52. *Rosenbloom v. Metromedia*, 91 S.Ct. 1811 (1971).

53. *Gertz v. Welch*, 94 S.Ct. 2997, 3025 (1974), Justice White, dissenting.

54. *Time v. Firestone*, 96 S.Ct. 958, 968 (1976), Justice Rehnquist, Court opinion. In a footnote Rehnquist noted that *Time v. Pape* [mentioned above] did not apply in this case, because the presence of a private figure in this case meant the actual malice standard would not be used.

55. *Wolston v. Reader's Digest*, 99 S.Ct. 2701, 2709 (1979), Justice Blackmun, concurring.

56. *Bose Corp. v. Consumers Union of United States*, 104 S.Ct. 1949, 1966 (1984), Justice Stevens, Court opinion.

57. *Dun & Bradstreet v. Greenmoss Builders*, 105 S.Ct. 2939, 2948 (1985), Chief Justice Burger, concurring.

58. *Dun & Bradstreet v. Greenmoss Builders*, 105 S.Ct. 2939, 2948 (1985), Justice White, concurring.

59. *Dun & Bradstreet v. Greenmoss Builders*, 105 S.Ct. 2939, 2951 (1985), Justice White, concurring.

60. *Philadelphia Newspapers v. Hepps*, 106 S.Ct. 1558, 1566–68 (1986), Justice Stevens, dissenting.

61. *Milkovich v. Lorain Journal*, 110 S.Ct. 2695 (1990).

62. *Masson v. New Yorker Magazine, Inc.*, 110 S.Ct. 2419, 2432 (1991), Justice Kennedy, Court opinion.

63. *Time v. Hill*, 87 S.Ct. 534, 553–54 (1967), Justice Harlan, concurring and dissenting.

64. *Curtis Publishing Co. v. Butts*, 87 S.Ct. 1975, 1991 (1967). The majority later repudiated this as a test for determining when public officials and figures could win libel cases.

65. *Pennekamp v. Florida*, 66 S.Ct. 1029, 1037 (1946), Justice Reed, Court opinion.

66. *Beauharnais v. Illinois*, 72 S.Ct. 725 (1952), Justice Jackson, dissenting.

67. *Times Film Corp. v. City of Chicago*, 81 S.Ct. 391, 412 (1961), Justice Douglas, dissenting, quoting Murray, *We Hold These Truths*, 1960, 164–65.

68. *Harte-Hanks Communications v. Connaughton, Inc.*, 109 S.Ct. 2678, 2683 (1989), Justice Stevens, Court opinion.

69. *Harte-Hanks Communications v. Connaughton, Inc.*, 109 S.Ct. 2678, 2693 (1989), Justice Stevens, Court opinion.

70. *Harte-Hanks Communications v. Connaughton, Inc.*, 109 S.Ct. 2678, 2694 (1989), Justice Stevens, Court opinion.

71. *Harte-Hanks Communications v. Connaughton, Inc.*, 109 S.Ct. 2678, 2698 (1989), Justice Stevens, Court opinion.

72. *Estes v. Texas*, 85 S.Ct. 1628, 1651 (1965), Chief Justice Warren, concurring.

73. *Harper and Row v. Nation Enterprises*, 105 S.Ct. 2218, 2231 (1985), Justice O'Connor, Court opinion.

74. *Bridges v. California*, 62 S.Ct. 190, 203 (1941), Justice Frankfurter, dissenting.

75. *Wood v. Georgia*, 82 S.Ct. 1364, 1378 (1962), Justice Harlan, dissenting.

76. *Associated Press v. United States*, 65 S.Ct. 1416, 1424–25 (1945), Justice Black, Court opinion.

77. *Gertz v. Welch*, 94 S.Ct., 2997, 3025 (1974), Justice White, dissenting.

78. *Gertz v. Welch*, 94 S.Ct., 2997, 3036 (1974), Justice White, dissenting.

79. *Masson v. New Yorker Magazine, Inc.*, 110 S.Ct. 2419, 2434 (1991), Justice Kennedy, Court opinion.

80. *Red Lion Broadcasting v. Federal Communications Commission*, 89 S.Ct. 1794 (1969).

81. *Red Lion Broadcasting Co. v. Federal Communications Commission*, 89 S.Ct. 1794, 1806 (1969), Justice White, Court opinion.

82. *Red Lion Broadcasting Co. v. Federal Communications Commission*, 89 S.Ct. 1794, 1806–07 (1969), Justice White, Court opinion.

83. *Columbia Broadcasting System v. Democratic National Committee*, 93 S.Ct. 2080, 2090 (1973), Chief Justice Burger, Court opinion.

84. *Columbia Broadcasting System v. Democratic National Committee*, 93 S.Ct. 2080, 2094 (1973), Chief Justice Burger, Court opinion.

85. *Columbia Broadcasting System v. Democratic National Committee*, 93 S.Ct. 2080, 2095 (1973), Chief Justice Burger, Court opinion.

86. *Columbia Broadcasting System v. Democratic National Committee*, 93 S.Ct. 2080, 2121 (1973), Justice Brennan, dissenting.

87. *Columbia Broadcasting System v. Democratic National Committee*, 93 S.Ct. 2080, 2130 (1973), Justice Brennan, dissenting.

88. *Columbia Broadcasting System v. F.C.C.*, 101 S.Ct. 2813, 2825–26 (1981), Chief Justice Burger, Court opinion.

89. See William Hocking, *Freedom of the Press: A Framework of Principle* (Chicago: University of Chicago Press, 1947).

90. Many have argued that media rights belong not to the institution but to practitioners and media owners. The Court, however, has described this as an institutional right.

Chapter Two

The Early Years, 1931–1953

The political and educational functions and the truth telling and stewardship canons each have provided the Supreme Court ways to explain its views on the media and their connection to society. This chapter and the next three examine the Court's views from the perspective of time. Select media cases are discussed in chronological order, with an emphasis on the views of both the Court as a body and several individual justices. These chapters address the questions of how and if the overall conflict between individualism and collectivism—as demonstrated in the libertarian/social responsibility, liberal/conservative, natural law/legal positivism, and negative/affirmative freedoms debates—affected Court conceptions of media responsibility, and whether any dominant view of media responsibility prevailed over time.

First, changes in the Court's conceptions over time were analyzed, with particular attention to the conservative-liberal-conservative shift the Court made from the 1930s to the 1990s. Second, cases were grouped by topic within those eras, because often the Court decided a number of similar cases within a short period of time. Third, the philosophies of a few individual justices were examined, as were those of cohesive groups of justices. The purpose was to discover long- and short-term trends in the justices' conceptions of media responsibility by considering the impact of their judicial and political philosophies as well as the characteristics of the Court during the eras under study.

These four chapters are organized around definable eras of the Court. Chapter Two focuses on the early years of the Court's examination of media roles and responsibilities, encompassing the years 1931 to 1953. Within this two-decade period there was dramatic change in American society and within Court philosophy, change reflected in the justices' decisions on media responsibility. Chapter Three covers the period 1953 to 1969, the "Warren Court" era, which has been characterized as the most liberal era of the Supreme Court. Chapter Four begins with the dawn of the "third conservative era" of the Court, as defined by historian Russell Galloway, and takes the Court from 1969 to the beginning of the Reagan presidency in 1981. Finally, Chapter Five examines the years from 1981 to 1996, encompassing the first decade of the Rehnquist Court and the recent appointments of more liberal justices.

THE END OF LAISSEZ FAIRE, 1931–1937

The "second conservative era" of the Supreme Court, lasting from about 1890 to the majority's apparently sudden acceptance of Franklin Roosevelt's New Deal programs in 1937,[1] was characterized by the development of a laissez-faire interpretation of the Constitution, in which Court majorities continually thwarted governmental attempts to regulate business and economics. Judicial emphasis on laissez-faire policy was nearing its end by 1931, and throughout the 1930s the Court was in transition to the next stage, the second liberal period. Nevertheless, until 1937 traditional conservatives tended to dominate the Court, favoring the right to property and frowning upon government intervention in the business of business.

The Court actually was split into three factions. Willis Van Devanter, James McReynolds, George Sutherland, and Pierce Butler (known collectively as the "Four Horsemen") comprised the "conservative" wing, and were pro-laissez faire. Louis Brandeis, Harlan Fiske Stone, and Benjamin Cardozo (called the "Three Musketeers") were the "liberals," who approved of federal economic regulation; Chief Justice Charles Evans Hughes and Owen Roberts provided the swing votes. Their differences were not party-related, for Van Devanter, Sutherland, Stone, Hughes, and Roberts were Republicans, while McReynolds, Butler, Brandeis, and Cardozo were Democrats. Instead, the difference was geographical, according to Court historian C. Herman Pritchett, who explained:

Van Devanter from Wyoming, McReynolds from Tennessee, Sutherland from Utah, Butler from Minnesota—all had 'grown up and made great careers for themselves out of the pioneer life of the frontier.' . . . In contrast, the other five justices had built their careers in Boston, Philadelphia, New York—far from the frontier, where men were more accustomed to the limitations imposed by a settled community and to the use of public instrumentalities for community purposes.[2]

In addition, the Four Horsemen shared more than a frontier heritage. Each had been involved, before his term on the Court, in reform movements: Sutherland and Butler in worker's compensation, McReynolds in trust busting, and Van Devanter in public-land management. And they were connected by "the ideological convictions of their early maturity." All were born around the time of the Civil War (the earliest in 1859, the last in 1866) and educated in the 1880s during the rise of the laissez-faire legal tradition: For them, "the universe was governed by inexorable laws; certain rights were inalienable; the Constitution was an unchanging document; the judiciary was a refuge against the excesses of the populace."[3]

The split in judicial philosophy on the Court was deep. The conservatives used their votes to overturn most federal legislation that aided the working class or protected individual rights against those of business. These activist justices, however, viewed *state* intervention in business as acceptable and allowed states a freer rein over regulation of the business class. Still, even at the level of state regulation, these four did not necessarily favor individual rights—other than the right to property. The three liberals, on the other hand, saw state and federal intervention as necessary, for only through legislation would business agree to provide wage minimums, work-hour maximums, and other pro-worker concessions. Thus, these justices viewed individual rights other than that of property as paramount.

While the period from 1931 to 1937 marked a transition on the Court, the limited number of cases in these six years involving discussion of media responsibility preclude drawing any definitive conclusions about the Court's views on the topic. Nevertheless, three cases provide interesting debate on the issue, at least indirectly, for all dealt with the meaning of the right of press freedom: *Near v. Minnesota* and *Associated Press v. National Labor Relations Board*, and to a lesser extent an early broadcast case, *Federal Radio Commission v. Nelson Brothers Bond and Mortgage Co.*, demonstrated the deep division within the Court.

Near v. Minnesota marks the beginning of the Court's attempts to define media freedom, both generally and with regard to media responsibility, and it provides an excellent example of the liberal/conservative conflict. The liberals, joined by the two moderates, voted to protect the individual right to publish. The conservatives, however, voted against that right, choosing instead to favor a collectivist interpretation of the first amendment and a particular conception of the good—that is, a definite idea of what values society should hold. Minneapolis publisher Jay Near, whose newspaper had been shut down when he violated a state "nuisance" law by publishing "malicious, scandalous, and defamatory" information, appealed the case with the help and financing of the *Chicago Tribune*'s publisher. Chief Justice Hughes and Justice Roberts joined the Court's three liberals—Brandeis, Stone, and Holmes—to rule that Minnesota had to uphold the first amendment's protections. Near, who indeed published scandalous and malicious material, thus gained the right to print freely.

In this case, therefore, the majority allowed irresponsible behavior by the media, finding that the principle of freedom overruled a desire by society to inhibit this type of publication. Hughes acknowledged this dilemma in his opinion for the Court: "[T]he authority of the state to enact laws to promote the health, safety, morals, and general welfare of its people is necessarily admitted. . . . Liberty of speech and of the press is also not an absolute right, and the state may punish its abuse."[4] But some irresponsible behavior had to be tolerated, Hughes continued, and Near's actions were no worse than actions of printers in the days of the first amendment's passage: "While reckless assaults upon public men, and efforts to bring obloquy upon those who are endeavoring faithfully to discharge official duties, exert a baleful influence and deserve to severest condemnation in public opinion, it cannot be said that this abuse is greater, and it is believed to be less, than that which characterized the period in which our institutions took shape."[5] For the majority, then, some irresponsibility on the part of the media was an inevitable, though undesirable, consequence of media freedom.

The four conservatives disagreed. The right of the state to govern as it chose had been violated, they argued, in a classic conservative statement: "It is of the greatest importance that the states shall be untrammeled and free to employ all just and appropriate measures to prevent abuses of the liberty of the press,"[6] wrote Justice Butler. Near's actions had harmed "the morals, peace, and good order" of society, and the state should have been allowed to silence him. The conservatives, then, were articulating a conception of the good (a typically conservative gesture), or at least were arguing that the state should be permitted to do so. Press freedom had limits: When it conflicted with the needs of society to maintain public morals, whatever those might be, it could be subordinated to society's needs.

The second case of this time period, *Federal Radio Commission v. Nelson Brothers Bond and Mortgage Co.*, brought the nine justices together in a statement subordinating the rights of broadcasters to the needs of the community. The Commission had terminated Nelson Brothers' license to operate a Chicago radio station because a station in nearby Gary, Indiana, had wanted that particular radio frequency. The Gary station provided service to new immigrants, including education and information in various non-English languages represented by Gary's largely immigrant population. It was the only station in Gary, and because of its service to its community and the fact that Chicago residents could receive the same material from other stations that they had received from Nelson Brothers, the Commission ruled for the Gary owners. The Supreme Court agreed, focusing on the power of Congress and the Commission to delete stations and assign radio frequencies. Nelson Brothers had no right to a particular frequency, the Court ruled, for government regulation of broadcasting was acceptable and could override owners' wishes: "Those who operated broadcasting stations had no right superior to the exercise of [the power of Congress to regulate broadcasting]. They necessarily made their investments and their contracts in light of, and subject to, this paramount authority."[7] Though it seems logical for the Court liberals to agree with this outcome, allowing government intervention to serve the needs of immigrant groups, it is surprising that the conservatives agreed. The absence of concurring opinions, however, makes it impossible to suggest why they permitted the federal government to interfere with private businesses.

Shortly after the justices decided *Nelson Brothers*, the first of the "New Deal cases" began to arrive on the Court's docket, exacerbating the Court's split. These cases tested the constitutionality of President Roosevelt's federal New

Deal legislation. True to their political philosophy, the Four Horsemen resisted federal and some state attempts at business regulation, while the three liberals generally supported those attempts. The first test of "legislation having a New Deal tinge"[8] came in *Home Building and Loan Association v. Blaisdell*,[9] the so-called "Minnesota Moratorium case." The state of Minnesota had allowed moratoriums to be placed on foreclosures, allowing debtors up to two years to pay off creditors. Chief Justice Hughes, writing for the Court, upheld the statute as a constitutional state action (Sutherland, Van Devanter, Butler, and McReynolds dissented). The same year, in *Nebbia v. New York*,[10] the Court majority (Stone, Brandeis, and Cardozo, joined by Hughes and Roberts) upheld a New York statute establishing minimum prices for milk. The split among the three factions is clear in these cases. Fence-sitters Hughes and Roberts joined the "liberal" faction to uphold state statutes.

When national legislation appeared before the Court, however, Hughes and Roberts changed their positions. In 1935 the Court declared the National Industrial Recovery Act (NIRA) unconstitutional in *Schechter Poultry Corporation v. United States*,[11] arguing that "Congress afforded no constitutional justification for NIRA . . . [and that] NIRA delegated legislative power unconstitutionally."[12] In 1936 the Court overturned the Bituminous Coal Conservation Act, "legislation designed to bring order to one of the most chaotic industries in the United States,"[13] in *Carter v. Carter Coal Company*;[14] in that same year the Court set aside the Agricultural Adjustment Act in *United States v. Butler*.[15] So by 1936 the split was 6–3, with Hughes and Roberts joining the "conservative" faction against national New Deal legislation.

Before the 1936 election, therefore, the Court was divided over New Deal legislation, with Stone, Cardozo, and Brandeis favoring it in dissent time after time. President Roosevelt, whose hands were tied by the Court, unveiled a plan he thought would enable New Deal legislation to pass judicial review. On February 5, 1937, three months after his landslide reelection, he announced a proposal to appoint one justice to the Court for every justice who reached the age of seventy but did not retire, up to a limit of fifteen justices total. Because six justices were already over seventy, he immediately would have been able to appoint six justices and gain a majority favoring the New Deal. On March 27, the Court upheld a Washington state minimum wage law, reversing a ruling from the previous year.[16] Then on April 12, the Court upheld the National Labor Relations Act,[17] which it had declared unconstitutional in *Carter v. Carter Coal Company*. These decisions proved to be the end of the "Court-packing" plan, for it appeared that Roosevelt had won, and within two years he had a majority on the Court.[18]

The change had come without any change in personnel on the Court. The two extreme factions maintained their positions; instead, it was Chief Justice Hughes and, more importantly, Justice Roberts who performed the so-called "switch in time that saved nine." While many historians attribute the switch to Roosevelt's Court-packing plan, Murphy, Fleming, and Harris argue that the change actually came before the plan was announced in February 1937. The justices, they contend, saw the 1936 election as a popular mandate for the New Deal and decided that the citizens of the United States clearly wanted Roosevelt's plans implemented:

By early December 1936, the justices began to capitulate. Roberts changed his mind first on the constitutionality of state regulation of wages (*West Coast Hotel v. Parrish*, 1937), then on the reach of the commerce clause, and later on the authority of the federal government to tax in order to regulate. Because these changes began in December 1936 in the justices' secret conferences, months before they were publicly announced, Roosevelt had no way of knowing that he was winning the war. In February 1937 he launched his plan. . . . Ultimately, the Court-packing bill failed to pass either house of Congress; but when the Court's shift became public that spring, it seemed that the justices had retreated under fire.[19]

Finally—or at least for the duration of Roosevelt's presidency—the Court had begun to abandon laissez faire.

The conservative wing was in form in the next media case, however. In April 1937, just after the "Court-packing" incident, the Court split 5–4 in *Associated Press v. National Labor Relations Board* (N.L.R.B.), with the liberal wing upholding workers' rights and holding business (in this case, the Associated Press) accountable to those rights, while the conservatives favored business rights. In this case, therefore, the traditional views of the liberals and conservatives led the former to require press responsibility and the latter to deny it. The Associated Press had dismissed an employee involved in labor organizing, but denying that as the reason for his dismissal. The N.L.R.B. consequently ordered the Associated Press to rehire the employee with back pay. However, the Associated Press had argued that the N.L.R.B.'s interference with its decisions about whom to employ violated its freedom. Because of his union activity, Associated Press maintained, the employee could not be objective in his work (he was an editor); thus, to keep him employed would harm the quality of the Associated Press' news product. But the Court majority did not agree. The two moderates, Hughes and Roberts, joined with the liberal wing to hold that the Associated Press could not discriminate based on union activity. The Associated Press had to uphold laws, just like any other business, wrote Justice Roberts: "The business of the Associated Press is not immune from regulation because it is an agency of the press. The publisher of a newspaper has no special immunity from the application of general laws. He has no special privileges to invade the rights and liberties of others."[20] The press, the majority warned, would be held to the same standards of accountability as would any business.

The conservatives, on the other hand, articulated a classical laissez-faire argument against government interference in business, using the first amendment to bolster their views. The first amendment does not allow exceptions to its prohibition against government intervention, wrote Justice Sutherland. Freedom of the press is one of the "fundamental" freedoms protected by the Bill of Rights, he argued, and government interference with it would render it meaningless. "If freedom of the press does not include the right to adopt and pursue a policy without government restriction, it is a misnomer to call it freedom."[21] To the conservatives, the first amendment required that the press be free to manage its own affairs, including the hiring and firing of employees. The press, therefore, was also free to be irresponsible, if it so chose.

Though one cannot generalize from only three cases, these early media decisions show the split within the Court over the roles and responsibilities of the media. In *Near,* the conservatives voted for press responsibility while the liberals argued for media freedom, whereas in *Associated Press* the liberals demanded accountability and the conservatives used media freedom to argue for protection of a business.

There are several possible reasons for this apparent reversal of expectations among justices. First, as Paul Murphy has pointed out,[22] in *Near* the conservatives were protecting business—not the media, but the "legitimate" businesses that Near's paper had vilified—whereas the liberals were protecting individual freedom. Second, the *Near* case involved state legislation, which the conservatives, who favored states rights over the reach of the federal government, were less inclined to overturn, while the statute in *Associated Press* was federal. In addition, the liberals in *Associated Press* were protecting the individual rights of the employee from the threat of big business. When seen this way, these cases make more sense together. In both situations, the Court's liberal faction promoted equality of the individual, though it used different methods to achieve that value, while the conservatives promoted the independence of "decent" businesses. Responsibility, however, was not a unifying factor. In these cases, the more fundamental values of the liberals (promoting equality) and of the conservatives (promoting laissez faire) had priority over media responsibility. Here, the justices' conceptions of media responsibility, or lack thereof, were a result of their overall philosophies.

THE TRANSITION YEARS, 1937–1953

The U.S. Supreme Court's "second liberal era," heralded in such cases as *Near* as well as in the switch from a laissez-faire perspective on government intervention in the economy, began in earnest as the result of an effort by Associate (later Chief) Justice Harlan Fiske Stone, who in 1938 in a footnote in an otherwise uneventful case outlined what later became the "preferred freedoms" or "reinforcing representative democracy" theory of the Constitution. This footnote suggested that though most legislation would continue to be presumed constitutional by the Court, legislation that infringed upon certain rights—speech, press, religion, assembly, and other rights protected by the first ten amendments—would have to meet stricter standards to be considered constitutional.

Stone's footnote symbolically ushered the Supreme Court into a new age, one in which individual rights and equality were valued more highly than the rights of property. Though there were times of conservatism during this era (for example, the Japanese internment and Cold War cases), the overall emphasis over the next several decades was one of expanding rights and liberties, including the right of a free press. This era encompassed U.S. involvement in three wars and the beginning of the Cold War, the rise and threat of totalitarianism in Europe, the Civil Rights Movement in the United States, five presidents, four chief justices, and hundreds of Supreme Court cases. This era reached its peak in the years of the Warren Court (1953–1969) and is perhaps best characterized by the unanimous ruling in *Brown v. Board of Education*, in which the Court overturned the separate-but-equal doctrine as unconstitutional, at least with regard to public schooling. The liberal era began to decline with the resignations of Chief Justice Earl Warren and Associate Justice Abe Fortas and the election of Richard Nixon as president in 1969.

If the 1937 shift in emphasis by the Court signaled the end of one era, Stone's articulation of the preferred freedoms doctrine in 1938 signaled the beginning of the next. Footnote number four in *Carolene Products v. United States*[23] came shortly after the Court's about-face in the Court-packing incident. The result of that incident was a tendency on the part of the Court to presume state and federal statutes constitutional. The justices faced a dilemma, explain Murphy, Fleming, and Harris: "If they were to presume economic regulation constitutional, why not all regulation? On what principles could they draw lines?"[24] The footnote, which became the Court's attempt to draw those lines, states:

4. There may be narrower scope for operation of the presumption of constitutionality when legislation appears on its face to be within a specific prohibition of the Constitution, such as those of the first ten amendments, which are deemed equally specific when held to be embraced within the Fourteenth. See Stromberg v. California (1931); Lovell v. Griffin (1938).

It is unnecessary to consider now whether legislation which restricts those political processes which can ordinarily be expected to bring about repeal of undesirable legislation, is to be subjected to more exacting judicial scrutiny under the general prohibitions of the Fourteenth Amendment than are most types of legislation. On restrictions upon the right to vote, see Nixon v. Herndon [1927]; Nixon v. Condon [1932]; on restraints upon the dissemination of information, see Near v. Minnesota [1931]; Grosjean v. American Press Co. [1936]; Lovell v. Griffin [1938]; on interferences with political organizations, see Stromberg v. California [1931]; Fiske v. Kansas [1927]; Whitney v. California [1927]; Herndon v. Lowry [1937]; and see Holmes, J. in Gitlow v. New York [1925]; as to peaceable assembly, see De Jonge v. Oregon [1937].

Nor need we inquire whether similar considerations enter into the review of statutes directed at particular religious, Pierce v. Society of Sisters [1925]; or national, Meyer v. Nebraska [1923]; Bartels v. Iowa [1923]; Farrington v. Tokushige [1927]; or racial minorities, Nixon v. Herndon [1927]; Nixon v. Condon [1932]; whether prejudices against discrete and insular minorities may be a special condition, which tends seriously to curtail the operation of those political processes ordinarily thought to be relied upon to protect minorities, and which may call for a correspondingly more searching judicial inquiry.[25]

In essence, the "preferred freedoms" doctrine (or "reinforcing representative democracy" doctrine, as it later came to be known), explained that the United States is a representative democracy in which the people have a right to govern themselves through their elected representatives. Therefore, the courts should presume that legislation enacted by the people through their representatives is constitutional, because the people are the ultimate interpreters of the Constitution. This is the essence of the democratic theory of constitutional interpretation. But there was still a problem: The majority could conceivably revoke the rights of the minority, if representative democracy were taken to an extreme.[26] Therefore, the argument was made, there are certain situations in which constitutionality cannot be presumed, including "when legislation restricts rights to free political communication and open political processes; and second, when legislation singles out for disadvantage minorities who lack political power."[27]

The footnote, which "has become the centerpiece of latter-day constitutional interpretation,"[28] gave for the first time *special* constitutional protection to the rights of free speech and press. According to current constitutional interpretation, rights, including speech and press, are protected by the doctrine of "strict judicial scrutiny." This means the Court applies a two-part test to any legislation appearing to inhibit these "fundamental" rights: first, any infringement on fundamental rights must be because of a "compelling"—as opposed to a "reasonable"—state interest. Second, if the state's interest is compelling, it must accomplish its goals through the least restrictive means possible. Here, in *Carolene Products*, the Court finally began to give fundamental rights the protection Dworkin argues for when he makes his principles/policy distinction; and this made possible later influential decisions on the role of the press in American society.

The 1930s were crucial years for the press clause of the first amendment. Most obvious, of course, is the Court's commitment to a free press as a "fundamental" right, as outlined in *Carolene Products*. This conception of the right of free press has been apparent in many cases through the years, as the Court began balancing the rights of free press and speech against other rights, with the weight in favor of speech and press. During the 1930s, freedom of the press began to be seen less strictly as a policy right—overridable if need be—and potentially as a principle right—overridable only in extreme circumstances. The Court actually seldom regarded freedom of the press as a principle in practice, but the possibility of viewing it that way exists because of *Carolene Products*.

The second liberal period began, then, with an abrupt, significant change in constitutional doctrine as applied to press freedom. Individual freedoms, including that of the press, would be given special consideration. Though the 1938 Court had articulated the new doctrine, it remained for later Courts to interpret and apply it. The Hughes, Vinson, and Warren courts did that, with ever-greater emphasis on protection of individual rights.

The Stone Court, 1941–1946

President Herbert Hoover appointed Charles Evans Hughes Chief Justice of the United States in 1930. He had already spent six years as an associate justice—President William H. Taft had named him to the Court in 1910, but he resigned to run as the Republican presidential candidate in 1916. In the meantime Hughes had served as Secretary of State from 1921 to 1925. His primary goal as chief justice was to put forth the image of a stable, moderate Court; he wanted to hide the growing split between the liberal and conservative factions. As time passed, however, the Court's stability decreased, partly because of events beyond its walls. Between 1931 and 1937, only one seat on the Court changed, when Benjamin Cardozo replaced Oliver Wendell Holmes in 1932. But in those same six years, America's economic woes worsened, Franklin Roosevelt and his New Deal were voted into office twice, and fascism gained a hold in Europe. The world changed, but an elderly Court—only one of whom had graduated from law school in the twentieth century—marched on under nineteenth-century assumptions and views.[29] Eventually the world and the Court clashed.

The initial result of this clash was the switch in 1937 and the increased emphasis on preferred freedoms in 1938. The liberals on the Court rapidly gained strength after 1938; between the beginning of the 1937 term (fall, 1937) and the middle of the 1939 term five justices retired and were replaced by Roosevelt appointees. The spring following the switch, Willis Van Devanter retired and was replaced by the liberal Hugo Black. The following winter (January 1938), Stanley Reed replaced another of the Four Horsemen, George Sutherland. One year later, in January 1939, Felix Frankfurter replaced Benjamin Cardozo, who died during summer 1938. Three months later (April 1939), William O. Douglas joined the Court, replacing Louis Brandeis, and in January 1940 Frank Murphy took the seat of Pierce Butler. So within three years of the switch, only one of the Four Horsemen remained, and he, James McReynolds, retired not long after, in 1941.

So by 1941, when Harlan Fiske Stone replaced Hughes as chief justice, the Court had undergone a transformation, of which Stone was an integral part. The Court had, in answer to the legislative response to the Depression, discarded nearly half a century of doctrine and returned to the states and Congress the freedom to enact economic legislation with little resistance from the courts. The doctrine of liberty of contract had all but disappeared, and the taxing, commerce, and spending powers of Congress had been reaffirmed.[30] "[I]n short, the Roosevelt Court withdrew from the role of constitutional censor of socio-economic legislation, adopting instead the posture of judicial restraint characteristic of Holmesian liberalism."[31]

In addition to this new view of economic legislation, the Court had put forth a new vision of rights—individual rights were to be given a high priority. Where economic rights had been considered "inalienable" before, individual rights how occupied that position. And within American society at large, a new emphasis on rights was becoming stronger, as demonstrated by the growth of the American Civil Liberties Union and the founding of the NAACP Legal Defense Fund, both of which would become prominent in the 1950s and 1960s.

Former Associate Justice Harlan Fiske Stone took over the Court on the eve of the United States' entry into World War II and died five years later, eight months after the end of the war. The Court with which he served was undeniably liberal, at least in comparison with recent Courts; yet, there were still internal divisions. The Court made great strides in protecting some forms of individual liberty, but failed in others. In freedoms of speech, press, and religion, the Court relied on the preferred freedoms doctrine (though Stone eventually deserted his own creation); yet, with regard to the war and procedural rights, the Court was less inclined to favor individual freedoms.

By 1943 the nine justices made up the "most liberal Court in history,"[32] according to Galloway. Chief Justice Stone and Justices Roberts, Hugo Black, Stanley Reed, Felix Frankfurter, William O. Douglas, and Frank Murphy had been joined in 1941 by Robert H. Jackson, who took Stone's associate seat, and Wiley Rutledge, who replaced James Byrnes (who had replaced James McReynolds and served only one term). Of the nine, at that point only Roberts could be considered a moderate; the rest were liberal in the sense that they favored economic legislation.

Despite their similarities, the justices did not agree on many issues. In fact, in the 1941 term the rate of dissenting opinions rose to 36 percent,[33] and there were distinct divisions within the liberal wing (if eight justices can be called a "wing"): Douglas, Black, Murphy, and Reed comprised a solid left-wing group, while Frankfurter and Stone were more conservative, joining often with Roberts. Reed, Jackson, and Byrnes held the middle-liberal ground.[34] This split, Pritchett suggests, occurred for several reasons. First, because the liberals no longer had to join against the conservatives, the divisions within their group could become apparent—without a group of conservatives to align against, the liberals had no need to appear united. Second, Chief Justice Stone lacked the leadership ability Hughes had shown in his later years, and was unable to bring the Court together.[35]

The splits among the Court liberals had shifted again by 1943, and it became clearer that the rift was between judicial activists and those who believed in restraint. Black, Douglas, Murphy, and Rutledge thought the Court should overturn legislation, while Frankfurter, Reed, Stone, and Jackson were less sure.[36] Again, Roberts occupied the "conservative" camp alone. Overall, during this period the Court viewed media freedom as a social goal, not as a right. While the justices protected that freedom for the most part, at times they were willing to subordinate it to other social needs, requiring media responsibility in the process. In particular, several justices applied affirmative and social responsibility conceptions of responsibility to the media.

The first media decision after the beginning of the second liberal era was *Bridges v. California* in 1941, a combination of two cases, discussed earlier, involving citations for contempt of court against the media. *Bridges* is a classic example of ongoing tension between Justices Black and Frankfurter. Though both were liberals in one sense, they divided on how to achieve liberal goals and policies, with Black upholding a libertarian perspective and Frankfurter adopting a social responsibility stance. Black, who wrote the Court opinion in *Bridges*, was at that time an activist, willing to interfere with state and federal legislation to bring about what he saw as justice. In addition, he occasionally subscribed to what later would be called the social responsibility theory of the press, although as his time on the Court passed, he became more and more libertarian. In *Bridges* he and four colleagues overturned contempt citations against the press, arguing that the media in question had a right to comment upon ongoing legal cases in the California court system.

Here, for the first time, Black maintained in an opinion that the first amendment was close to absolute. The amendment, he wrote, "does not speak equivocally. It prohibits any law 'abridging the freedom of speech, or of the press.' . . . No suggestion can be found in the Constitution that the freedom there guaranteed for speech and the press bears an inverse relation to the timeliness and importance of the ideas seeking expression."[37] The media had the right to publish discussion of court cases, for to deny that right would be to harm the political function of the media and consequently democracy itself. Black's libertarian views, though he would not permanently settle into them until later, are clear here, with their consequent meaning for media responsibility.

Justice Frankfurter disagreed. Dissenting with three colleagues, he argued that California had a right to administer its justice system by holding the press in contempt. Though civil liberties are important, he admitted, so is the maintenance of the federal system, which gives certain powers to the states. And in this case California, exercising its rights under that federal system, had tried to hold the media accountable for their actions by balancing the media's freedom with society's need to maintain a fair justice system. Media freedom could not be absolute, Frankfurter contended in a policy-based argument for social responsibility; that interpretation of the first amendment would remove from the states any power to balance media freedom with other freedoms and rights. To deny the states that ability would "paral[yze] the means for effective protection of all the freedoms secured by the Bill of Rights,"[38] Frankfurter wrote. In addition, to grant absolute privilege to the press could create a situation in which the press would never have to choose to act responsibly. "Doctrinaire overstatements" of the reach of press freedom, according to Frankfurter, could greatly harm society's ability to balance the various rights provided in the Constitution. Here, therefore, Frankfurter's tendency toward collectivism led him to allow states to punish the media for irresponsible behavior.

In another important case during this period, Justice Frankfurter's collectivist tendencies led him again to advocate socially responsible media.[39] In *National Broadcasting Co. v. United States* in 1943, the NBC and CBS networks had asked the Court to stop enforcement of several Federal Communications

Commission policies regulating chain broadcasting. The F.C.C. had ruled that certain practices of network-affiliated radio stations[40] violated the stations' commitment to act "in the public interest, convenience, and necessity."[41] Frankfurter reasoned that because of this requirement, outlined originally by Congress, radio stations and networks were obligated to act in a socially responsible way. The first amendment did not protect them from the F.C.C.'s regulations, for owners and operators of radio stations had a special obligation to society. Because of their use of a scarce public resource—the airwaves—they could be required to act for the benefit of all. Freedom to use the airwaves was naturally abridged, Frankfurter explained: "Unlike other modes of expression, radio inherently is not available to all. That is its unique characteristic, and that is why, unlike other modes of expression it is subject to governmental regulation. Because it cannot be used by all, some who wish to use it must be denied. . . . Denial of a station license . . . if valid under the [Communications] Act, is not a denial of free speech."[42] Though the result of this case was to require responsible behavior by radio station owners and operators, the Court based its rationale on the right of Congress to regulate broadcasting, rather than specifically on a notion of the social responsibility of the press.

The concept of social responsibility received a solid endorsement from the Court two years later, however, when the justices agreed that the Associated Press had conspired to violate the Sherman Anti-Trust Act. In *Associated Press v. United States*, Justice Black, who authored the Court's opinion, clearly took an affirmative, pro-social responsibility stance. The first amendment, he wrote, promoted press responsibility because it required application of the Sherman Act to the Associated Press, which had allowed its member organizations to keep their direct competition from joining the organization and thus benefiting from its services. The press, in the form of the Associated Press, could not act to keep nonmember organizations out, for to do so would disrupt "the widest possible dissemination of information from diverse and antagonistic sources [that] is essential to the welfare of the public."[43]

The Sherman Act could be used positively to promote a diversity of views in the mass media, Black suggested in a truly liberal argument. Thus an affirmative view of the role of government in promoting the social responsibility of the press was acceptable to a majority of the Court, at least in 1945. It is perhaps ironic, however, that Justice Black was the one articulating an affirmative, socially responsible conception of the first amendment, because later he became one of the Court's most consistent libertarians.

Other justices had reactions to this case as well. Justice Frankfurter for once agreed with Black, writing, "A public interest so essential to the vitality of our democratic government may be defeated by private restraints no less than by public censorship."[44] But Justices Roberts and Murphy offered more libertarian views. In his partial dissent, Roberts (joined by Chief Justice Stone) argued that the majority was making the Associated Press into "a public utility subject to duty to serve all on equal terms," which he called the "first step in the shackling of the press," leading to a time when "the state will be supreme and freedom of the state will have superseded freedom of the individual to print."[45]

Justice Murphy complained of the affirmative view of press freedom taken by the majority. Reacting specifically to recent events in Europe—Germany had surrendered to the Allies just six weeks before this case was handed down— Murphy wrote,

Today is also the first time the Sherman Act has been used as a vehicle for affirmative intervention by the Government in the realm of dissemination of information. . . . The tragic history of recent years demonstrates far too well how despotic governments may interfere with the press and other means of communication in their efforts to corrupt public opinion and to destroy individual freedom. Experience teaches us to hesitate before creating a precedent in which might lurk even the slightest justification by the Government in these matters.[46]

Clearly the conflicts between affirmative and negative views of media freedom and between the social responsibility and libertarian concepts of the media caused tension among the justices, whose judicial philosophies led them to view media responsibility in profoundly different ways. For Black and those who joined the majority (Reed, Frankfurter, Douglas, and Rutledge),[47] media responsibility implied a duty by the media to present a diversity of viewpoints and to avoid private decisions harming that obligation. But for Roberts, Stone, and Murphy, the requirement that the media fulfill that duty involved too great a danger to media freedom—and consequently to democracy. Here, therefore, liberal and libertarian conceptions of media responsibility were in conflict.

Among other cases involving media responsibility during these years, in *Valentine v. Chrestensen*[48] in 1942 all nine justices refused to extend first amendment protection to commercial speech, thus allowing local governments to place restrictions on the behavior of advertisers. In 1946 Justice Douglas wrote for seven of his colleagues (Jackson took no part in this case) in *Hannegan v. Esquire* that the Postmaster General could not revoke *Esquire* magazine's second-class mailing privileges based on the magazine's "objectionable" content. Making a decidedly liberal argument against a particular conception of the good, Douglas commented that government should not be allowed to decide what expression was acceptable, for "[W]hat is good literature, what has educational value, what is refined public information, what is good art, varies with individuals as it does from one generation to another."[49]

In a 1946 speech case, *Marsh v. Alabama*,[50] Black again argued for an affirmative view of the first amendment. Grace Marsh, a Jehovah's Witness, had been convicted for distributing religious literature in a company-owned town. The town's "owners," Black wrote for the Court, had to uphold the first amendment and could not impede Marsh's press freedom. Freedom of the press and of religion, he maintained, occupied a "preferred position" over property rights in the constitutional hierarchy. However, Justice Reed, joined by Justice Harold Burton and Chief Justice Stone, disagreed with that balance of rights. In their dissent they presented a negative, collectivist view of the first amendment, arguing that the property rights of the town owners were not outweighed by the press and religion rights of the individual, and that the government and courts could not interfere.

The question of balancing various rights characterized the last media case of Stone's tenure, *Pennekamp v. Florida* in 1946. Like *Bridges v. California*, *Pennekamp* involved contempt of court by the media. But, unlike *Bridges*, in *Pennekamp* the justices were unanimous in their support of the media's right to criticize pending trials.[51] The justices agreed that though there conceivably could be limits on permissible expression in similar situations, in this case the right of "free discussion of the problems of society" outweighed the need for "fair and orderly judicial administration."[52] The media's political and educational functions, therefore, outweighed their responsibility.

Though he agreed with the case's outcome, Justice Frankfurter concurred separately, outlining his ideas on the role of media responsibility in the administration of justice. The ultimate end promoted by the Constitution, he explained, is a free society. Both media freedom and the justice system are merely means to that end; thus, both can be regulated if that will better achieve a free society. The judicial system, he suggested, cannot perform its role if the press acts "to disturb the judicial judgment in its duty and capacity to act solely on the basis of what is before the court."[53] The media must recognize their obligations to society, Frankfurter suggested, in a conservative argument: "[F]reedom carries with it responsibility even for the press; freedom of the press is not a freedom from responsibility in its exercise."[54] If the press did not uphold its responsibilities, Frankfurter feared, it could easily change from being a crucial segment of a democratic society to a "powerful instrument of injustice," and he was not willing to let that happen. Freedom of the press, in his opinion, is not absolute; if the press genuinely violates its obligations, it can, and must, be stopped and punished.

The transition years of the liberal era, 1938 to 1946, were characterized by the Court's acknowledgment that though media freedom was valuable and "preferred" under constitutional interpretation, the media could and should be accountable to society's goals and needs. The "right" of press freedom, then, was viewed as a policy, to use Dworkin's term. In particular, the justices believed the media should present a diversity of viewpoints. The Court was willing to protect the media so they could perform that function—as in *Bridges, Hannegan*, and *Pennekamp*—but was also willing to require that behavior if the media did not serve this role on their own. Several of the justices, including Black and Frankfurter, articulated and applied both affirmative understandings of media freedom and the social responsibility concept of the media, though negative and libertarian interpretations were also apparent in other justices during this time. These divisions in the Court continued throughout the next period of the Court's history.

The Vinson Court, 1946–1953

Fred Vinson, who took over the Court upon Stone's death in 1946, presided over a rather significant shift to the right. Though not as abrupt as the Court's switch in 1937, this change in focus in the late 1940s signaled the Court's willingness to emphasize law and order over some civil rights. This change occurred primarily for two reasons: First, the country as a whole changed, becoming more conservative as the Cold War developed; and second, changes in the Court personnel gave Justice Frankfurter more allies in his quest for collectivism.

Vinson was more conservative than his predecessor. He had been a member of Congress, the Director of Economic Stabilization during World War II, and was Secretary of the Treasury when President Truman nominated him to the high court.[55] He was appointed in part "for his lack of strong commitments" and to smooth over the divisions in the Court left from the Stone legacy, Murphy writes, and he "sought in every way possible to accommodate the Court to the tensions of the times, to avoid public controversy, and to minimize the Court's role as a policy-making and power body."[56] Yet almost immediately the percentage of nonunanimous opinions began to grow, from 64 percent in Vinson's first term (1946), to 74 percent by 1948 and 81 percent in 1951.[57]

This increase came in part because of the growing split between the judicial philosophies of Justices Black and Frankfurter. The Black libertarian faction took a blow with the deaths of Murphy and Rutledge in 1949. Truman replaced them with former Attorney General Tom C. Clark and Sherman Minton, neither of whom "had a distinguished legal mind" and both of whom, like the chief justice, viewed civil liberties as expendable "in the face of the pressure of national security and, so some critics maintained, of political assault."[58] While Frankfurter himself did not necessarily see civil liberties as expendable, his views on collectivism required him to bend to the will of legislatures—to avoid any appearance of making public policy. His perspective on the role of the Court made him particularly hostile to the preferred freedoms doctrine.[59]

Black, on the other hand, maintained his support of civil rights, which he saw as even more crucial in the face of the political tenor of the times. In a 1948 dissent in a non-media case he made a natural law claim in arguing that the entire Bill of Rights should be incorporated into the due process clause of the fourteenth amendment:[60] "[T]his Court is endowed by the Constitution with boundless power under 'natural law' periodically to expand and contract constitutional standards to conform to the Court's conception of what, at a particular time, constitutes 'civilized decency' and 'fundamental liberty and justice.'"[61]

The political tenor of the times had a great, if indirect, impact on the Court. Shortly after the end of World War II, the country began a swing to the right. In the 1946 elections, Republicans gained control of both houses of Congress and began to chip away at New Deal reforms. In addition, the "heating up" of the

Cold War and the war in Korea made national security an issue, and anti-Communist forces gained prominence.

The justices saw this change in public opinion, and reacted accordingly. Vinson in particular did not want to call attention to the Court, and Frankfurter's restraintist attitude, as well as the moderates' views on social order, led to some anti-Communist decisions. For example, as Murphy points out,[62] on one day in 1951 the Court protected the freedom of individuals to speak on religious issues in two cases, but ruled against a pro-Communist speaker in a third. In 1952 the Court ruled that teachers who were members of groups advocating violent overthrow of the government could be fired,[63] and also upheld the deportation of three aliens who were former, but not current, Communists.[64]

The conflict between collectivist and individualist perspectives, and that between libertarian views versus those advocating responsible behavior, spilled into the Court's media cases as well. The first major media case decision of this period was *Craig v. Harney*, which was handed down near the end of the 1946–1947 term. It included several interpretations of the media's role in a democracy. Like *Bridges* and *Pennekamp* before, *Craig* involved a newspaper charged with contempt of court for reporting negatively on ongoing legal proceedings. And as in *Bridges* and *Pennekamp*, the justices decided in favor of the press. In the Court opinion, Justice Douglas admitted that the Corpus Christi, Texas, newspaper had likely acted unfairly. But even unfair criticism of the justice system must be viewed in context, Douglas maintained, and in this context the press' actions were protected under the first amendment.

Justice Murphy, who often exhibited a libertarian philosophy, agreed with the ruling. In concurring, he acknowledged the importance of a free press to the functioning of democracy and suggested that "any inroad made upon the constitutional protection of a free press tends to undermine the freedom of all men to print and to read the truth."[65] To Murphy, the newspaper had every right to publish at will, and the local judge could not use contempt power against it.

Three justices dissented, though for two very different reasons. Justice Frankfurter, joined by the new chief justice, agreed in principle with the majority's assertion that the press had the right to criticize judicial action. But Frankfurter's collectivist views would not let him vote with Douglas and the others. Texas had the constitutional right, Frankfurter argued, to administer its justice system without interference from the Supreme Court. The state court knew the specific facts of the case better than he, wrote Frankfurter; thus, the state should be permitted to act as it saw fit. Justice Jackson, also dissenting, took another path. The press, he contended, had gone beyond the boundaries of responsible behavior and had interfered with the fairness of a trial. In addition, Jackson wrote, by permitting this interference, the Supreme Court sent a signal that the press would not be held accountable for such irresponsible action in the future.

With the various opinions in *Craig v. Harney*, the divisions on the Vinson court became clear. Divisions over the role of the Court and views of media responsibility continued for the next six years, through a series of minor but relevant media cases. For example, the affirmative and libertarian views of the first amendment clashed in *Donaldson v. Read Magazine* in 1948. *Read Magazine* had published a puzzle contest promoting book sales that led readers to believe they could win merely by solving puzzles and paying an entry fee of $3.00, when in fact they had to pay more and write an essay as well. Justice Black, writing for himself and six colleagues, maintained that the magazine had a responsibility to its readers not to mislead them in this instance. The U.S. Postmaster General, therefore, had an obligation to stop the contest. The government, the majority ruled, could step in to ensure responsibility in the advertisements of contests sponsored by the media. As Black explained, "People have a right to assume that fraudulent advertising traps will not be laid to ensnare them."[66]

But the two dissenters, Justices Burton and Douglas, disagreed. The government, in the form of the Postmaster General, did not have the right to interfere in the promotion. Rather than requiring the media to be accountable, Burton and Douglas argued that the contest participants had a responsibility: "Anyone who entered this contest to win substantial prizes by doing so little to win them should at least examine the exact terms of the contest and make himself responsible for meeting the rules prescribed."[67] Under this libertarian interpretation, the responsibility belonged to the consumer, rather than the producer.

Other cases also demonstrated conflict among the justices over defining press responsibility. A few weeks after *Donaldson*, in a case foreshadowing the many obscenity cases of later years, the Court divided over whether conceptions of good deserved any place in first amendment interpretation. A bookseller had been convicted of a New York state ordinance forbidding selling publications "devoted to . . . and principally made up of criminal deeds, or pictures, or stories of deeds of bloodshed, lust, or crime."[68] While the six-justice majority admitted that some actions do violate community morals and are subject to legal sanction, the first amendment, they argued, substantially limits what communities can do to enforce morality. "What is one man's amusement," wrote Justice Reed for the majority, "teaches another's doctrine. Though we can see nothing of any possible value to society in these magazines, they are as much entitled to the protection of free speech as the best literature."[69] Justice Frankfurter, however, suggested in dissent that the state had a right to legislate morality, particularly in situations in which there was not only "nothing of any possible value," but in which the publication would cause "mischief." The consequence of people reading these publications would be a decline in public morals and increase in crime; thus, the state could prohibit the sale of such magazines and books. To Frankfurter (and Jackson and Burton, who joined the dissent), there was a conception of the good that the media should, and could be required to, uphold.

The conflict between requirements of responsibility and libertarian views appeared again several years later, in 1951 in *Breard v. Alexandria*. Breard, a door-to-door magazine subscription salesman, was arrested because homeowners he visited had not consented to his solicitations. Though Breard had some protection from the first amendment, acknowledged the majority, he could not violate the privacy of city residents because of that protection. He could not use freedom of the press to "smooth [his] path by crushing the living rights of others to privacy and repose."[70] The city could balance competing rights, the Court concluded, and individuals could still receive these magazines by ordering them, ensuring both "full liberty of expression and an orderly life."[71]

This conclusion aroused anger on the libertarian side of the bench. Justices Black and Douglas dissented, arguing that the majority had forgotten the "preferred position" occupied by first amendment freedoms.[72] Black, who authored the dissent, seemed to forget his earlier acceptance of government intervention,[73] for he wrote, "It is my belief that the freedom of the people cannot survive even a little governmental hobbling of religious or political ideals, whether they be communicated orally or through the press."[74] Homeowners had a right to refuse solicitation, Black admitted, but the city could not make that decision for individual residents. The first amendment's protection of media freedom was much too strong for this kind of interference.

Finally, in 1952 the Vinson Court decided one of its most significant media responsibility cases, a group libel case. In *Beauharnais v. Illinois,* the Court concluded that a lithograph portraying African-Americans as "depraved, criminals, unchaste, and without virtue"[75] did not deserve first amendment protection. In addition to publishing the lithograph, Beauharnais had asked Chicago public officials to "halt the further encroachment, harassment, and invasion of white people, their property, neighborhoods and persons by the Negro." Justice Frankfurter, using a states-rights argument to call for responsibility, concluded that if the Court allowed states to punish libel against individuals, it must allow states to punish libel against groups. The subject of the libel was particularly painful for Frankfurter,[76] who noted that the Illinois law was enacted to stop "willful purveyors of falsehood concerning racial and religious groups [that] promote strife and tend powerfully to obstruct the manifold adjustments required for a free, ordered life in a metropolitan, polyglot community."[77]

Frankfurter's opinion provoked dissents from four justices, two of whom made strong libertarian arguments, and one of whom argued for a more limited responsibility than provided for in the Illinois group libel statute.[78] Justice Black, who was by this time beginning his move toward libertarianism, concluded that Beauharnais had been exercising his right to petition the government, but the state had censored his opinion. The Illinois statute and the Court's response to it could lead, he suggested, to "a practice of meticulously scrutinizing" all publications for group libel, a situation that would greatly harm the first amendment. Justice Douglas also made a libertarian argument against the statute, concluding that the first amendment rights—speech, press, and religion, in particular—are absolute and, thus, cannot be regulated under any circumstances. He noted with despair the growing tendency of the Court to allow the state and federal governments some opportunity to regulate speech and suggested that the marketplace of ideas had consequently disappeared. In its place, he complained, was "a new orthodoxy—an orthodoxy that changes with the whims of the age or the day, an orthodoxy which the majority by solemn judgment proclaims to be essential to the safety, welfare, security, morality, or health of society."[79] Despite his fears for the fate of the first amendment, Douglas left open the possibility of punishment for group libel. If, he suggested, conduct directed at a particular race or group were harmful, that conduct could be punished. Picketing, for example, was not absolutely protected speech; it was, in Douglas' words, "speech plus" that could be regulated. So, although Douglas was a libertarian in one sense, arguing for complete protection for speech and press, he was willing to require responsibility once the expression in question took on any aspects of conduct or action.

Justice Jackson also dissented in *Beauharnais*, but for somewhat different reasons. Jackson essentially agreed with requiring media responsibility, but he was not willing to do so in this case. Governmental expectations of press responsibility, wrote Jackson, were recognized by those who wrote and ratified the fourteenth amendment, which eventually became the vehicle for applying to the states the protections offered by the Bill of Rights. When the fourteenth amendment was ratified in 1868 many states already required press responsibility; he suggested, therefore, that amendment could not have been meant to deny that requirement. State expectations of press responsibility could coexist with the first amendment. In fact, he wrote, "Group libel statutes represent a commendable desire to reduce sinister abuses of our freedoms of expression—abuses which I have had occasion to learn can tear apart a society, brutalize its dominant elements, and persecute, even to extermination, its minorities."[80] Despite accepting expectations of press responsibility, Jackson ruled in favor of the press here, for the expression involved, he argued, did not present a clear and present danger to any individual or to the general peace of society. Had there been evidence of specific harm to society or any individuals, however, Beauharnais' punishment would have been acceptable.

Though the Vinson Court has been characterized by historians as somewhat conservative—compared to Supreme Courts before and after it—there was in no sense a unified conservative theme to its media decisions. Instead, the Vinson years are more aptly described as divided. The libertarians (who at this point were primarily liberal in their views) and conservatives clashed during this period over whether the media could be held accountable. For the "conservatives"—including Justice Frankfurter—the media at times did need to be held accountable for their actions, and on occasion the government needed to promote a particular conception of the good. The libertarians, however, argued that media freedom meant no requirements of responsibility and no government intervention in the media's business. During this period, then, the conflict between media freedom and responsibility continued in Court opinions, though Justice Jackson made an attempt to reconcile the two in his discussion of the fourteenth amendment and state requirements of press responsibility.

The years 1937 to 1953, therefore, provided a transition between the laissez-faire attitudes of the late nineteenth and early twentieth centuries on the Court and the liberal, individualist period that followed. Over time, the Stone and Vinson courts grew increasingly liberal in their general attitudes, but conflict between collective and individualist interpretations of the first amendment continued throughout the period. That conflict, demonstrated in discussions and decisions using libertarian and social-responsibility conceptions of the first amendment, as well as a growing liberal emphasis by the Court, became even more apparent during the Warren Court years that followed.

NOTES

1. The "First Conservative Era" of the Court ran from its inception to 1835, the end of John Marshall's tenure as chief justice, whereas the "First Liberal Era" began in 1835 and concluded in about 1890, with the rise of what Galloway calls the "first age of laissez faire." See Russell Galloway, *The Rich and the Poor in Supreme Court History, 1790–1982* (Greenbrae, Calif.: Paradigm Press, 1982).

2. C. Herman Pritchett, *The Roosevelt Court: A Study in Judicial Politics and Values, 1937–1947* (New York: Macmillan, 1948), 4.

3. G. Edward White, *The American Judicial Tradition: Profiles of Leading American Judges*, expanded edition (New York: Oxford University Press, 1988), 188.

4. *Near v. Minnesota*, 51 S.Ct. 625, 628 (1931), Chief Justice Hughes, Court opinion.

5. *Near v. Minnesota*, 51 S.Ct. 625, 632 (1931), Chief Justice Hughes, Court opinion.

6. *Near v. Minnesota*, 51 S.Ct. 625, 637 (1931), Justice Butler, dissenting.

7. *Federal Radio Commission v. Nelson Brothers Bond and Mortgage Co.*, 53 S.Ct. 627, 635 (1933), Chief Justice Hughes, Court opinion.

8. Alpheus Thomas Mason, *The Supreme Court from Taft to Burger* (Baton Rouge: Louisiana State University Press, 1979), 85.

9. 290 U.S. 398 (1934).

10. 291 U.S. 502 (1934).

11. 295 U.S. 495 (1935).

12. Edward S. Corwin, *Constitutional Revolution, Ltd.* (Claremont, Calif.: Claremont Colleges, 1941), 48.

13. Mason, 91.

14. 298 U.S. 238 (1936).

15. 297 U.S. 1 (1936).

16. *West Coast Hotel v. Parrish*, 300 U.S. 379 (1937) reversed *Morehead v. New York*, 298 U.S. 587 (1936).

17. *N.L.R.B. v. Jones and Laughlin Corp.*, 301 U.S. 1 (1937).

18. Information on the New Deal cases comes from Pritchett, Corwin, and Walter F. Murphy, James E. Fleming, and William F. Harris, II, *American Constitutional Interpretation* (Mineola, N. Y.: The Foundation Press, Inc., 1986).

19. Murphy, Fleming, and Harris, 945–46.

20. *Associated Press v. National Labor Relations Board*, 57 S.Ct. 650, 656 (1937), Justice Roberts, Court opinion.

21. *Associated Press v. National Labor Relations Board*, 57 S.Ct. 650, 657 (1937), Justice Sutherland, dissenting.

22. Paul Murphy, "*Near v. Minnesota* in the Context of Historical Developments," *Minnesota Law Review* 66(1981): 95–160.

23. 304 U.S. 144 (1938).

24. Murphy, Fleming, and Harris, 473.

25. *Carolene Products v. United States*, 304 U.S. 144 (1938), footnote #4.

26. This occurred during the rise of Hitler in Germany, and the understanding that a western, lawful democracy could remove the rights of its citizens likely influenced the Court, at least subconsciously.

27. Murphy, Fleming, and Harris, 474.

28. Murphy, Fleming, and Harris, 474.

29. White, 210.

30. Galloway, 139–40.

31. Galloway, 140.

32. Galloway, 145.

33. Pritchett, 39.

34. Pritchett, 39.

35. Pritchett, 40.

36. Galloway, 148.

37. *Bridges v. California*, 62 S.Ct. 194, 196 (1941), Justice Black, Court opinion.

38. *Bridges v. California*, 62 S.Ct. 190, 194, 203 (1941), Justice Frankfurter, dissenting.

39. While the "social responsibility" theory of the press did not technically come into being until the Hutchins Commission's reports in the late 1940s, the Supreme Court before that articulated principles that would become part of the Commission's understanding of media responsibility.

40. For example: network requirements that affiliates use network programming exclusively harmed community needs; network affiliation requirements of five years, even though F.C.C. licenses were granted only for three years; network ownership of eighteen of the most powerful stations in the country; network agreements not to sell programming to stations that might compete with affiliates.

41. This language is found in the Communications Act of 1934.

42. *National Broadcasting Co. v. United States*, 63 S.Ct. 997, 1014 (1943), Justice Frankfurter, Court opinion.

43. *Associated Press v. United States*, 65 S.Ct. 1416, 1424–25 (1945), Justice Black, Court opinion.

44. *Associated Press v. United States*, 65 S.Ct. 1416, 1428 (1945), Justice Frankfurter, concurring.

45. *Associated Press v. United States*, 65 S.Ct. 1416, 1436–37 (1945), Justice Roberts, dissenting in part.

46. *Associated Press v. United States*, 65 S.Ct. 1416, 1439 (1945), Justice Murphy, dissenting.

47. Only eight justices took part in this case. Justice Jackson was at the time the U.S. representative to the International Military Tribunal trying Nazi war criminals at Nuremberg, Germany.

48. *Valentine v. Chrestensen*, 62 S.Ct. 920 (1942).

49. *Hannegan v. Esquire*, 66 S.Ct. 456, 462 (1946), Justice Douglas, Court opinion.

50. *Marsh v. Alabama*, 66 S.Ct. 276 (1946).

51. At this point, in June 1946, there were only eight justices serving on the Court. Chief Justice Stone had died in April 1946.

52. *Pennekamp v. Florida*, 66 S.Ct. 1029, 1037 (1946), Justice Reed, Court opinion.

53. *Pennekamp v. Florida*, 66 S.Ct. 1029, 1041 (1946), Justice Frankfurter, concurring.

54. *Pennekamp v. Florida*, 66 S.Ct. 1029, 1042 (1946), Justice Frankfurter, concurring.

55. Robert G. McCloskey, *The Modern Supreme Court* (Cambridge: Harvard University Press, 1972), 57.

56. Paul L. Murphy, *The Constitution in Crisis Times, 1918–1969* (New York: Harper and Row, 1972), 263.

57. McCloskey, 57.

58. Murphy, *Crisis* 263–64.

59. Murphy, *Crisis* 266.

60. Until and past this point, the various guarantees in the Bill of Rights had been incorporated one at a time, as in *Near v. Minnesota*, which incorporated only the press clause.

61. *Adamson v. California*, 332 U.S. 46 (1948) at 69. Quoted in Murphy, *Crisis*, 264.

62. Murphy, *Crisis*, 295.

63. *Adler v. Board of Education*, 342 U.S. 485 (1952).

64. *Harisiades v. Shaughnessy*, 342 U.S. 580 (1952).

65. *Craig v. Harney*, 67 S.Ct. 1249, 1258 (1947), Justice Murphy, concurring.

66. *Donaldson v. Read Magazine*, 68 S.Ct. 591, 597 (1948), Justice Black, Court opinion.

67. *Donaldson v. Read Magazine*, 68 S.Ct. 591, 600 (1948), Justice Burton, dissenting.

68. *Winters v. New York*, 68 S.Ct. 665 (1948).

69. *Winters v. New York*, 68 S.Ct. 665, 667 (1948), Justice Reed, Court opinion.

70. *Breard v. Alexandria,* 71 S.Ct. 920, 923 (1951), Justice Reed, Court opinion.

71. *Breard v. Alexandria,* 71 S.Ct. 920, 932 (1951), Justice Reed, Court opinion.

72. Chief Justice Vinson also dissented, but his disagreement with the majority stemmed from his belief that the decision interfered with interstate commerce.

73. Admittedly, however, Black only argued for government intervention when it would increase the diversity of viewpoints to which people had access.

74. *Breard v. Alexandria,* 71 S.Ct. 920, 936 (1951), Justice Black, dissenting.

75. *Beauharnais v. Illinois*, 72 S.Ct. 725, 728 (1952), Justice Frankfurter, Court opinion.

76. In other cases Frankfurter, a Jew, had mentioned his own status as a member of a minority group often the subject of unreasonable hatred.

77. *Beauharnais v. Illinois*, 72 S.Ct. 725, 731 (1952), Justice Frankfurter, Court opinion.

78. Justice Reed also dissented, but primarily because he thought the wording of the statute was vague.

79. *Beauharnais v. Illinois*, 72 S.Ct. 725, 745 (1952), Justice Douglas, dissenting.

80. *Beauharnais v. Illinois*, 72 S.Ct. 725, 754–55 (1952), Justice Jackson, dissenting. Jackson was referring here to his participation in the Nazi war crimes trials at Nuremberg.

Chapter Three

The Warren Court Years, 1953–1969

Republican Earl Warren, former vice presidential candidate (1948) and governor of California, became chief justice on October 5, 1953, less than a month after Chief Justice Fred Vinson's death. He had no judicial experience; his appointment was "purely political," meant to appease liberal Republicans criticizing President Eisenhower's links with more conservative party members.[1] His views on social issues and the judiciary were not well known, other than his pro-state sovereignty statements as California governor (which he later came to regret) and his work as a district attorney concerned with law enforcement.[2] He was meant to be a moderate chief justice, White writes, but "came . . . possessed of a strong belief in the worth of active government. . . . The fact that he had no well-developed philosophy of judging was in his case of no consequence; he had instead a well-developed philosophy of governing."[3] Warren's belief in the ultimate value of fairness and equality guided him, and the Court under his direction, for fourteen years.

Warren served with sixteen associate justices over the fourteen years, a group that included some of the most brilliant justices of the century. Hugo Black and Felix Frankfurter continued their battles of earlier years, William O. Douglas fought for libertarian ideals, and John Marshall Harlan, II, took up Frankfurter's restraintist banner, but with more conservative colors. By the mid-1950s, the Court was evenly split between liberals and conservatives, with Warren, Douglas, Black, and William Brennan on one side and Harlan, Frankfurter, Harold Burton, and Stanley Reed on the other. Tom Clark occupied a moderate position.[4] The Warren Court underwent several phases, from this even split in the early years, to a retreat to (moderate) conservatism in the late 1950s, to a definite liberal phase in the mid and late 1960s. Throughout it all, however, the conflicts formed in earlier years continued.

The main conflict within the Warren Court, as within the Stone and Vinson Courts, was between collectivism and individualism, demonstrated in the justices' balancing of individual rights and social goals and their views on judicial activism and restraint. Within the Warren Court that conflict took the form of "process liberalism" versus "substantive liberalism." Both methods of interpretation value individual rights; the difference lies in which rights and whether or not to take means into account in achieving ends.

Believers in substantive liberalism, including Warren, Douglas, and to some extent Black, argued that equality was the highest value within the Constitution, and they focused their interpretation in that manner. Thus, their primary goal was to use the Constitution to erase inequality in American society, both socially and economically—to create opportunities for people, to create "freedom for."[5] Process liberalism, the domain of Frankfurter and Harlan, saw equality as one of many values contained within the Constitution. Frankfurter and Harlan reacted against the substantive liberals and eventually became associated with "conservative" viewpoints. For example, they voted for "the autonomy of law enforcement (against increased protection for criminal suspects), freedom of association (against equal access to facilities by all races), [and] federalism (against uniform courtroom procedures across the nation)." The difference, primarily, was between balancing rights and valuing equality more highly than other individual rights.[6]

John Harlan, like Frankfurter a process liberal in conservative clothing, accused the Court of "unrestrained egalitarianism"[7] and called for more state and federal sovereignty. The judiciary was, for the most part, to stay away from government regulation of rights. He argued that the Warren majority's focus on equality was harming the states' ability to enforce laws and run their criminal justice systems. In addition to valuing law enforcement, Harlan saw the need to allow local democracies to function unhindered by the federal court system. He also valued individual privacy and suggested that government should stay out of private affairs. In their quest for equality, Harlan thought, Warren, Black, and the others were trampling on individual rights.[8]

Douglas, a Roosevelt appointee, fell in line with Warren most of the time, but for his own idiosyncratic reasons. Douglas was a realist, a subscriber to a twentieth-century judicial philosophy that "stressed the impermanence, flexibility, artificiality, and uncertainty of legal rules and principles."[9] The realist movement, in the words of one of its founders, Karl Llewellyn, suggested that the law is a creation of judges (as opposed to existing independently "out there"); the law is a means to social ends rather than an end in itself and is never quite caught up with changes in society. Realists, Llewellyn explained, distrust legal rules as descriptions of what courts do and are determined to evaluate laws in terms of their effects.[10] So for Douglas, the crucial aspects of a case were its result and the political philosophy behind that result. He cared little for the doctrinal arguments used to justify results; instead, he focused on the implications of cases.[11]

When Douglas joined the Court in 1939, his colleagues were just beginning to work out a new rationale for decision-making after the demise of liberty of contract two years earlier. He remained on the Court as it, and he, changed emphasis from due-process issues to those of equal protection. During the Warren Court years the freedoms outlined in the Constitution were interpreted more under the concept of equality than under liberty—the Court was putting forth a "affirmative" view of freedom. For the Court in these years, freedom meant opportunity, "freedom for," rather than the more traditional (in the historical sense) "freedom from." Douglas and his like-minded colleagues saw as their mission to make the government responsible for upholding the ideal of equality. At the same time, Douglas saw that individual choice—liberty—was a value inherent in the Constitution. This tension between equality and liberty was very apparent in many of the Warren Court's decisions.

At various times Douglas saw both liberty and equality as fundamental. In the 1940s, well before the Warren Court's focus on equality, Douglas had linked economic opportunity with personal liberty, thus smoothing the conflict between the two values. And in the middle Warren years, he began publicly to call privacy and liberty "natural rights." In 1958 he argued in a clear approval of natural law and rights theory, foreshadowing the privacy case of 1965,[12] that the right of liberty had been "written explicitly into the Constitution. Other [rights] are to be implied. The penumbra of the Bill of Rights reflects human rights which, though not explicit, are implied from the very nature of man as a child of God."[13] And in 1973, near the end of his tenure on the bench, he further outlined his views on natural rights. In a concurrence in *Doe v. Bolton*, a companion case to *Roe v. Wade*, Douglas wrote that the right to abortion was one of

a catalogue of . . . customary, traditional, and time-honored rights, amenities, privileges, and immunities that come within the sweep of 'the Blessings of Liberty' mentioned in the preamble to the Constitution, [many of which] come within the meaning of the term 'liberty' as used in the Fourteenth Amendment. . . . First is the autonomous control over the development of one's intellect, interests, tastes, and personality. Second is freedom of choice in the basic decisions of one's life respecting marriage, divorce, procreation, contraception, and the education and upbringing of children. Third is the freedom to care for one's health and person, freedom from bodily restraint or compulsion, freedom to walk, stroll, or loaf.[14]

For Douglas these were absolute, or fundamental, rights with which the state could not interfere without compelling reason.

Though the Warren Court struggled with the conflict between liberty and equal protection, it found more often for equality than Courts before or since. But this emphasis on equality did not come all at once, nor was it the product of a steadily growing doctrine. Instead, the Warren Court underwent at least three distinct phases over the fourteen years. In its earliest stage, exemplified in decisions outlawing segregation in public schools and protecting political thought and speech,[15] the Court gained its reputation for liberalism and a willingness to challenge social values. Reaction to the 1957 political beliefs cases included a movement to impeach Warren and censure of the Supreme Court's activism by justices of the state supreme courts, and led to the second period, in which the Court seemed to allow more conservative public opinion to influence its decisions. This was due in part to a switch by Justice Frankfurter, who until 1957 had voted with Warren and Douglas on many liberal issues. Sensitive to public opinion and the view that the Court was thwarting the will of the legislative branch, Frankfurter began voting against Warren and Douglas in 1957. And finally, the move toward liberalism in the country in general, characterized by the social programs of Presidents Kennedy and Johnson as well as the Civil Rights Movement, was matched by changes in Court personnel and rulings. In 1962 Byron White, a moderate with liberal views on civil rights, replaced Charles Whittaker (who had taken Reed's seat in 1957), and liberal Arthur Goldberg replaced the retiring Frankfurter. With Goldberg (and occasionally White), Warren, Black, Douglas, and Brennan could now count on a five-vote majority most of the time. With these changes the truly activist, liberal phase of the Warren Court began.

THE WARREN COURT EARLY YEARS, 1953–1964

The Warren era officially began with the fall 1953 term, though the justices did not decide a media case until early 1957. By this time Black was the senior associate justice, and the conservative Harlan and the liberal Brennan had joined the court, in 1955 and 1956, respectively. Harlan, who favored state power over that of the federal government, quickly became an ally of Frankfurter, whereas Brennan joined often with Black and Douglas. By 1957 the Court, though filled with liberals, was evenly split between the "substantive liberal" group (Black, Douglas, Brennan, and Warren) and the "process liberal" group (Frankfurter, Harlan, Reed, and Burton), with Tom Clark occupying a more moderate position. For the substantive liberals, equality was the most important right protected by the Constitution, and the Court's role was to ensure equality, even if that meant taking an activist stance. Process liberals, on the other hand, valued equality as one of many important rights, and were more willing to allow legislatures to define rights in their own way. This position led many to see Frankfurter and the other process liberals as conservative, at least in contrast to the substantive liberals. These two positions were clearly visible in the Court's decisions on the media.

The first significant media case decided by the Warren Court was *Roth v. United States* at the end of the 1956–1957 term. *Roth*, like the many obscenity cases that followed it, did not deal directly with the traditional media, but it did provide discussion of the responsibilities of those desiring protection under the first amendment. The majority saw a role for community definitions of morality and the good, while the libertarian dissenters argued against that, suggesting instead a standard of responsibility applying only to action, not expression. *Roth* was actually two cases decided jointly, one concerning a federal obscenity statute, the other a California obscenity law. Despite upholding both statutes, the seven-justice majority outlined a fairly libertarian rationale in its opinion authored by Justice Brennan, in his first year on the Court. "All ideas having even the slightest redeeming social importance," wrote Brennan, "unorthodox ideas, controversial ideas, even ideas hateful to the prevailing climate of opinion—have the full protection of the guaranties" of the first amendment. Despite this statement acknowledging great protection of ideas, Brennan continued with a disclaimer: All ideas would be protected "unless [they were] excludable because they encroach upon the limited area of more important interests." And obscenity was excludable: "[I]mplicit in the history of the First Amendment is the rejection of obscenity as utterly without redeeming social importance."[16] Obscenity could be defined, Brennan continued, by the following test: "whether to the average person, applying contemporary community standards, the dominant theme of the material taken as a whole appeals to prurient interest."[17]

Therefore, while most ideas and opinions would receive full protection from the Warren Court, Brennan suggested, expression violating community morals through its appeal to obsessive interest in sex and its lack of redeeming social qualities would not be protected. The Court, thus, viewed first amendment protection of any expression as a policy or collective goal, limiting protection of ideas "encroach[ing] upon the limited area of more important interests." In the case of obscenity, the Court's conception of morality—of the good—became the social need outweighing freedom of expression. A minimum level of responsibility on the part of publishers of pornography was thus determined.

Three justices dissented in *Roth*[18] for two completely different reasons. Justice Harlan, showing states'-rights tendencies, argued that the federal obscenity law should be overturned in favor of individual state statutes. Regulating obscenity was acceptable to Harlan, but it should be done at the state level to protect expression against "uniform, nation-wide suppression" of particular works. However, regulation was not acceptable to the Court's two libertarians, who argued against enacting moral standards into first amendment protection. Protected expression, wrote Douglas, with Black joining, should not be defined by what a particular community would find offensive: "Any test that turns on what is offensive to the community's standards is too loose, too capricious, too destructive of freedom of expression to be squared with the First Amendment."[19] In addition, Douglas and Black argued, protected expression could not be defined by courts attempting to determine "redeeming social importance." Instead, the only acceptable demarcation between protected and unprotected expression, they maintained, was that between expression not associated with illegal action and expression closely tied to illegal action. Expression should receive absolute protection, then, unless it was clearly inseparable from action that the government could prohibit. Thus, this expression/action distinction became the point at which Black and Douglas were willing to require responsible behavior. In outlining this idea of limited responsibility, these two justices mapped out the most libertarian view put forth by any justice to this point.

The Warren Court continued to seek the line between acceptable and inappropriate censorship throughout its first decade and beyond. In a rare unanimous decision, the Court agreed in 1959 that a New York statute requiring denial of licenses for exhibition of motion pictures portraying immorality interfered with the first amendment rights of motion picture distributors. Justice Potter Stewart, who joined the Court in October 1958, declared for his colleagues that New York could not forbid advocacy of ideas—in this case advocacy of adultery. Though the Court agreed that the movie in question—"Lady Chatterley's Lover"—could be considered immoral, that determination ultimately was irrelevant. As long as it was not obscene, the movie could not be banned. In separate concurrences, Justices Black and Douglas argued that the question of morality should not matter. This was an example of prior restraint and thus was unconstitutional, they maintained. Justice Frankfurter, however, did not agree with the libertarians. In his own concurring opinion demonstrating his views of media freedom as a policy, Frankfurter noted that while he agreed with the majority in this particular case, he thought states could protect themselves and their citizens against evil, as long as that protection did not harm "the necessary dependence of a free society upon the fullest scope of free expression."[20]

The debate over where to draw the line between protected and unprotected speech, and consequently when to expect responsible behavior, appeared again in another 1959 obscenity case, *Smith v. California*. Here the conviction of a bookseller was overturned because he had no way of knowing whether the material sold would be considered obscene under California law. In the various opinions in this case, the different perspectives of the justices are clear. Brennan again wrote the Court opinion, in which he argued that to uphold the conviction would effectively make booksellers censors of their own material, something unacceptable under the first amendment. Black concurred, but used his opinion to return to the majority's statement in *Roth* that some "more important interests" could outweigh first amendment protections. What were those interests, he wondered, and who would define them? Congress did not have that right under the Constitution, he argued; neither could the Supreme Court act as a board of censors, determining if expression "might adversely affect the morals of people throughout the many diversified local communities in this vast country." Black viewed his role as not defining the good for society. It was not for him or anyone else to decide what individuals could and could not read and see. Douglas, like Black, concurred with the result of *Smith*, repeating his views from his *Roth* dissent. Obscenity must be included under the first amendment umbrella, he argued, and no one could be punished for creating or distributing it. Frankfurter also concurred, but noted that this case favoring obscene material did not imply that all laws against expression were unconstitutional. Defamation, for example, and "inciting crime by speech" could both be held accountable under law—responsible behavior was expected in these situations. And finally, Harlan both concurred and dissented. He commented, as he had in *Roth*, that state laws on obscenity should be given more latitude than federal laws. In this case, however, he admitted that local communities could not arbitrarily consider some expression to be obscene.

The final censorship case decided prior to 1964 involved a denial by Chicago city officials of permission to show a particular motion picture. Again, the majority concluded that local communities could define morality for themselves. A split Court held that the first amendment did not grant absolute freedom to exhibit motion pictures, so the officials' action did not constitute prior restraint. Justice Clark, joined by Justices Frankfurter, Harlan, Whittaker, and Stewart, maintained that the city of Chicago had a right to protect its citizens from "the dangers of obscenity in the public exhibition of motion pictures."[21] In supporting his argument, Clark referred to often-quoted words from *Chaplinsky v. New Hampshire*, in which the Court outlined the categories of expression not protected under the first amendment:

[There are] certain well-defined and narrowly limited classes of speech, the prevention and punishment of which never have been thought to raise any Constitutional problem. These include the lewd and obscene, the profane, the libelous, and the insulting or 'fighting' words—those which by their very utterance inflict injury or tend to incite an immediate breach of the peace.[22]

In each of these types of expression, whether spoken, written, or broadcast, the requirements of media responsibility would outweigh the protection offered by the first amendment. And in this case, according to a majority of the Court, Chicago had a right to demand that minimum level of media responsibility in order to retain a certain level of decency in society.

The four "substantive" liberals, however, vehemently dissented. Chief Justice Warren, joined by Justices Black, Douglas, and Brennan, feared that the Court's apparent acceptance of a licensing system for motion pictures could lead to licensing—and demands of accountability—of all forms of media. All films in Chicago had to obtain a permit for exhibition, he pointed out, and while Chicago was not trying to license other media, there was no difference in principle between allowing one type of content-based licensing and not another. Interestingly, Justice Douglas, normally an ardent libertarian, wrote a separate dissenting opinion, joined by Warren and Black. Stressing that the government could not support the views of any particular religion or political philosophy, he quoted a "noted Jesuit," explaining that government could require responsibility after publication, though not before: "Antecedently," quoted Douglas, "it is presumed that a man will make a morally and socially responsible use of his freedom of expression; hence there is to be no prior restraint on it. However, if his use of freedom is irresponsible, he is summoned after the fact to responsibility before the judgment of the law."[23] Though this was all Douglas said on the issue at this point, it appears that he, and those who joined his opinion, were amenable to punishing media irresponsibility after publication but not requiring media responsibility before.

During the early Warren years, the justices decided two libel cases, both favoring media freedom and limiting media responsibility. *Barr v. Mateo* in 1959 involved a press release issued by a government official, in which he disclosed his intention to suspend certain employees. The official argued that he had absolute or qualified privilege to comment upon his employees, and five justices agreed. Justice Harlan, writing for himself and three others (Justice Black concurred separately) held that because Barr had written the press release "in the line of duty," he was entitled to absolute privilege—meaning he could not be sued for libel, even if he had released the information maliciously. This ruling was necessary, suggested Harlan, to protect public officials from "harassment and hazards of vindictive or illfounded damage suits" related to their official actions.[24] Four justices dissented for various reasons, including Chief Justice Warren, who argued that another, equally crucial interest was involved: the right to criticize, through libel suits if necessary, the actions of public officials. By removing the right of the public to sue officials for libel, Warren suggested, the Court majority had given too much power to officials, who were therefore free to say or print anything they wished within the jurisdiction of their offices. Public officials, Warren maintained, should receive no more than a qualified privilege to comment upon issues related to their work.

The second libel suit also protected publications—even irresponsible ones—from libel suits. In *Farmers Educational and Cooperative Union of America v. WDAY*, decided the same day as *Barr v. Mateo*, a five-justice majority held that broadcast stations could not be held liable for libelous statements made over the air by candidates for public office, if the station had been barred from removing the statements by the Federal Communications Act. Section 315 of that Act required broadcasters to give air time to legally qualified candidates for public office, and it had been interpreted to deny broadcasters the power of censorship over the candidates' statements. When a North Dakota senatorial candidate accused the farmers cooperative of conspiring to promote Communism, the cooperative sued the Fargo station broadcasting the comments. Justice Black, writing for the majority, argued that stations could not be held accountable for the statements of candidates, for they would act as censors, depriving their listeners of discussion on public issues. Thus, in this situation, requiring responsible behavior was seen as harming the political and educational functions of the media.

During the early Warren years, the Court also began dealing extensively with conflicts between the media and the justice system. Of course, earlier cases such as *Bridges* and *Pennekamp* had provided protection for the media to comment on and criticize judicial action, but the issue of the effect of news reporting on sensational trials had not yet reached the Court. It did, however, in two instances in the early 1960s, though in neither case did the justices comment on the media's responsibility in these situations. *Irvin v. Dowd*[25] involved a convicted murderer whose trial had been extensively covered by the news media. According to

Justice Clark's opinion for the unanimous Court, before the trial the media had interviewed people on the street, asking their opinions about Irvin's guilt or innocence and what sentence he should receive. The media had also detailed his background, including previous convictions for arson and burglary and a court martial. They announced that he refused to confess, that he had taken a lie detector test, and that he eventually did confess. Partly because of this pretrial publicity, 268 of the 430 persons interviewed for jury slots were excused because they already had an opinion about his guilt or innocence. However, despite all of this prejudicial coverage and evidence of its impact, in overturning the conviction the Court made no mention of media responsibility. In other words, even though Irvin's conviction was reversed specifically because the jury could not be impartial, the justices saw no need to comment upon the responsibility of the media in the case.

A similar situation arose two years later in *Rideau v. Louisiana*.[26] A film of Rideau's jail interview and confession to murder was broadcast several times, to audiences of up to 150,000 people. The trial court denied his request for a change of venue, so the Supreme Court overturned his conviction, again making no mention of media responsibility. It seems, then, at least for this group of justices, that media would not be held accountable for even the most sensationalized coverage.

The trend of the early Warren years is clear—in the areas of libel, pretrial publicity, and protected expression that did not qualify as obscenity, the responsibilities of publishers and broadcasters were minimal. The media, broadly defined to include public officials issuing press releases, booksellers, and so on, were remarkably free to write, say, and sell what they wished. Though there were dissenters among the justices, media freedom seemed always to muster a majority, thanks in part to the unwavering support of Justices Black and Douglas. But, though the holdings of the cases provided ample protection for the media against demands of responsibility, there was occasional discussion of the roles and responsibilities of the media.

One final case from this period provides an example of this. In *Talley v. California* in 1960, handbills were distributed calling for a boycott of merchants carrying products whose manufacturers would not give equal opportunity to African-Americans, Hispanics, or Asian-Americans. Though the handbills included an address and the identification "National Consumers Mobilization," no individual was listed as responsible for their distribution, a violation of a Los Angeles ordinance. The six-justice majority, led by Black, concluded that Los Angeles' requirement of identification would restrict freedom of expression, even though its intent was to identify purveyors of fraud, false advertising, and libel. Three justices, however, dissented. Clark, writing for himself, Frankfurter, and Whittaker, agreed that while Talley had a right to distribute the handbills, he did not have a right to anonymity. Los Angeles had a legitimate reason for the statute, Clark explained, for it wanted to protect its citizens from fraudulent or false statements. Newspapers and magazines had to reveal the names of publishers, he pointed out, in order to receive second class mailing privileges. It was clearly a minimum responsibility of anyone distributing information to acknowledge his or her role in that distribution:

All that Los Angeles requires is that one who exercises his right of free speech through writing or distributing handbills identify himself just as does one who speaks from the platform. The ordinance makes for the responsibility in writing that is present in public utterance. When and if the application of such an ordinance in a given case encroaches on First Amendment freedoms, then will be soon enough to strike that application down. But no such restraint has been shown here. . . . Before we may expect international responsibility among nations, might not it be well to require individual responsibility at home? Los Angeles' ordinance does no more.[27]

The first years of the Warren Court, then, set the stage for the unprecedented protection offered the media in 1964, as well as the ongoing discussion of media responsibility that occurred until the end of the liberal period in 1969. From the time of Earl Warren's appointment as chief justice in 1953, through the 1950s and early 1960s the Court consistently granted protection to the media and minimized demands of media responsibility. Despite this trend, there always existed a vocal minority on the bench, arguing for, at minimum, a recognition that the media could and should be accountable for some of their actions. It is not surprising, then, that after the unanimous vote protecting criticism of public officials in 1964, the Court divided again over the issue of media responsibility. That unanimity and division are the subject of the next section.

THE WARREN COURT LATER YEARS, 1964–1969

The cases decided in the later years of the Warren Court cluster in two primary areas, libel and obscenity, but discussions of media responsibility also occurred in privacy and broadcasting cases. These years, along with the first few of the following conservative era, were in some ways a time of turmoil with regard to definitions of media responsibility. In 1964 the Court articulated a strong, principled conception of media freedom and responsibility in *New York Times v. Sullivan*. It spent the next ten years reexamining and refining that principle, while sometimes granting more protection to the media. This continual reexamination yielded a remarkable array of definitions of media responsibility, as the justices shifted from giving near absolute protection to upholding an affirmative, liberal interpretation of media freedom and responsibility. This turmoil did not begin to subside until 1974, when the Court reversed an earlier decision, lessened protection of the media, and increased its demands of responsibility by the media.

In the meantime, however, throughout most of the final Warren years, libertarians Douglas and Black continued their arguments against any requirement of media responsibility. The first amendment protected the media absolutely, they concluded; therefore, the government is prohibited from interfering with, or demanding responsibility of, the media. But Douglas' and Black's philosophy never gained the full support of their colleagues, and they were left to expound their beliefs in concurring and dissenting opinions.

Another principled view of media freedom and responsibility did gain support, however briefly. Justice Harlan's "reasonableness" standard, defining acceptable behavior as how a "reasonable" or "responsible" publisher would act, became the standard in libel law from 1967 to 1971. Harlan also made the only natural-law-based argument for freedom of expression found in the cases studied. Freedom of the press belongs to all, he suggested, and is, as described in the Declaration of Independence, "unalienable."[28]

Finally, the period ended with a remarkable display of unity: The entire Court voted in *Red Lion Broadcasting Co. v. F.C.C.* to uphold the affirmative interpretation of the first amendment as applied to broadcasting. In a clearly liberal argument, the Court required broadcasters to provide equal opportunity for expression of diverse views. In addition, the Court maintained that individuals do not have a "right" to a broadcast license. Licenses are received as a privilege and include the obligation to act as a fiduciary, or steward, for the rest of society. The final part of the liberal era included, therefore, both cases granting strong protection of media freedom and requiring significant media responsibility.

This section begins with an overview of *New York Times v. Sullivan*, arguably one of the two most important press cases (with *Near v. Minnesota*) the Court has ever decided, and one in which the Court demanded little media responsibility. Despite the Court's strong statements protecting the media's right to criticize public officials in *New York Times*, the remainder of this era of the Court's history clearly demonstrates the division among the justices over how much expression to protect and what kinds of obligations to require of the media. Following the explanation of *New York Times* is a summary of the Court's growing disarray, first over obscenity law; and second, in three significant cases demonstrating the justices' differing opinions on media responsibility.

New York Times v. Sullivan, which outlined a new principle of media freedom and responsibility, involved a libel suit brought by a Montgomery, Alabama, commissioner against the *New York Times*. The unanimous Supreme Court overturned the libel verdict, arguing that Alabama's libel law did not sufficiently protect freedom of the press. In doing so, it acknowledged some irresponsible behavior on the part of the *Times*, but concluded that the level of irresponsibility was not enough to negate the newspaper's first amendment protection. Justice Brennan, writing for the Court, maintained that even though the *Times* had correct information in its own files and did not use them to check the accuracy of the defamatory statements, the *Times* did not act with "actual malice," the Court's new standard for irresponsible behavior regarding statements about public officials. The media were free, the Court ruled, to publish unkind, untrue, even damaging statements about officials as long as they did not know the statements were false or demonstrate "reckless disregard of whether [they were] false or not."[29]

For the first time in its history, the Court had set into law a definition of irresponsible behavior by the media. Some false statements were inevitable in discussion of public issues, the justices argued, so the media would be held accountable under law only when they were remarkably careless or knowingly lied. The Court had laid down new law and in the process defined one aspect of media responsibility. Despite the unanimous vote in the disposition of the case, Justice Black, joined by Justice Douglas, expressed reservations about the new standard. In his concurring opinion, Black argued what would become a recurring theme in his jurisprudence: The first amendment protects the media from abridgment by government; period. Thus, no law or standard—including the Court's new actual malice standard—could be used to punish the media for their published statements. Though they joined in the result of the case, Black and Douglas did not approve of the concept of actual malice and feared the Court had limited the protection granted by the first amendment. Malice, wrote Black,

is an elusive, abstract concept, hard to prove and hard to disprove. The requirement that malice be proved provides at best an evanescent protection for the right critically to discuss public affairs and certainly does not measure up to the sturdy safeguard embodied in the First Amendment. Unlike the Court, therefore, I vote to reverse exclusively on the ground that the *Times* and the individual defendants had an absolute, unconditional constitutional right to publish in the *Times* advertisement their criticisms of the Montgomery agencies and officials. . . . [T]he Federal Constitution has . . . [granted] the press an absolute immunity for criticism of the way public officials do their duty. . . . Stopgap measures like those the Court adopts are in my judgment not enough.[30]

In sum, despite granting the media the most protection they had ever had, the justices disagreed over where to draw the line between acceptable and unacceptable behavior by the media. Six justices believed the actual malice standard provided an appropriate line, while three justices argued that the first amendment demanded that there be no line at all.[31] This discussion was to continue throughout the remainder of the Court's liberal era.

The various obscenity cases decided between 1964 and 1969 provided additional examples of the continuing conflict between the libertarians, who argued for no demands of media responsibility, and the rest of the Court, which acknowledged the needs of communities to set—within certain limitations—their own standards of morality in expression. Of the seven obscenity cases decided during these five years, only one was the result a unanimous vote. Votes in the other six ranged from 7–2 (one case) to 6–3 (four cases) to 5–4 (one case).[32] In each of the nonunanimous cases, Justice Brennan authored the Court's opinion, each time trying to define more precisely the meaning of obscenity and the outer limits of protected expression. And in each case Black and Douglas—sometimes independently, sometimes together—argued that any definition of obscenity led inevitably to censorship and thus was unconstitutional. The dividing line between responsible and irresponsible publication was again drawn.

By taking on the task of defining and redefining obscenity, the Court put itself in the position of ruling on the character of individual publications, much as a trial court might do. For example, in *Jacobellis v. Ohio* in 1964, Brennan and two others held that a particular film was not obscene. These three were joined by Douglas and Black, who made their standard anti-censorship argument, to create a majority favoring the film. In *Mishkin v. New York* (1966) Brennan and five others held that fifty books could be considered obscene under New York's obscenity statute. Libertarians Black and Douglas, of course, dissented. While Black and Douglas maintained their principled view that all speech and press should be protected, the other seven justices were forced continually to reexamine the line between responsible and irresponsible publication, a line that ultimately depended upon how many other justices Brennan could convince to join him.

Justice Harlan outlined a more principled—though doomed—definition of media responsibility in his opinions in *Time v. Hill* and *Curtis Publishing Co. v. Butts/Associated Press v. Walker*.[33] In both cases, decided in 1967, Harlan argued for a "reasonableness" standard of press responsibility. That is, the media should and would be protected as long as they acted reasonably and within the standards of everyday journalism. When the media went beyond those standards, Harlan suggested, they could be punished. In the first case, *Time v. Hill*, Harlan alone maintained his idea, but in *Curtis v. Butts/Associated Press v. Walker*, he was able to muster enough votes to author the Court opinion.

Time v. Hill involved a *Life Magazine* article and photo essay about a Pennsylvania family held hostage by escaped convicts. The photos were taken of a fictionalized play about the incident, which had changed the circumstances of the situation to portray the family members as more heroic and the convicts as more violent than had been true. The play had changed the family's names, but *Life* used their real names. The family was awarded damages from *Life*'s parent company for invasion of privacy based on the false portrayal of the hostage situation. The Supreme Court, however, overturned that award, maintaining that the actual malice standard from *New York Times* should apply to "false light" privacy cases as well. The protections of the first amendment, wrote Justice Brennan for the majority, apply not only to matters of political interest; they apply also to matters of purely public interest: "One need only pick up any newspaper or magazine," he wrote, "to comprehend the vast range of published matter which exposes persons to public view, both private citizens and public officials. Exposure of self to others in varying degrees is a concomitant of life in a civilized community. This risk of exposure is an essential incident of life in a society which places a primary value on freedom of speech and press."[34] Thus, as long as *Life* did not act with actual malice as defined in *New York Times*, it could not be held liable for its "false reports of matters of public interest."[35] Brennan and the majority, therefore, were willing to apply the protection of the first amendment to admittedly false, though not malicious, statements.

Justice Harlan, however, disagreed with this application of the actual malice standard. In his concurring/dissenting opinion,[36] Harlan argued that there exists a key difference between protecting the media in publishing information about public officials and in allowing them to harm private individuals caught in a public controversy. Public officials, he noted, have the resources to respond to attacks in the media, whereas private individuals typically do not. In addition, public officials choose to enter public life, whereas innocents like the Hill family are thrust into the spotlight without their consent. In cases involving private individuals caught in the public glare, Harlan suggested, states should be allowed to require that the media make "a reasonable investigation of the underlying facts" of the situation.[37] The media, he contended, could be held accountable for their actions in situations like these, much as doctors and lawyers are held accountable under law for their actions:

Other professional activity of great social value is carried on under a duty of reasonable care and there is no reason to suspect the press would be less hardy than medical practitioners or attorneys for example. The 'freedom of the press' guaranteed by the First Amendment, and as reflected in the Fourteenth, cannot be thought to insulate all press conduct from review and responsibility for harm inflicted. The majority would allow sanctions against such conduct only when it is morally culpable. I insist that it can also be reached when it creates a severe risk of irremediable harm to individuals involuntarily exposed to it and powerless to protect themselves against it. . . . A constitutional doctrine which relieves the press of even this minimal responsibility in cases of this sort seems to me unnecessary and ultimately harmful to the permanent good health of the press itself.[38]

The reasonableness standard, therefore, Harlan argued, should be applied when the media caused "irremediable" harm to private individuals caught in the limelight. The media should be held to a higher standard of accountability in cases like these than in situations involving public officials.

Despite this impassioned argument, none of Harlan's colleagues joined his opinion in *Time v. Hill*. That changed several months later, however, when Harlan was able to convince Justices Clark, Stewart, and Fortas to join him in *Curtis v. Butts/Associated Press v. Walker*. Because Chief Justice Warren concurred with these four in their conclusions, though not their arguments, Harlan was able to write the Court's opinion for a 5–4 majority. His reasonableness standard became the official Court definition of media responsibility, if only briefly. *Curtis Publishing Co. v. Butts* and *Associated Press v. Walker* were companion cases in which the Court explicitly extended first amendment protection to the press in libel cases involving public figures, those people who intentionally thrust themselves into public controversies. *Curtis v. Butts* involved a claim by the *Saturday Evening Post* that University of Georgia athletic director Wally Butts and University of Alabama football coach "Bear" Bryant had conspired to fix a football game between the two schools. *Associated Press v. Walker* involved a supposed "charge" led by a former Army officer against federal marshals trying to enforce a court order integrating the University of Mississippi in 1962. In the first case, the Court upheld the jury ruling against the *Saturday*

Evening Post because of clear violations of accepted standards of reporting. In the second case, however, the Court found that the Associated Press had acted reasonably in its report on the situation in Mississippi.

Harlan's argument in the *Curtis/Associated Press* cases recognized the difficulty of balancing the right of freedom of expression with the danger of harming individuals' reputations. Freedom of expression, he pointed out, belongs not just to the media, and it is guaranteed for more than social needs. It also belongs to individuals, who have the right simply to speak their minds, he explained in a classic natural rights, principled argument: "[I]t is as much a guarantee to individuals of their personal right to make their thoughts public. . . . as it is a social necessity required for the maintenance of our political system and an open society. . . . The dissemination of the individual's opinions on matters of public interest is for us, in the historic words of the Declaration of Independence, an 'unalienable right' that 'governments are instituted among men to secure.'"[39]

Individuals, as well as the media, have a natural right to speak their opinions, according to Harlan. Nevertheless, that right has limits. By its very existence, libel law—even in the form of the actual malice standard—acknowledges those limits. And for Harlan, the limits of the right of free expression could be found at the outer edges of journalistic standards of the day. In the case of public figures claiming to have been libeled, recovery for damages could only occur, held Harlan and the three justices joining his opinion, if the media had abandoned the standards held by responsible journalists. Specifically, Harlan wrote, "We . . . would hold that a 'public figure' who is not a public official may also recover damages for a defamatory falsehood whose substance makes substantial danger to reputation apparent, on a showing of highly unreasonable conduct constituting an extreme departure from the standards of investigation and reporting ordinarily adhered to by responsible publishers."[40]

In outlining this new definition of media responsibility, Harlan and the others set the reasonableness standard into constitutional law, but in the process created a tautology: Media responsibility was defined as actions that responsible journalists would take. This new standard was clarified somewhat by these two cases, for the *Saturday Evening Post*'s conduct was viewed as departing from standards of responsibility, whereas that of the Associated Press was viewed as reasonable, given the situation.

Harlan had, therefore, created a new Supreme Court conception of media responsibility, vague though it was. But this new conception never had the approval of a majority of the Court. Chief Justice Warren, who joined Harlan and the other three in the result, but not the reasoning, of the two cases, specifically pointed out the confusing nature of Harlan's new standard. The "reasonableness" standard, Warren argued, would not aid juries in deciding whether statements on public figures were in fact constitutionally protected, and thus would not sufficiently protect the media's freedom. The outer limit of responsibility, he argued, should be the actual malice standard from *New York Times v. Sullivan*. That test would adequately protect both the media's freedom and the reputations of public figures, Warren maintained. And in the case of the *Saturday Evening Post*, in his opinion, the actual malice standard had been met.

Although Harlan's reasonableness standard was presented in a Court opinion, it never had the support of more than four justices at one time, so it never truly became Supreme Court doctrine. Instead, the *New York Times* actual malice test ultimately became the rule regarding libel of public figures and officials, and Harlan's standard was expressly repudiated in later libel cases.[41]

Nevertheless, Justice Harlan had articulated, however unsuccessfully, a standard of responsibility that would offer more protection to individuals covered in the media while still protecting media freedom. Though his standard suffered from circular reasoning, it is possible that had it gained the support of a majority of the justices it might have become refined into a viable definition of media responsibility. As it is, the Court chose to use the more protective actual malice standard, and in so doing demonstrated that it would hold the media to a truly minimum level of responsibility, at least in the area of libel of public figures and officials.

While the Court, over the long term, was willing to require only a minimum threshold of media responsibility in the area of libel, it did conclude that more responsibility could be required of the broadcast media. In 1969, in the last media case of the Warren years, the Supreme Court handed down one of the most liberal (though not libertarian) media cases in its history. *Red Lion Broadcasting Co. v. Federal Communications Commission* provided the single best example of both the social responsibility and affirmative views of the first amendment, for it was in *Red Lion* that the unanimous Court[42] permitted the federal government, in the form of the F.C.C., to require a right of reply for individuals attacked on broadcast stations. In addition, during this decision the Court ruled that the Fairness Doctrine, a policy of the F.C.C., not only did not violate the first amendment, but actually enhanced the amendment's freedoms.

Red Lion involved two cases having to do with F.C.C. rules regarding individuals' right of reply. Specifically, the F.C.C. required that stations carrying a personal attack had to notify the attacked individual of the time and date of the broadcast, provide the individual with a tape or script of the attack, and offer time to respond. The rules did not apply to attacks by legally qualified candidates or their spokespersons, bona fide news coverage, or attacks on foreign individuals. In both cases the Supreme Court held that the F.C.C. rules promoted the values of the first amendment.

Justice White, who was later to become one of the Court's strongest proponents of media responsibility, wrote the opinion. Broadcasters, he and the rest of the Court contended, had an affirmative obligation to society to provide "both" sides of public issues. But White was careful in the early part of his opinion to note that Congress itself had recognized this affirmative obligation of broadcasters. In 1957, he pointed out, Congress had modified part of the Communications Act of 1934, expressly noting the obligation of broadcasters "to operate in the public interest and to afford reasonable opportunity for the discussion of conflicting views on issues of public importance."[43] This statement validated, in the Court's view, the responsibility of broadcasters to promote diverse perspectives on public issues. Therefore, the Court itself felt free to include that responsibility in its own decisions.

But the 1957 statement by Congress did not provide the only rationale for the Court's ruling in *Red Lion*. Justice White also relied upon what had become known as the "scarcity principle"—the notion that because the number of broadcast frequencies is finite, the government can place restrictions upon their use, including requiring presentation of various sides of issues. Broadcasting, White admitted, does have some first amendment protection, but because of broadcasting's unique nature as a limited resource, the government may apply different standards to it. Broadcasting could be compared to loudspeakers on a sound truck, he explained, which the Court had limited in an earlier case. "Just as the Government may limit the use of sound-amplifying equipment potentially so noisy that it drowns out civilized private speech, so may the Government limit the use of broadcast equipment," White wrote. And in a direct example of the affirmative view of the first amendment, he continued: "The right of free speech of a broadcaster, the user of a sound truck, or any other individual does not embrace a right to snuff out the free speech of others."[44]

But this was not all. Broadcasters are granted licenses by the federal government, and in accepting those licenses they also accept certain obligations. One of those obligations, White contended in a collectivist argument, is to act not in self-interest, but in the interests of society. Licensees, he wrote, have no right to exclude points of view with which they do not agree. And the first amendment does not forbid the government from requiring broadcasters to act as public trustees who must represent fairly "those views and voices" of their community.[45] The broadcaster was to act as a steward of the valuable resource, sharing the airwaves with others. Broadcast frequencies, the Court ruled, belong to all people, not just those to whom the government has granted licenses.

In one of its strongest affirmative statements ever on freedom of the press, the Court returned to a fundamental understanding of the role of the media in U.S. society and politics. In order for the political and social systems to function as they should, each person should have access to as much information as possible, so that she or he can make competent decisions concerning everyday life. The media play a crucial role in the spread of this information, and, for the most part, they are protected from all government intervention so that they may pursue that role fully. But the broadcasters' role as fiduciary or steward of broadcast frequencies places upon them a special obligation. Unlike the print media, broadcasters have a specific responsibility to the public, a responsibility that the federal government and the Supreme Court enforced. Ultimately, broadcasting is a privilege, Justice White noted, not a right, and with that privilege comes the responsibility to promote equality of opportunity and serve the marketplace of ideas.

It seems appropriate that this announcement of the unique responsibility of one part of the media industry came when it did, for *Red Lion* marked the symbolic, if not the actual, end of the liberal era of the Supreme Court. It was the final media case the Warren Court decided, and certainly one could argue it was one of the most demanding on the issue of media responsibility. As a final example of Chief Justice Warren's, and his colleagues', desire to use the government to promote equality, it illustrates what Dworkin argues separates late-twentieth-century liberals from their conservative counterparts. *Red Lion*, therefore, marks the high (or low, depending on one's perspective) point of liberal rulings on media responsibility, for it contains expectations that the media can, and should, be used to promote equality within U.S. society. Within a few years, however, as the Court began its shift to more conservative views, this conception of the media and equality faded.

NOTES

1. Paul L. Murphy, *The Constitution in Crisis Times, 1918–1969* (New York: Harper and Row, 1972), 310.

2. Murphy, *Crisis*, 310.

3. G. Edward White, *The American Judicial Tradition: Profiles of Leading American Judges*, expanded ed. (New York: Oxford University Press, 1988), 337.

4. Russell Galloway, *The Rich and the Poor in Supreme Court History, 1790–1982* (Greenbrae, Calif.: Paradigm Press, 1982), 156.

5. White, 324.

6. White, 324.

7. Quoted at White, 342.

8. White, 344–45.

9. Kermit C. Hall, *The Magic Mirror: Law in American History* (New York: Oxford University Press, 1989), 270.

10. Karl N. Llewellyn, "Some Realism about Realism—Responding to Dean Pound" in Stephen B. Presser and Jamil S. Zainaldin, *Law and Jurisprudence in American History* (St. Paul, Minnesota: West Publishing, 1989). 782–83.

11. White, 389.

12. *Griswold v. Connecticut*, 381 U.S. 478 (1965).

13. *Public Utilities Commission of the District of Columbia v. Pollack*, 343 U.S. 451 (1952) at 467–69. Quoted in Michael Kammen, *Sovereignty and Liberty: Constitutional Discourse in American Culture* (Madison: University of Wisconsin Press, 1988), 94.

14. 410 U.S. 179 (1973) at 211–13. Quoted at White, 411.

15. *Brown v. Board of Higher Education*, 347 U.S. 483 (1954); *Watkins v. United States*, 354 U.S. 178 (1957); *Sweezy v. New Hampshire*, 354 U.S. 234 (1957); *Yates v. United States*, 354 U.S. 298 (1957).

16. *Roth v. United States*, 77 S.Ct. 1304, 1309 (1957), Justice Brennan, Court opinion.

17. *Roth v. United States*, 77 S.Ct. 1304, 1311 (1957), Justice Brennan, Court opinion.

18. Justice Harlan dissented in *Roth*, but joined the majority in the companion case, *Alberts v. California*.

19. *Roth v. United States*, 77 S.Ct. 1304, 1323 (1957), Justice Douglas, dissenting.

20. *Kingsley International Pictures Corp. v. Regents of the University of the State of New York*, 79 S.Ct. 1362, 1368 (1959), Justice Frankfurter, concurring.

21. *Times Film Corp. v. City of Chicago*, 81 S.Ct. 391, 395 (1961), Justice Clark, Court opinion.

22. *Times Film Corp. v. City of Chicago*, 81 S.Ct. 391, 394 (1961), Justice Clark, Court opinion. Quoting *Chaplinsky v. New Hampshire*, 62 S.Ct. 766, 769 (1942).

23. *Times Film Corp. v. City of Chicago*, 81 S.Ct. 391, 412 (1961), Justice Douglas, dissenting. Quoting Murray, *We Hold These Truths*, 1960, 164–65.

24. *Barr v. Mateo*, 79 S.Ct. 1335 (1959), Justice Harlan, Court opinion.

25. *Irvin v. Dowd*, 81 S.Ct. 1639 (1961).

26. *Rideau v. Louisiana*, 83 S.Ct. 1417 (1963).

27. *Talley v. California*, 80 S.Ct. 536, 542 (1960), Justice Clark, dissenting.

28. *Curtis Publishing Co. v. Butts*, 87 S.Ct. 1975 (1967), Justice Harlan, Court opinion.

29. *New York Times v. Sullivan*, 84 S.Ct. 710, 726 (1964), Justice Brennan, Court opinion.

30. *New York Times v. Sullivan*, 84 S.Ct. 710, 733–34 (1964), Justice Black, concurring.

31. Justice Goldberg also concurred, writing "In my view, the First and Fourteenth Amendments to the Constitution afford to the citizen and the press an absolute, unconditional privilege to criticize official conduct despite the harm which may flow from excesses and abuses." *New York Times v. Sullivan*, 84 S.Ct. 710, 735 (1964), Justice Goldberg, concurring.

32. The seven cases are *A Quantity of Copies of Books v. Kansas*, 84 S.Ct. 1723 (1964); *Jacobellis v. Ohio*, 84 S.Ct. 1676 (1964); *Ginzburg v. United States*, 86 S.Ct. 942 (1966); *Mishkin v. New York*, 86 S.Ct. 958 (1966); *A Book Named John Cleland's Memoirs of a Woman of Pleasure v. Attorney General of the Commonwealth of Massachusetts*, 86 S.Ct. 975 (1966); *Ginsberg v. New York*, 88 S.Ct. 1274 (1968); and *Stanley v. Georgia*, 89 S.Ct. 1243 (1969).

33. These two cases were decided together.

34. *Time v. Hill*, 87 S.Ct. 534, 542 (1967), Justice Brennan, Court opinion.

35. *Time v. Hill*, 87 S.Ct. 534, 542 (1967), Justice Brennan, Court opinion.

36. He concurred with the majority's remanding of the case, but disagreed with the majority's command that the lower court apply the actual malice standard to the case; he preferred the less protective negligence standard.

37. *Time v. Hill*, 87 S.Ct. 534, 553 (1967), Justice Harlan, concurring/dissenting.

38. *Time v. Hill*, 87 S.Ct. 534, 553–54 (1967), Justice Harlan, concurring/dissenting.

39. *Curtis Publishing Co. v. Butts*, 87 S.Ct. 1975, 1988 (1967), Justice Harlan, Court opinion.

40. *Curtis Publishing Co. v. Butts*, 87 S.Ct. 1975, 1991 (1967), Justice Harlan, Court opinion.

41. See, for example, *Rosenbloom v. Metromedia*, 91 S.Ct. 1811 (1971) and *Gertz v. Welch*, 94 S.Ct. 2997 (1974).

42. The vote was 8–0; Justice Douglas took no part in the case.

43. *Red Lion Broadcasting Co. v. Federal Communications Commission*, 89 S.Ct. 1794, 1801 (1969), Justice White, Court opinion, quoting 1957 congressional amendment of section 315 of the Communications Act.

44. *Red Lion Broadcasting Co. v. Federal Communications Commission*, 89 S.Ct. 1794, 1805 (1969), Justice White, Court opinion.

45. *Red Lion Broadcasting Co. v. Federal Communications Commission*, 89 S.Ct. 1794, 1806 (1969), Justice White, Court opinion.

Chapter Four

The Centrist Years, 1969–1981

Though the change from Earl Warren to Warren Burger was not as abrupt as the change the Court underwent in 1937–1938, the shift in chief justices in 1969 did herald another era of the Court's history. The "third conservative era" of the U.S. Supreme Court,[1] which began symbolically with Burger's arrival, in fact, appeared gradually over a number of years, and in three marked phases. The first phase, from 1969 until about 1975, contained some remnants of the Warren period. The Warren liberals were often able to convince one or more of the moderates to join them in expansive readings of the rights provisions in the Constitution. *Roe v. Wade* symbolizes this period. A nearly perfect balance on the Court characterizes the second phase, from 1975 to 1981: There were two confirmed liberals, two equally dedicated conservatives, and five centrists moving back and forth. Finally, the shift to the conservative side became more pronounced in the third period, beginning in 1981.

The Burger Court era began with a shift in the country's political leanings. The increasingly bitter and violent political conflicts of 1968 had brought Richard Nixon to the presidency, beginning a period of over two decades of Republican control of the White House (with the exception of Jimmy Carter, who made no appointments to the Court). Throughout Burger's tenure, the country became more conservative, with the policies of Lyndon Johnson's Great Society and welfare liberalism falling further and further from favor. By 1980 and the election of Ronald Reagan, the Republican party had left behind the emphasis on equality present in American politics since the New Deal.[2] Burger and his colleagues, therefore, received clear signals from the occupants of the White House: They were to tone down, and even remove, the "excesses" of the Warren Court years.

However, this was not to be, at least not entirely, and not during the 1970s. Burger could not often command a majority until later in his tenure, and he suffered from a lack of ability, both intellectually and personally, to lead the Court. He was interested less in the legal aspects of his job and more in the ceremony and esteem reserved for the Supreme Court. He effectively alienated several of his colleagues, who occasionally resorted to working behind his back to form coalitions and rewrite his opinions. Justice Douglas evidently believed that Burger often switched his vote to the majority view to deny Douglas the opportunity to assign opinions.[3] He was, in one observer's words, "out of his depth."[4]

Not all of Burger's leadership problems were his fault, however. Earl Warren, particularly in his later years, had a solid majority to lead, but Burger never did. Though in the first three years of his presidency, Nixon had already made four appointments to the Court (Burger, Harry Blackmun for Abe Fortas' seat in June 1970, and both Lewis Powell and William Rehnquist in January 1972, to replace Hugo Black and John Marshall Harlan, who both resigned in September 1971), the four did not necessarily command a majority. Three strong Warren liberals— William O. Douglas, William Brennan, and Thurgood Marshall—remained and were joined regularly by some of the centrists—Potter Stewart, Byron White, Blackmun, and Powell. The three liberals needed to gain only two votes, while Burger and Rehnquist had to convince three colleagues to vote with them.

Perhaps the key characteristic of the early and middle Burger years was the presence of between three and five moderates on the Court, justices who individually decided cases based on specific facts rather than overall principles, and who collectively controlled the outcomes of many decisions. Stewart, White, Blackmun, Powell, and John Paul Stevens (who replaced Douglas in 1975), though they had varying backgrounds, were appointed by different presidents, and served during very different eras, were all "lawyer's judges,"[5] who examined each case independently, relying on precedent and the facts at hand rather than a grand vision of the purposes of the Constitution. They were, in a word, pragmatists.

Stewart had been appointed in 1958 by Dwight Eisenhower, and during the latter Warren years he appeared more conservative in relation to his liberal colleagues. But as the Court shifted gently to the right, Stewart occupied the middle. He had no "deep-seated philosophy regarding the proper relationship between the state and its citizens," but he was the justice "most interested in the technical aspects of the Court's work."[6]

White, a 1962 Kennedy appointee, was remarkably qualified for the Supreme Court. He graduated first in his college class, was elected Phi Beta Kappa as a junior, won ten varsity letters, was All-America in football, and won a Rhodes Scholarship, which he delayed to play professional football for a year. After his work at Oxford, he attended Yale Law School, but dropped out to play for the Detroit Lions and serve in World War II. He returned to Yale and graduated *magna cum laude*. After law school he clerked for Chief Justice Fred Vinson and eventually went into private practice. At the time of his appointment, he was deputy attorney general, working directly under Robert Kennedy. Though known for favoring civil rights claims, White was more conservative on issues of criminal procedure; in Blasi's words, he "prefer[red] that social problems be solved by other branches of the federal government and by the states."[7] He was pragmatic and given to narrow, rather than sweeping, opinions. Perhaps because of this pragmatism, White "has not left a strong mark on the development of legal doctrine"[8] Blasi concluded.

Blackmun, known early as a "Minnesota Twin" because of his long friendship with, and apparent judicial likeness to, Warren Burger, moved out from under Burger's wing in 1973 when he authored *Roe v. Wade*. As time went on, Blackmun's opinions became increasingly liberal, and by the end of his tenure he was considered one of the most liberal justices.

Powell, a Richmond lawyer and former head of the American Bar Association, arrived in 1971 and soon carved out a space on the right side of the centrist justices. He "avoided doctrinaire positions and hard-edged ideological decisions and gained a reputation as a moderate though he voted more often with Chief Justice Burger than some of the others in the center bloc."[9] In several key decisions, Powell cast the fifth vote and wrote a concurring opinion. Thus, he was able with his single vote to lessen the impact of the majority opinion. For example, in *Branzburg v. Hayes*, in which the Court concluded that journalists do not have a constitutional right to refuse to testify before grand juries, Powell provided the fifth vote. His concurring opinion (he did not join the majority opinion) suggested that while journalists did not have a constitutional right not to testify, courts should "[strike] a proper balance between freedom of the press and the obligation of all citizens to give relevant testimony with respect to criminal conduct."[10] This narrowing of the majority opinion opened the door for a dissenting Justice Stewart to suggest a three-step process for courts to use to determine that balance. Stewart's three-step suggestion has been adopted in many jurisdictions. Thus, Powell was able to so completely limit the Court ruling that, in fact, the dissenting view eventually became predominant.

The arrival of Stevens in 1975 marked the beginning of the second phase of the Burger Court shift to conservatism. Stevens replaced Douglas, the Court's longest-serving and most libertarian justice, and changed the balance of the Court to two liberals, two conservatives, and five moderates. The moderates now could be a majority by themselves, and on occasion they were, leaving the four ideologues to dissent. This new configuration, as well as Burger's inability to lead, had a direct impact on the Court's decisions. Any majority now needed some of the moderates, and case opinions tended toward "narrow and cautious dispositions of issues."[11] The new balance also changed the roles of some justices. For example, Brennan's once-considerable liberal influence declined, whereas Stewart and White gained power they did not have in the Warren years.[12]

The Court composition changed again in 1981 when Sandra Day O'Connor became the first "sister" to join the "brethren,"[13] replacing moderate Stewart. O'Connor, third in her class at Stanford Law School (Rehnquist was first in the same class), was a conservative in comparison to most of her colleagues in the early 1980s and tended to vote with the chief justice and Rehnquist. Her arrival, then, marked the third phase of the Burger Court, the point at which it became easier for conservatives to gain a majority. By this time equality as a constitutional principle was less valued than it had been in the Warren years.

Throughout the years of the Burger Court, then, the centrists had a significant amount of control. They could command a majority of their own, use their influence to narrow rulings that were too liberal or too conservative, and could force justices on the ends of the spectrum to tailor their own opinions to gain a majority. The five centrists did not have a collective view of the Constitution. Instead, they took cases individually; thus, the Court, particularly in its middle years, appeared often to be rudderless and without an overall philosophy.

But some justices had definite philosophies. On either end of the judicial spectrum, Brennan and Marshall, Rehnquist and Burger fought for their conceptions of the Constitution. Brennan and Marshall, holdovers from the heyday of the Warren years who lasted well into the Rehnquist Court, were determined to continue the work of the Warren Court, valuing equality over liberty, freedom *for* over freedom *from*. For them, "the primary role of the courts was to serve as protectors of individual rights."[14] Yet, according to Blasi, they were not up to the task. They could not "articulat[e] in compelling and pure form the liberal theory of the Constitution. Both are pragmatic men, more clever than profound. They lack the elemental force and vision of a Holmes, or Brandeis, or Black, or Douglas, or Warren."[15] Blasi has similar comments for the conservative side of the Burger Court:

The Chief Justice is a man of limited capacity and no discernible coherent philosophy. . . . William Rehnquist has the intelligence, energy, charm, and a very conservative judicial philosophy, but he is more of a debater than a thinker, more a lawyer than a statesman. He has not even approached his predecessors Frankfurter, Jackson, and Harlan in articulating a conservative constitutional philosophy. In fact, Justices Rehnquist and Brennan could be viewed as twin aliens of the right and left . . . who could serve better as coalition builders operating at the center of the Court's divisions. Brennan performed that role to perfection during the heyday of the Warren Court. Rehnquist may have a chance to do so in the future.[16]

The Burger Court, then, throughout its seventeen years, was dominated by moderates, but did move from left to right over time. It was indeed a time of transition from the Warren liberalism to the Rehnquist conservatism.[17] This can be seen clearly in the various doctrinal developments of the time, for in some cases the Burger Court advanced the Warren Court program, in some cases there was little change, and in some cases the Warren precedents were narrowed.

THE BURGER COURT EARLY YEARS, 1969–1975

The period from fall 1969 to the end of 1975 included significant change in the Court, both in personnel and ideology. The first third of Chief Justice Burger's tenure saw five new justices (including Burger), the beginning disintegration of the liberals' power, and the Court's shift toward conservatism, with consequent changes in views on media responsibility. The arrival of conservatives Burger and Rehnquist (1972), apparent conservative Blackmun (1971), and moderates Powell (1972) and Stevens (1975), replacing Justices Warren, Harlan, Fortas, Black, and Douglas, respectively, seemed likely to move the Court sharply to the right. The Court did indeed move away from the extreme liberalism of the later Warren years, but it did not immediately reflect a conservative ideology. During this and the ensuing period, divisions among the justices were too great for the Court to find a coherent philosophical perspective. Justices Brennan, Marshall, and Douglas continued until 1975 to form a solid liberal bloc, needing only two votes to gain a majority, while Burger and Rehnquist occupied the opposite side of the political philosophical spectrum. Justices Stewart, White, and Powell were pragmatic moderates, voting with either side, and Justice Blackmun, originally seen as conservative, moved more toward the liberals over time. During these early Burger years, then, the influence of the Warren liberals remained strong, but liberal decisions were no longer guaranteed.

The divisions among the justices and the diminishing liberal power added to the turmoil visible in media cases after 1964. After unanimously outlining the actual malice standard in *New York Times v. Sullivan* that year, the Court spent the next decade struggling to define the parameters of that standard. During the first Burger Court years, a plurality of three justices extended the standard to include discussion on issues of public importance, but the Court reversed that three years later in a decision that began the trend toward greater demands for media responsibility that continued until—and perhaps past—the late 1990s.

While the liberals' power was diminishing, the Court's caseload was growing. From fall 1969 to the end of 1975, the justices ruled on thirty-five media cases[18] in a number of areas, including libel, obscenity, national defense, commercial speech, privacy, special press rights, and public access to the media.

Three areas provided ongoing discussion of media responsibility. First, throughout the early 1970s the Court continued its attempt to define the line between libelous statements needing protection and those beyond acceptable legal standards, by protecting accurate and defamatory discussion of public issues, but also by narrowing the boundaries of protected expression and increasing media responsibility for the first time since 1964. Second, in several cases the justices confronted the question of whether the first amendment grants special privileges to the media beyond those given to the public at large and concluded that it does not. Third, the Court returned to the issue put forth in *Red Lion* of whether the media could be required to grant space or time to private individuals or groups. While the majority held on two cases that it could not, one of those cases produced discussion of the merits of liberal, social responsibility, negative, and affirmative interpretations of media freedom and responsibility. The other showed a full Court unwilling to use an affirmative interpretation to require print media to provide access to alternative voices. Discussion of these three areas follows.

The Supreme Court decided six libel cases during the early years of Burger's tenure, four of which did little to change the law. The first of these, *Greenbelt*

Cooperative Publishing Association v. Bresler[19] in 1970, did, however, provide some indirect discussion of media responsibility. A newspaper had been sued over its reports on heated discussion in several city council meetings, where the term "blackmail" had been used in reference to Bresler, a land developer, and had been duly reported. Bresler sued for libel and won. In overturning the jury verdict, the Court held that the term was neither libel nor slander, given the context of heated public debate. In addition, Justice Stewart, writing for all of his colleagues, argued that the newspaper could not be held liable anyway, for it was merely reporting what happened at the city council meetings. The articles in question, Stewart wrote, were "accurate and truthful reports of what had been said at the public hearings before the city council."[20] This meant that not only could the newspaper not be found liable, but in fact it was acting responsibly. In Stewart's words, the newspaper was "performing its wholly legitimate function as a community newspaper."[21]

The important point in Stewart's opinion, for present purposes, is his emphasis on the accuracy of the reports. Had the term blackmail been taken out of context, Stewart notes, "this would be a different case," implying that perhaps this situation would be unacceptable behavior in the Court's view. Responsibility in this case, then, might be limited to full, accurate reporting of hyperbole.

The next three libel cases were decided on a single day in 1971, all in favor of the media organizations involved. *Monitor Patriot v. Roy*[22] and *Ocala Star-Banner v. Damron*[23] both concerned charges of criminal conduct levied against candidates for public office; *Time v. Pape*[24] dealt with a magazine article taken primarily from a federal government report. In *Monitor Patriot*, Justice Stewart writing for the entire Court held that charges of criminal conduct were never irrelevant to a candidate's suitability for public office; thus, a claim that a senatorial candidate was a bootlegger could not be libel as long as it was not published with actual malice. In *Ocala*, a newspaper mistakenly reported that a mayoral candidate had been arrested for perjury. The newspaper admitted that the story was false and that an editor was at fault. But because actual malice was not involved, and because the charge related to the candidate's qualifications for office, the Court ruled for the newspaper.

The Court also required minimal responsibility in the third of these cases. A writer for *Time* magazine had to choose from among several possible versions of the "truth." Although she ultimately chose the wrong interpretation, the magazine could not be punished, for, as Justice Stewart explained, it had "maintain[ed] a standard of care" to avoid actual malice. *Time*, therefore, was safe from liability because it had exercised its journalistic discretion—it had behaved, as Justice Harlan had argued in other cases, as a reasonable, responsible publisher would.

The final two libel cases decided between 1969 and 1975, unlike the first four, added significantly to libel law and the Court's interpretation of its rule of actual malice. In addition, opinions in both *Rosenbloom v. Metromedia* and *Gertz v. Welch* further illuminated the various justices' views of media responsibility within the realm of libel.

The *Rosenbloom* case provided the most protection given the media in the sixty-five years studied and outlined the most lenient demands of media responsibility. Because the holding was not from a majority, however, it lacked the impact of *New York Times v. Sullivan*. In *Rosenbloom* a plurality of three justices (Brennan, Burger, and Blackmun) held that private libel plaintiffs, like public officials and public figures, had to prove actual malice if they were libeled in the course of a discussion on public issues.[25] Writing for the plurality, Justice Brennan admitted that the holding could encourage irresponsible behavior by the media but said he was willing to risk that result to protect public debate. Further, he explicitly rejected Harlan's "reasonable care" standard. To expect the media to act with "reasonable care" would significantly damage their freedom, Brennan argued, for it would not allow publishers enough "breathing room"—in other words, they would be too cautious in reporting of public issues, fearing retribution.[26]

Here, then, the Court finally abandoned the reasonable care standard of responsibility outlined in *Curtis Publishing v. Butts*. Justice Harlan, however, was unwilling to give it up, and argued again, dissenting in *Rosenbloom*, for his definition of media responsibility. First, he contended, expecting the media to act as a reasonable person would does not harm first amendment freedoms. Everyone in the United States, he pointed out, is generally responsible for the consequences of his or her actions, and to hold the media similarly accountable would not create additional or unique burdens on them. Second, Harlan wrote, the government has an interest both in helping speakers and publishers to find the truth before they communicate and in protecting individuals harmed by that communication. Therefore, according to Harlan, it is reasonable to expect care on the part of the media and to side with those harmed if the media careless or act unreasonably.

Rosenbloom, with its extension of the actual malice standard to all statements on public issues, became the high point in legal protection of the press in the area of libel, and it consequently marked the low point of the Court's demands for media responsibility. Only three years later, however, the justices lessened the extensive protection given the media in *Rosenbloom*, when in *Gertz v. Welch* they agreed that a private individual would not have to prove actual malice to win a libel suit, even if he or she were libeled in the context of discussion on a public issue.[27] A five-justice majority held that because private individuals are limited in their ability to respond to libelous statements in the media, the state could and should give them more protection. Thus, the Court allowed individual states to determine the level of responsibility required of the press in cases like this, as long as private individuals were required to prove some type of fault on the part of the media. So, beyond requiring that the press be found at fault in libel cases, the Court left to the states the determination of press responsibility in this area. The *Gertz* ruling marked the first time since *New York Times v. Sullivan* in 1964 that the Court's holdings—the legal rule arising from a case— increased the responsibility required of the media in libel cases.

While attempting to clarify the meaning of media responsibility in the area of libel, the Court was also determining the extent of special rights extended to the media and debating whether those carried consequent obligations. In several cases during the early Burger years, the press asked the Court to use the first amendment to give them special privileges not granted to the public at large. In each case the Court refused this request, but in doing so studied closely the role and responsibilities of the media.

The first of these cases proved to be the most significant, both in terms of long-term results and in discussion of media responsibility. *Branzburg v. Hayes* in 1972 was actually three cases considered together[28] concerning whether requiring journalists to appear before grand juries violated the first amendment. Justice White, who wrote the Court opinion, argued the Constitution did not give immunity to journalists and they would, therefore, be held to the same standards regarding testimony as any individual. Further, he noted that the media are subject to any law applied to all individuals or businesses, including, for example, the National Labor Relations Act, the Sherman Act, and taxes.[29] Not only must the media uphold laws applied to everyone, they also receive no special consideration not granted to all. "It has been generally held," wrote White, "that the first amendment does not guarantee a constitutional right of special access to information not available to the public generally."[30] The media, therefore, receive no special privileges, and they are held to the same standards of accountability as any individual or collective. Though White did not explicitly mention the media's responsibility in this context, it is clear that the Court expected the media to be as legally responsible as any person or group.

Despite this apparent general view of media responsibility, the Court did leave a way for states to grant special privileges to the media. At the end of his opinion, White admitted that state legislatures and courts could recognize a journalists' privilege, as long as they did so within the confines of the first amendment. Justice Powell, who provided the crucial fifth vote against the press in *Branzburg*, agreed in his concurring opinion. State courts, he wrote, should grant special protection to the media when situations warranted such protection. And Justice Stewart, in a dissent joined by Justices Brennan and Marshall, insisted that courts must recognize a right of the media to gather news. Taken together, these three statements encouraged state legislatures and courts over the next few years to fashion policies about journalists' responsibilities concerning testimony to grand juries. Ultimately, while requiring the media to be as responsible as any individual or collective, the Court allowed the creation of a special privilege and added to the affirmative rights enjoyed by the media.[31]

The other two cases involving special press rights during these years, decided the same day in 1974, concerned media access to prisons and prisoners. Justice Stewart wrote the Court opinions in both *Pell v. Procunier* and *Saxbe v. Washington Post*,[32] in which the justices refused to grant the media access to state and federal prisons beyond that enjoyed by the general public. In *Pell*, the Court upheld California's rule that the media could not interview specific prisoners, and in *Saxbe* sustained a similar federal rule. Referring to the *Branzburg* ruling, Stewart argued that the media have no more rights than members of the public. Neither the Constitution nor the Supreme Court, he continued, grants the media positive rights to gather information.

Several justices disagreed. Powell, dissenting in *Saxbe* and joined by Brennan and Marshall, argued that the media, because part of their responsibility is to examine government institutions to ensure they are administered justly, must be able to gather the information they need. While Powell agreed with Stewart that the media deserve no special privileges beyond those of the general public, he acknowledged the special role the media play as agents of the public. All members of the public could not possibly be allowed into prisons to see first-hand their conditions, so the media act as the public's "eyes." If the media are denied access to prisons, they cannot fulfill that responsibility. Justice Douglas, also dissenting and joined by Brennan and Marshall, took the responsibility concept one step further. The public has a responsibility to ensure just and effective government, he argued, and to fulfill that responsibility the media should have access to prisons and specific prisoners.

The media do not, according to the Supreme Court, have a right to interview specific prisoners or refuse to testify before a grand jury. Despite the ultimate result of the 1972 *Branzburg* ruling, a majority of the Burger Court was not willing to view the first amendment as granting these affirmative rights. But affirmative interpretations of the first amendment received more attention in two other early Burger Court cases, in which members of the public sued for the right to publish or broadcast their ideas in the mass media. In both cases, again, a majority of the justices refused.

In the 1973 case *Columbia Broadcasting System, Inc. v. Democratic National Committee*, the Democratic party organization and another group had filed a complaint about an F.C.C. rule allowing broadcasters to refuse editorial advertisements. The F.C.C. had ruled that the "public interest" clause of the federal Communications Act did not require broadcasters to sell time to outside groups as long as those broadcasters fulfilled their public obligations in other ways. Chief Justice Burger and six of his colleagues refused, in a classic libertarian argument, to accept the suggestion of the Democratic National Committee that "responsible" individuals and groups had a right to buy time to provide their views on public issues. Burger agreed that the broadcast media have special responsibilities based on their use of scarce public resources, but he noted that Congress, in enacting the Communications Act and subsequent revisions, intended to give discretion to broadcasters in their choice of material to air. The "initial and primary responsibility for fairness, balance, and objectivity," wrote Burger, "rests with the [broadcast] licensee."[33] And broadcasters, he continued, must have a certain amount of freedom to fulfill this responsibility.

Here Burger attempted to find a balance between the affirmative and more libertarian views of media responsibility under the first amendment, but in doing so he landed solidly on the libertarian side. Broadcast media, by virtue of the

Communications Act's requirement of acting in the public interest, in some sense have an affirmative responsibility to provide discussion of various views on public issues, a role the Court acknowledged in *Red Lion v. F.C.C.* At the same time, however, broadcasters are protected from government intervention by the first amendment. Only their overall programming, Burger explained, is subject to oversight by the government. As long as they uphold generally the requirements of the Communications Act, they are free to choose what material to broadcast, how to treat that material, and to whom they provide air time. It is up to the individual broadcaster, the Court maintained, "to balance what it might prefer to do as a private entrepreneur with what it is required to do as a 'public trustee.'"[34] Thus, the Court, and broadcasters, must find a middle ground between affirmative and libertarian understandings of the first amendment, between "freedom for" and "freedom from." In this way broadcasters' first amendment freedom is different than that of the print media, whose "power to advance [their] own political, social, and economic views is bounded by only two factors: first, the acceptance of a sufficient number of readers—and hence advertisers—to assure financial success; and second, the journalistic integrity of [their] editors and publishers."[35] Chief Justice Burger and the majority believed they had found the balance in this case by denying the Democratic Party's assertion of its right to purchase editorial time from CBS and CBS' responsibility to sell the time. In this instance, anyway, the weight was given to the libertarian side of the scale.

But Brennan and Marshall, for once departing from their liberal colleague Justice Douglas,[36] dissented, taking up the affirmative stance. Referring to the F.C.C. rule as an "exclusionary policy," Brennan concluded that the majority's holding harmed public debate by giving too much discretion, therefore power, to broadcasters. Under the F.C.C.'s conception of the "public interest" standard, which was accepted by the Court majority, broadcasters could meet their obligations by "presentation of carefully edited news programs, panel discussions, interviews, and documentaries." This resulted in complete broadcaster control over content—the issues covered, "the manner of presentation, and perhaps most important, who shall speak."[37] Ultimately, Brennan complained, broadcasters would not provide a forum for truly unpopular ideas. Those who hold such ideas, he argued, have as much right to speak them as broadcasters have to voice their own ideas. Freedom of speech, Brennan argued, "can flourish only if it is allowed to operate in an effective forum. . . . For in the absence of an effective means of communication, the right to speak would be hollow indeed."[38] The Court's holding, to Brennan and Marshall, precluded the effective communication of a great many "novel, unorthodox, and unrepresentative"[39] ideas, thus denying the possibility of full public debate.

Burger's and Brennan's opinions in *Columbia Broadcasting System, Inc. v. Democratic National Committee* provide a wonderful example of the clash between the libertarian and affirmative views of the first amendment. Both justices believed they were arguing for freedom and the first amendment, yet their views differed dramatically. The chief justice offered a traditional libertarian viewpoint—at least as much as possible within the context of the "public interest" standard. To him and the Court majority, media freedom meant the freedom to choose material to present and how to present it, with minimal interference from the government and little requirement of responsibility. To Justice Brennan, however, the media's responsibility in fulfilling their functions was much more specific. The media, in this instance broadcasters, should provide full debate on public issues, including representing unpopular ideas. To that end, broadcasters should sell air time to nonmedia speakers, even those with whom they disagreed.

Here Brennan demonstrated an affirmative view of the first amendment, one which sees media freedom as including obligations to society. This is classic Brennan, for it reflects his position as a substantive liberal of the Warren era, using the government to promote equality and the rights of minority groups—in this case equality of speech rights and the rights of political and philosophical minorities. The broadcast media, for Brennan, have a responsibility to ensure equal opportunity through providing access to all viewpoints.

Despite his dissent in *CBS v. DNC* the following year Brennan joined Burger and the rest of the Court to deny public access to the print media, in *Miami Herald v. Tornillo*. *Tornillo* involved a Florida statute giving political candidates a right to reply to attacks in the print media by giving them an amount of space equal to that of the original attack. Writing for the Court, Chief Justice Burger argued that governmentally enforced access to print media involved coercion directly violating the first amendment. Requiring a right to reply would be no different than prior restraint, for enforced content takes space that normally would be devoted to other matter, meaning the other material could not be published. In addition, Burger argued, enforced reply could easily result not in more public debate but less, if publishers decided to avoid controversial topics altogether. In trying to enforce responsibility, the Court could do more damage than good, for the public ultimately would lose debate on some public issues. "A responsible press," Burger noted in a classic statement of legal positivism, "is an undoubtedly desirable goal, but press responsibility is not mandated by the Constitution and like many other virtues it cannot be legislated."[40]

Though the vote in *Tornillo* was unanimous and provided a strong declaration of a view of media responsibility, Justice White added his own thoughts in a concurring opinion that showed his unwillingness to allow the media absolute freedom to be irresponsible. While the media should not be required to be responsible in every situation, he admitted, they must always be liable for harmful publications. Individuals disparaged in the media should have the opportunity to redeem their reputation, either through libel verdicts or some other method. The first amendment, though it provides protection for full debate on public issues, does not give absolute freedom to the media. In White's words, "the press is the servant, not the master, of the citizenry, and its freedom does not carry with it an unrestricted hunting license to prey on the ordinary citizen."[41] Though in this case White did vote with the majority, he continued arguing for this perspective in later cases.

The Court handed down the *Miami Herald v. Tornillo* decision the day after its holdings in *Pell v. Procunier* and *Saxbe v. Washington Post*. These final three media cases of the early Burger era provided mixed messages concerning media responsibility. On one hand, in *Tornillo* newspapers were not required to be responsible for providing access to their pages. On the other, in *Pell* and *Saxbe* the Court denied the special access the media argued was needed to uphold their responsibility of informing the public. These mixed messages on responsibility proved a harbinger of cases to come, for the middle Burger years was a period of pragmatism, when the Court's five moderates held the votes and the power.

THE BURGER COURT MIDDLE YEARS, 1976–1981

The Court decided thirty-five press cases during the middle Burger years. The Court's five moderates, pragmatists all, were able to control the opinions, slowing the general trend toward conservatism throughout the last half of this decade. Justices Stewart, Powell, and Stevens occupied the true center of the Court, while Justices White and Blackmun provided the moderates with slight conservative and liberal leanings, respectively. This left Rehnquist and the chief justice on the right, and Brennan and Marshall on the left. Both pairs were ardent in their views, but they had to temper their opinions to gain a majority. The media cases showed evidence of this moderatism. In addition, the moderates tended to decide cases based strictly on the facts, with little or no regard for overall principle. In this period, therefore, no consistent theme emerged in the cases studied. For example, in libel cases, the Court's views on the media's responsibility were mixed; and in some broadcast cases, a majority of the justices put forth an affirmative view of the first amendment, whereas in others a more libertarian view prevailed. Overall, these six years offered no coherent conception of media responsibility.

During these six terms the Court decided four libel cases, three of which merely refined the definition of public figure—those who, like public officials, have to prove actual malice to win libel suits against the media.[42] In the fourth case, however, the majority held that libel plaintiffs who have to prove actual malice may inquire into the editorial process leading to alleged defamatory statements, concluding that this action would lead to a more responsible media. This 1979 case, *Herbert v. Lando*, provided useful discussion on how far the government can intrude into the editorial process to ensure that the media act responsibly. The CBS news show "60 Minutes" had aired a story on General Anthony Herbert, in which he was portrayed as a liar. Herbert agreed that he fit the definition of public figure, and that he, therefore, would have to prove that "60 Minutes" personnel acted with knowledge that the claims were false or made with "reckless disregard for the truth." Herbert argued that to do that he must be allowed to interview "60 Minutes" personnel under oath to determine their states of mind when they produced the story. Justice White, along with six of his colleagues, agreed with Herbert. An inevitable result of the protection the media received in *New York Times*, White admitted, was that the motivation of reporters, editors, and producers could be questioned in court. In fact, this type of inquiry could be beneficial, he suggested, by encouraging the media to be more responsible: "If such proof [of state of mind] results in liability for damages which in turn discourages the publication of erroneous information known to be false or probably false, this is no more than what our cases contemplate and does not abridge the freedom of speech or of the press."[43] The media, in the views of Justice White and the rest of the majority, had a responsibility to attempt to be truthful, so a ruling ensuring that responsibility was acceptable to most of the Court.

It was not acceptable, however, to Justices Brennan, Stewart, and Marshall. Brennan, dissenting in part, agreed that the editors' mental processes should not have absolute protection from court inquiry, but he argued that a privilege should exist unless a libel plaintiff could prove the statements at issue were in fact defamatory and false. In other words, plaintiffs would have to prove falsity and defamation *before* interviewing editors under oath. Yet, Brennan admitted, allowing questioning of the editorial process would ultimately harm the media's function as watchdog. If editors were afraid their deliberations could be subject to inquiry, he explained, they might not go after the major stories. Thus, according to Brennan, in the name of responsible media the Court was in fact creating irresponsible media—which might not uphold the constitutional watchdog function. To ensure that the media fulfill their obligation under the political function, they must be allowed to be irresponsible. "I fully concede," Brennan wrote, "that my reasoning is essentially paradoxical. For the sake of more accurate information, an editorial privilege would shield from disclosure the possible inaccuracies of the press; in the name of a more responsible press, the privilege would make more difficult of application the legal restraints by which the press is bound. . . . The paradox is unfortunately intrinsic to our social condition."[44] In requiring responsibility the Court left open the possibility of irresponsible behavior; by allowing irresponsible behavior, the Court allowed the media room to fulfill their responsibilities.

Brennan's paradox in *Herbert v. Lando* illustrates nicely the general views of the Court toward responsibility of the print media. More often than not in the cases examined, the justices protected freedom of the press in hopes that the press would uphold its obligations to society and the political system, but they knew that in doing so they were giving the press freedom also to act irresponsibly. The broadcast media, however, were viewed a bit differently—at least sometimes.

The Court decided three major broadcast cases during the middle Burger years. In two of these—*F.C.C. v. Pacifica Foundation* and *CBS v. F.C.C.*—the justices put forth an affirmative view of the first amendment, holding that government interference was allowable to promote a social good. But in the third, *F.C.C. v. WNCN Listeners Guild*, the Court outlined a traditional libertarian view and permitted radio stations to choose their own formats based on what market forces would allow. In addition to these conflicting rulings, the Court also vacillated over whether the first amendment should be construed to provide many voices or perspectives within public debate. In *CBS v. F.C.C.* the Court agreed that the F.C.C. has the right to require broadcast stations to provide time to federal candidates (consequently, providing more voices in public debate) but in *F.C.C. v. WNCN Listeners Guild* the Court ruled that stations cannot be required to continue particular formats (thus some voices would be lost).

F.C.C. v. Pacifica Foundation, handed down at the end of the 1977–1978 term, concerned whether the F.C.C. could prohibit broadcast stations from airing "indecent" language at certain times of the day. In a policy-based, 5–4 ruling advocating a conception of the good, the Court said that it could. Justice Stevens, writing for the plurality of three (Burger and Rehnquist joined him, while Powell, joined by Blackmun, concurred), argued that part of Congress' intent in the various acts concerning broadcasting was to allow the F.C.C. to regulate obscene, indecent, and profane language. Indecent material, Stevens explained, is that exhibiting "nonconformance with accepted standards of morality."[45] Though the words in question (a George Carlin monologue on the words one cannot say on the air) might be protected in another context, such as a broadcast political discussion, in this instance they were unacceptable, Stevens wrote. Thus, it was not so much the words themselves that the F.C.C. regulated; it was the situation. Broadcast, Stevens explained, "is uniquely accessible to children, even those too young to read. . . . The ease with which children may obtain access to broadcast material . . . amply justif[ies] special treatment of indecent broadcasting."[46] The F.C.C., then, has an obligation to monitor and regulate such speech to promote the particular social good of protecting children.

Though five justices agreed that the social good outweighed the right of free speech in this instance, the other four disagreed. Brennan and Marshall, ever the liberals, vehemently argued that the Court was imposing its own conception of the good onto not only broadcasters but all of American society:

I find the Court's misapplication of fundamental first amendment principles so patent, and its attempt to impose its notions of propriety on the whole of the American people so misguided, that I am unable to remain silent. . . . For the second time in two years the Court refuses to embrace the notion, completely antithetical to basic first amendment values, that the degree of protection the first amendment affords protected speech varies with the social value ascribed to that speech by five Members of this Court.[47]

By requiring this particular responsibility of the broadcast media, Brennan maintained, the Court violated the first amendment's primary goal of providing open debate on all matters of public importance. In addition, Brennan continued, there might be many listeners who wanted to receive that particular broadcast or one similar to it, but who no longer could because of the F.C.C. and Supreme Court decisions. And in a traditionally libertarian argument, Brennan refuted the majority's affirmative stance: It is not the role of either the F.C.C. or the Supreme Court, he argued, to decide what material is inappropriate for broadcast. Rather, that decision rests with the listening public. "I would place the responsibility and the right to weed worthless and offensive communications from the public airwaves where it belongs and where, until today, it resided: in a public free to choose those communications worthy of its attention from a marketplace unsullied by the censor's hand."[48] Therefore the marketplace, not the Supreme Court, should decide the "good" in this situation.

This, of course, conflicted with Brennan's earlier statements on the role of the Court and government, when as a member of the Warren Court he argued for certain conceptions of good in the area of equality and equal opportunity. The Court liberals at that time saw a specific purpose for themselves—to lead the country toward equal treatment for all people by setting forth an affirmative view of government's role in society. Brennan, normally one of the Court's most consistent liberals, at times such as this made the shift to a more libertarian philosophy, in which he considered the evil of government intervention with the press greater than the potential of equality provided by that intervention.

The affirmative view outlined by the Court's two conservatives and three of its moderates in *Pacifica* won again in *CBS v. F.C.C.*, though this time the two liberals joined the chief justice and Blackmun, Powell, and Stewart to form a majority. In this case, the F.C.C. had ruled that the three major broadcast networks had violated the Communications Act as amended in 1971[49] by refusing to sell time to the Carter-Mondale Presidential Committee in October 1979. The Court ruled for the F.C.C., finding that the Commission had congressional authority to enforce access to broadcast by federal candidates and to "preserve the balance between essential public accountability and desired private control of the media."[50]

Chief Justice Burger arrived at an affirmative reading of the first amendment—usually a liberal conception of media freedom—by a traditionally conservative path: The Court was not creating this required access, he argued; rather, it was merely enforcing Congress' clear intent in the Communications Act. "Congress did not prescribe merely a general duty to afford some measure of political programming [on the part of the broadcaster], which the public interest obligation of broadcasters already provided for. . . . [Section] 312(a)(7) [of the 1934 Communications Act] created a right of access that enlarged the political broadcasting responsibilities of licensees,"[51] responsibilities that could be enforced by the government. Additionally, Burger noted, federal candidates' rights of access are limited. They cannot demand air time before a campaign begins,[52] nor could the time allotted to candidates overall be allowed to "disrupt" regular programming. As long as broadcasters could demonstrate "reasonable and good-faith attention to access requests from 'legally qualified' candidates for federal elective office,"[53] Burger was willing to allow the networks editorial discretion. He also noted that while broadcasters have special obligations to provide access that the print media do not and are "granted the free and exclusive use of a limited and

valuable part of the public domain . . . burdened by enforceable public obligations,"[54] he and the rest of the Court were not creating a general right of access
to the broadcast media. The Court's ruling in the current case, he wrote, per-
tained only to the issue of the right of legally qualified candidates for federal offices to request air time once campaigns had begun. Though the Court was allowing a right of access to the media, that access was narrow.

Despite the limited nature of the majority's ruling, three justices dissented.
White, joined by Rehnquist and Stevens, argued that Congress had not meant to
grant the F.C.C. "the authority to insist on its own views as to reasonable access even though this entailed rejection of media judgments representing different
but nevertheless reasonable reactions to access requests."[55] In other words, section 312(a)(7) did not create a right of access by federal candidates, and in enforcing such a right the F.C.C. had overstepped its boundaries. There was no con-
gressionally approved affirmative interpretation of the first amendment, and the
Court should not create one.

Justice White again refused to adhere to an affirmative interpretation of the
first amendment in another broadcast case that term, *F.C.C. v. WNCN Listeners
Guild*. Writing for himself and six others, White upheld an F.C.C. policy that
market forces and economic competition, not the F.C.C., should determine the
formats of individual radio stations. The policy statement had been created in response to various rulings at the federal appeals level, which held that if an economically viable format were about to disappear in a particular community, and
if a "significant" number of people in the community had an interest in that
format, then the public interest clause of the Communications Act required
preservation of that format. The WNCN Listeners Guild and its co-respondent
the Office of Communication of the United Church of Christ had asked for a review of the F.C.C.'s policy statement, because they wanted to preserve a particular radio entertainment format they argued would be lost without F.C.C. intervention. They based their argument on the need for many "voices" within communities, voices needed to provide diversity. But the Supreme Court did not
agree. In a classic libertarian argument, the majority of seven agreed with the
F.C.C. that market forces were a sufficient measure of what entertainment formats should exist and thus the marketplace would provide all the diversity
needed. The first amendment, according to White, does not "grant individual listeners the right to have the Commission review the abandonment of their fa-
vorite entertainment programs."[56]

Marshall and Brennan, in keeping with their liberal desire to promote diversity
within public debate, dissented. Although they agreed that the F.C.C. should not
have to review every format change made by any radio station in the country for
its impact on the diversity of voices, they argued that the Commission's policy
statement was too rigid and could harm the focus on public interest required by
the Communications Act. The Act, Marshall noted, obligates the F.C.C. to ensure that the public interest is met, and permits Commission intervention if necessary. This policy statement, he continued, would not allow that intervention.

The phrase "public interest" clearly means "concern for diversity in entertainment programming,"[57] Marshall argued. Thus, the F.C.C. should not shut out the possibility of reviewing format changes for that purpose.

These three broadcast cases exemplified the middle Burger period, for they provided no overall theme for the media or lower courts to follow with regard to media responsibility. In all three cases, the Court dealt directly with affirmative views of the first amendment. Those affirmative views of government intervention prevailed in two (*Pacifica* and *CBS v. DNC*), while the libertarian perspective won in the third. Regarding the more specific issue of whether broadcasters have a responsibility to provide a diversity of opinions and voices, the Court again issued mixed rulings. In *CBS* the majority agreed that broadcasters could be required to give or sell time to federal candidates, while in *WNCN* the vote changed and a majority argued that radio stations were free to decide their own formats without regard for diversity. As in most cases during these years, the Court's five moderates provided the votes necessary to form a majority, so neither the liberals nor the conservatives could consistently control the holdings or provide a coherent conception of press responsibility.

That began to change, however, as the 1980s progressed, with a general move toward conservatism in the country and the arrival of several conservatives on the Court. Symbolically, at least, this change can be seen with the arrival of Justice Sandra Day O'Connor, who replaced Stewart in 1981. Though this was a change in only one seat, the balance of the Court switched to three apparent conservatives (Burger, Rehnquist, O'Connor), four moderates (White, Powell, Stevens, and Blackmun), and only two liberals (Brennan and Marshall). Slowly, the tenor of the Court continued to shift.

NOTES

1. Russell Galloway, *The Rich and the Poor in Supreme Court History, 1790–1982* (Greenbrae, Calif.: Paradigm Press, 1982).

2. White, G. Edward. *The American Judicial Tradition: Profiles of Leading American Judges,* expanded ed. (New York: Oxford University Press, 1988), 424.

3. For examples of all of these, see Bob Woodward and Scott Armstrong. *The Brethren: Inside the Supreme Court* (New York: Avon, 1979).

4. Bernard Schwartz, *The Ascent of Pragmatism: The Burger Court in Action* (Reading, Mass.: Addison-Wesley, 1990), 9.

5. Schwartz, 25.

6. Schwartz, 22–23.

7. Vincent Blasi, ed. *The Burger Court: The Counter-Revolution that Wasn't.* (New Haven: Yale University Press, 1983), 255.

8. Blasi, *Counter-Revolution*, 255.

9. Schwartz, 26.

10. 92 S.Ct. 2646 (1972) at 2670, Justice Powell, concurring.

11. White, 431.

12. White, 432.

13. The Court avoided an awkward moment when O'Connor arrived, for just a few years earlier they had stopped using the title "Mr. Justice _____" before their names, and had begun referring to themselves simply as "Justice _____."

14. Schwartz, 400.

15. Blasi, *Counter-Revolution*, 211.

16. Blasi, *Counter-Revolution*, 211.

17. For example, in the first five terms he was on the Court, Associate Justice Rehnquist, a conservative, wrote a total of 72 dissents, including 24 in which he was the lone dissenter. But in the 1985 term, his last as an associate, he dissented alone only once. (Robert J. Giuffra Jr., "The Rehnquist Court after Five Terms," *New York Law Journal*, 30 July 1991: 1).

18. In comparison, the Court heard six cases during the 12 terms from 1941 to 1953 (the Stone and Vinson eras), 14 from 1953 to early 1964, and 24 from early 1964 to 1969.

19. *Greenbelt Cooperative Publishing Association v. Bresler*, 90 S.Ct. 1537, (1970).

20. *Greenbelt Cooperative Publishing Association v. Bresler*, 90 S.Ct. 1537, 1541 (1970), Justice Stewart, Court opinion.

21. *Greenbelt Cooperative Publishing Association v. Bresler*, 90 S.Ct. 1537, 1541 (1970), Justice Stewart, Court opinion.

22. *Monitor Patriot v. Roy*, 91 S.Ct. 621 (1971).

23. *Ocala Star-Banner v. Damron*, 91 S.Ct. 628 (1971).

24. *Time v. Pape*, 91. S.Ct. 633 (1971)

25. Two more justices joined in the result, providing a majority to overturn a libel award. Black joined in the result because his libertarian views required the press never to be held accountable for libelous statements. White joined the result also, but wanted a ruling specific to the case, rather than the more general pronouncement of the plurality.

26. *Rosenbloom v. Metromedia*, 91 S.Ct. 1811, 1823 (1971), Justice Brennan, plurality opinion.

27. *Gertz v. Welch*, 94 S.Ct. 2997 (1974).

28. *Branzburg v. Hayes, In re Pappas, United States v. Caldwell*, 92 S.Ct. 2646 (1972).

29. *Branzburg v. Hayes*, 92 S.Ct. 2646, 2658 (1972), Justice White, Court opinion.

30. *Branzburg v. Hayes*, 92 S.Ct. 2646, 2658 (1972), Justice White, Court opinion.

31. Usually the affirmative interpretation of the first amendment is used to require the media to provide individual or group access to the press. Here, however, government intervention is used to give the media themselves special privileges.

32. *Pell v. Procunier*, 94 S.Ct. 2800 (1974); *Saxbe v. Washington Post*, 94 S.Ct. 2811 (1974).

33. *Columbia Broadcasting System v. Democratic National Committee*, 93 S.Ct. 2080, 2094 (1973), Chief Justice Burger, Court opinion.

34. *Columbia Broadcasting System v. Democratic National Committee*, 93 S.Ct. 2080, 2094 (1973), Chief Justice Burger, Court opinion.

35. *Columbia Broadcasting System v. Democratic National Committee*, 93 S.Ct. 2080, 2094 (1973), Chief Justice Burger, Court opinion.

36. Douglas, not surprisingly, held to his libertarian views that broadcast, like print, should be completely free from any government intervention. Thus, he agreed with the result of the case, but not with Burger's arguments.

37 *Columbia Broadcasting System v. Democratic National Committee*, 93 S.Ct. 2080, 2128–89 (1973), Justice Brennan, dissenting.

38. *Columbia Broadcasting System v. Democratic National Committee*, 93 S.Ct. 2080, 2132 (1973), Justice Brennan, dissenting.

39. *Columbia Broadcasting System v. Democratic National Committee*, 93 S.Ct. 2080, 2130 (1973), Justice Brennan, dissenting.

40. *Miami Herald v. Tornillo*, 94 S.Ct. 2831, 2839 (1974), Chief Justice Burger, Court opinion.

41. *Miami Herald v. Tornillo*, 94 S.Ct. 2831, 2842 (1974), Justice White, concurring.

42. In *Time v. Firestone* [96 S.Ct. 958 (1976)], the justices ruled that a Palm Springs socialite and member of the Firestone family was not a public figure. In *Wolston v. Reader's Digest* [99 S.Ct. 2701 (1979)], they held that an individual who had been newsworthy a number of years earlier, but who had returned to private life, was no longer a public figure. In *Hutchinson v. Proxmire* [99 S.Ct. 2675 (1979)], the Court held that a scientist singled out for ridicule by a U.S. Senator was not a public figure.

43. *Herbert v. Lando*, 99 S.Ct. 1635, 1646 (1979), Justice White, Court opinion.

44. *Herbert v. Lando*, 99 S.Ct. 1635, 1659 (1979), Justice Brennan, dissenting in part.

45. *F.C.C. v. Pacifica Foundation*, 98 S.Ct. 3026, 3035 (1978), Justice Stevens, plurality opinion.

46. *F.C.C. v. Pacifica Foundation*, 98 S.Ct. 3026, 3040–41 (1978), Justice Stevens, plurality opinion.

47. *F.C.C. v. Pacifica Foundation*, 98 S.Ct. 3026, 3047 (1978), Justice Brennan dissenting.

48. *F.C.C. v. Pacifica Foundation*, 98 S.Ct. 3026, 3052 (1978), Justice Brennan, dissenting.

49. In 1971 Congress added section 312(a)(7) to the Communications Act of 1934. The section allowed the F.C.C. to revoke broadcast licenses "for willful or repeated failure to allow reasonable access to or to permit purchase of reasonable amounts of time for the use of a broadcasting station by a legally qualified candidate for Federal elective office on behalf of his candidacy." Quoted in Marc A. Franklin and David A. Anderson, *Mass Media Law: Cases and Materials*, 4th ed. (Westbury, N.Y.: Foundation Press, Inc., 1990), 839.

50. *Columbia Broadcasting System v. F.C.C.*, 101 S.Ct. 2813 (1981), quote taken from synopsis of opinion provided by West Publishing.

51. *Columbia Broadcasting System v. F.C.C.*, 101 S.Ct. 2813, 2821 (1981), Chief Justice Burger, Court opinion.

52. One of the networks' arguments in this case was that President Carter requested time too far in advance of the 1980 general election.

53. *Columbia Broadcasting System v. F.C.C.*, 101 S.Ct. 2813, 2825 (1981), Chief Justice Burger, Court opinion.

54. *Columbia Broadcasting System v. F.C.C.*, 101 S.Ct. 2813, 2829 (1981), Chief Justice Burger, Court opinion, quoting from *Office of Communication of the United Church of Christ v. F.C.C.*, 123 U.S.App, D.C., 328 (1985).

55. *Columbia Broadcasting System v. F.C.C.*, 101 S.Ct. 2813, 2831 (1981), Justice White, dissenting.

56. *F.C.C. v. WNCN Listeners Guild*, 101 S.Ct. 1266, 1279 (1981), Justice White, Court opinion.

57. *F.C.C. v. WNCN Listeners Guild*, 101 S.Ct. 1266, 1281 (1981), Justice Marshall, dissent.

Chapter Five

The Move to Conservatism, 1981–1996

The 1970s proved to be a transition period for the United States Supreme Court. The decade began symbolically in June 1969 with Richard Nixon's appointment of Warren Burger as chief justice and ended in September 1981 when Sandra Day O'Connor, the first female justice, appointed by the newly elected Ronald Reagan, gave the conservatives a better hold on the Court. In between were twelve years of primarily pragmatic decisions from the Court moderates, which led to confusion regarding the Court's views on the media's roles and responsibilities.

The 1980s began with the "Reagan Revolution." Reagan's decisive victory over incumbent Jimmy Carter heralded twelve years of conservative dominance in the White House and a generally conservative era in America. This was reflected on the Court, for during the 1980s a stronger chief justice (William Rehnquist) took over and four more conservatives arrived on the bench, tipping the balance solidly to the right.

THE BURGER COURT LATER YEARS, 1981–1986

The final period of Burger's chief justiceship began symbolically with O'Connor's confirmation. Her arrival upset the 2–5–2 balance the Court had maintained the previous five years and gave Burger and Rehnquist another conservative to join their opinions.[1] Though the justices continued to rule in favor of the media (and against specific requirements of media responsibility) much of the time, the voices favoring responsible behavior by the media became stronger.

In a number of cases the justices discussed the media's roles and obligations, and although their opinions varied, a trend toward requiring more responsible behavior was clear. The media were not, for example, permitted to publish truthful information in two instances, and in a third Burger and Byron White argued for a stronger Court commitment to requirements of media responsibility. Perhaps most notable about this period, however, are the clearer individual philosophies put forth by the two most extreme (in terms of philosophy) justices, William Brennan and Rehnquist. In several cases Brennan articulated further his liberal conception of media responsibility, which included the requirement that broadcasters provide a diversity of viewpoints. On the other hand, Rehnquist put forth a conservative view, suggesting, among other things, that only political expression should enjoy absolute first amendment protection. All other expression, according to Rehnquist, could be balanced against competing social needs. Rehnquist's views led him, against traditional conservatism, on occasion, to favor government intervention in the media. Several cases involving general discussion of media responsibility are examined below followed by more specific attention to the views of Brennan and Rehnquist as they defined outer boundaries of what emerged as the Court's conception of media responsibility.

During the first half of the 1980s, the Court both approached new problems and revisited old ones. Among other issues, it reexamined whether the media should be allowed to publish information acquired in a court proceeding, dealt with copyright issues, and once again took up the challenge of finding a balance between protecting individual reputations and protecting the media from the chilling effect of large libel judgments. Although the cases involved in these issues do not encompass all of the media decisions during this period, they provide examples of issues confronting the Court. In both *Seattle Times v. Rhinehart*[2] in 1984 and *Harper and Row Publishers v. Nation Enterprises*[3] in 1985, the Court held against media attempting to publish true information. In the former, a newspaper was not allowed to publish information gathered as part of pretrial depositions in a case to which it was a party; in the latter, a magazine was forbidden from publishing key phrases and information from an as-yet unpublished presidential memoir. Concurring opinions in *Dun & Bradstreet v. Greenmoss Builders* in 1985 demonstrated that some justices were still using and favoring social responsibility arguments in the context of libel.

Seattle Times v. Rhinehart involved a libel case between the leader of an organization called the Aquarian Foundation and the *Seattle Times*. During preparation for the trial, the *Times* requested financial information from Rhinehart, who gave some information but refused to divulge the names of his donors, arguing that would violate their privacy and freedoms of religion and association. The trial judge granted the newspaper's request for information on donors, but also issued a protective order forbidding the *Times* from publishing that information. The Supreme Court was asked to rule on the constitutionality of that protective order. Justice Powell, writing for an unanimous Court, agreed that publication of names of donors would indeed violate their rights and upheld the order. Though admitting that the information was of public interest, the justices ruled that the *Seattle Times* could not publish it.

The newspaper's responsibility in this situation was to keep secret any information it obtained as the result of pretrial depositions when it was a party in the case, for to reveal that information would harm individual rights. In this ruling, the Court used an aspect of the social responsibility theory of media freedom, in which guarding individual rights is important. The Court did leave the *Times* a way out, however. If the newspaper could find another source of the same information, then it could publish. In other words, the limitations on publication existed only for information gained through the pretrial proceedings.

In *Harper and Row Publishers v. Nation Enterprises*, the Court was not as generous to the media. In this ruling, written by Justice O'Connor, seven justices admonished *The Nation* magazine and its editor, Victor Navasky, for what amounted to stealing first publication rights of former President Gerald Ford's memoirs from *Time* magazine. Ford's publisher, Harper and Row, sued *The Nation* for violation of copyright. The federal trial court found in favor of the publisher, but the appeals court reversed that decision, maintaining that *The Nation*'s use of 300 to 400 words from the manuscript constituted "fair use" of the material for news purposes. The Supreme Court disagreed and focused on *The Nation*'s actions:

Mr. Navasky knew that his possession of the manuscript was not authorized and that the manuscript must be returned quickly to his "source" to avoid discovery. . . . He hastily put together what he believed was "a real hot news story." . . . Mr. Navasky attempted no independent commentary, research, or criticism, in part because of the need for speed if he was to "make news" by "publish[ing] in advance of publication of the Ford book."[4]

Navasky meant, argued O'Connor, to "scoop" both Harper and Row and *Time*, which had agreed to pay the book publisher $25,000 for the right to publish excerpts from the memoirs first. However, *The Nation* argued that Ford's memoirs, in particular the story of his pardon of Richard Nixon, were genuinely newsworthy and that, therefore, their publication fell under the fair use area of copyright law. In rejecting that argument, O'Connor noted that fair use involves more than just newsworthiness. Courts must examine the purpose of the use of copyrighted information, as well as whether the use is commercial or nonprofit.[5] In addition, whether the work has already been published makes a difference, for authors retain a near-absolute right to control the first publication of their work. *The Nation* failed on all three counts—its purpose was merely to scoop other media, its use was commercial, and the work had not yet been published anywhere. O'Connor focused in particular on *The Nation*'s intent:

In evaluating character and purpose [of the use of the material] we cannot ignore *The Nation*'s stated purpose of scooping the forthcoming hardcover and *Time* abstracts. . . . *The Nation*'s use had not merely the incidental effect but the *intended purpose* of supplanting the copyright holder's commercially valuable right of first publication. . . . Also relevant to the "character" of the use is "the propriety of the defendant's conduct. . . . Fair use presupposes "good faith" and "fair dealing." . . . The trial court found that *The Nation* knowingly exploited a purloined manuscript.[6]

The Nation had not only published Ford's actual words without compensation, it had used a stolen manuscript, it had "stolen" *Time*'s right to publish the work first, and it had intended to "exploit the headline value of its infringement."[7] These actions proved too much for the Court. *The Nation*, seven justices ruled, had violated copyright law and the minimum level of responsibility involved in publishing the work of others. Ford's memoirs were indeed newsworthy, admitted the justices, but *The Nation*'s use of them was unacceptable. In the Court's conservative view, *The Nation* had disregarded its implicit responsibility to respect others' economic rights.

In addition to exploring new areas of media responsibility such as copyright, the Court during this time also revisited several "old" areas of the law, including libel. In *Dun & Bradstreet v. Greenmoss Builders*, also in 1985, the justices further refined the *New York Times* actual malice standard by holding that in cases involving private plaintiffs and nonpublic issues, the media could be sued for presumed and punitive damages without a showing of actual malice.[8] The important part of this case for present purposes is not the holding but the concurring opinions of Chief Justice Burger and Justice White, each of whom used a social responsibility argument to call for the Court to reexamine its interpretations of the first amendment with regard to libel.

The chief justice agreed with the majority that the libel judgment in *Dun & Bradstreet* should be upheld.[9] But he went further: *Gertz v. Welch*, he maintained, "was ill-conceived, and therefore I agree with Justice White that it should be overruled."[10] In addition, Burger, who had voted with the plurality in *Rosenbloom v. Metromedia* to extend protection to the media, ironically argued for the "reasonable care" standard that Justice Harlan had so fervently advocated for years. Actual malice, argued Burger in an apparent change of heart, should include actions taken by media defendants publishing "defamatory material which, in the exercise of reasonable care, would have been revealed as untrue."[11]

In his concurring opinion, Justice White also outlined his views of media responsibility. Though he had voted with the majority in *New York Times* and several subsequent cases, he had not joined the plurality in *Rosenbloom* and had dissented in *Gertz*. "I remain convinced that *Gertz* was erroneously decided," he wrote. "I have also become convinced that the Court struck an improvident balance in the *New York Times* case between the public's interest in being fully informed about public officials and public affairs and the competing interest of those who have been defamed in vindicating their reputation."[12] Like Burger, White seemed willing to use a reasonable care standard in deciding libel suits because the Court's actual malice standard went too far, in his estimation, in protecting irresponsible behavior. The actual malice standard, he explained, typically did not allow public figures to regain their reputations even if the publication defaming them was false. If the public figure could not meet the actual malice threshold, juries were required to return verdicts for the media; thus, the media would win cases involving false statements published without actual malice. This hurt not only public figures and officials unable to clear their names, White argued, but also the democratic process itself. "[T]he stream of information about public officials and public affairs is polluted," he wrote, "and often remains polluted by false information."[13]

In White's opinion, the Supreme Court had allowed an irresponsible media at the expense of the reputations of public officials and public figures. A more appropriate balance could be found, he suggested, by limiting large monetary judgments against the media while permitting public figures and officials recourse when they had been libeled. Public figures and officials could clear their names, yet the media would be protected from large damage awards. In any case, according to White, the media needed to be held more accountable for "misstatements of fact that seriously harm the reputation of another"[14] than was possible under the Court's current interpretation of the first amendment. Here White clearly showed his propensity, seen in many other cases, to require the media to be responsible.

White was not the only member of the Court to further outline views on media responsibility during the early 1980s. Two other justices in particular used their written opinions to characterize their perspectives on media responsibility. Brennan on the left and Rehnquist on the right each took several opportunities to argue about the media's roles and obligations. Brennan, who had seen his influence on the Court decline over the years, in one case explained carefully why broadcasting was regulated and how he and other liberals justified some intervention in order to preserve the broadest debate. In another case he argued against government intervention to achieve the same result. In addition, in passing, he briefly noted his views on constitutional interpretation and the balance of various rights against each other. Rehnquist, whose influence on the Court would soon become greater upon his elevation to the chief justiceship in 1986, demonstrated his view in several cases that the media should indeed be responsible. He suggested that those continually publishing false statements—even statements not meeting the definition of actual malice—should expect to be prosecuted. He argued that broadcasters could not use the first amendment's protection to relieve themselves of obligations arising from receipt of public funding. He began outlining his views on the difference between protected opinion and unprotected libel, and, finally, he argued that corporations should not be granted affirmative speech rights.

Throughout his years on the Court, Brennan was always an avowed liberal, joining with Burger, Douglas, Marshall and other liberals to promote both equality and individual rights, including freedom of expression. When those two broad areas came into conflict, he attempted to articulate principles for his decisions. In 1982, in *Globe Newspaper Co. v. Superior Court*, for example, he and the Court held that states could not automatically ban the media from access to the courtroom testimony of minor victims of sex crimes. Trial judges, Brennan argued, must consider closing courtrooms in these situations on a case-by-case basis. Although the first amendment does not specifically guarantee the media access to

criminal trials, he admitted, it—and the rest of the Constitution—was con-
structed to allow interpretation and creation of subsidiary rights:

[W]e have long eschewed any 'narrow, literal conception' of the Amendment's terms,
. . . for the Framers were concerned with broad principles, and wrote against a
background of shared values and practices. The First Amendment is thus broad enough
to encompass those rights that, while not unambiguously enumerated in the very
terms of the Amendment, are nonetheless necessary to the enjoyment of other First
Amendment rights.[15]

The first amendment and Constitution, therefore, could encompass both a right
of access to trials and a privacy right of children, carefully balanced.

In another case, however, Brennan once again balanced various rights but voted
against the first amendment. Concurring in *Seattle Times v. Rhinehart*, discussed earlier, Brennan agreed with the other eight justices that a newspaper was
forbidden from publishing information gathered as a result of pretrial discovery
in a libel suit to which it was a party. As always, Brennan acknowledged that
freedom of the press is vital to a democracy, but argued that sometimes other
rights are equally important. The media, he implied, cannot harm another's fundamental rights, and media freedom cannot extend to that point. In *Rhinehart*,
therefore, privacy and religious rights outweighed those of the media.

Though in both *Globe Newspaper* and *Rhinehart* Brennan voted against—or at
least did not support—media rights, in most cases throughout his tenure on the
Court he provided a strong voice for the media. For example, he dissented in
Harper and Row Publishers v. Nation Enterprises, also discussed earlier, arguing
that *The Nation*'s use of material from President Ford's memoirs did not violate
copyright laws. He concluded in his dissent, which Marshall and White joined,
that upholding the copyright holder's rights over those of the media would "stifle
the broad dissemination of ideas and information."[16] *The Nation* had not violated
copyright laws, he argued, because it had provided a synopsis of that part of
Ford's memoirs surrounding the pardon of Nixon, and descriptions of those
events could not be copyrighted. Brennan maintained that only literary form—
not general description of historical events—is copyrightable, and because *The
Nation* had copied only 300 words of the memoir, a tiny portion of the literary
form, it had not violated the law. In addition, *The Nation*'s "scoop" of both
Time and the memoir's publisher should not be condemned, suggested Brennan.
The Nation merely acted as most news organizations do in trying to compete:

A news business earns its reputation, and therefore its readership, through consistent
prompt publication of news—and often through scooping rivals. . . . *The Nation*'s
stated purpose of scooping the competition should . . . have no negative bearing on
the claim of fair use. Indeed, the Court's reliance on this factor would seem to amount
to little more than distaste for the standard journalistic practice of seeking to be the
first to publish news.[17]

The Nation, according to Brennan, had not violated its responsibilities; its actions were understandable and justifiable.

Perhaps the most intriguing of Brennan's opinions during this period was for the Court in *F.C.C. v. League of Women Voters of California*, in which five justices voted to overturn a ban on editorializing by public television stations receiving grants from the Corporation for Public Broadcasting. Brennan took this opportunity to explain his, and the Court's, justification for regulating broadcasting and requiring broadcasters to provide a diversity of views.

As a part of the Public Broadcasting Act of 1967, Congress had forbidden public stations receiving public funding from editorializing, so that the stations could not become "vehicles for government propagandizing or . . . convenient targets for capture by private interest groups wishing to express their own partisan viewpoints."[18] Congress had a right to regulate broadcasting generally, Brennan admitted, because the airwaves are a "scarce and valuable national resource,"[19] and to ensure that broadcasters presented information in a balanced way. In the view of Brennan and the Court, broadcasters were "fiduciaries for the public."[20] Yet, at the same time, they were media protected by the first amendment from government intervention, and they must be given as much editorial discretion as possible, consistent with congressional goals. Earlier broadcast cases, explained Brennan, had all attempted to find the balance between enough and too much government involvement with broadcasting. Sometimes this meant requirements of responsibility on the part of broadcasters, as in *Red Lion Broadcasting v. F.C.C.*, in which the Court upheld the F.C.C.'s "Fairness Doctrine," requiring stations to give time to the individual subjects of personal attacks on the air, and in *CBS v. F.C.C.*, in which the justices upheld a right of access to broadcast by federal candidates. Other times, however, the Court allowed broadcasters to make their own editorial judgments, as in *CBS v. Democratic National Committee*, in which the justices refused to require broadcasters to accept paid political advertising. The underlying principle involved in these decisions on the responsibility of broadcasters, wrote Brennan, was "to secure the public's first amendment interest in receiving a balanced presentation of views on diverse matters of public concern." This involved some restrictions on the freedom of broadcasters, but the justices allowed restrictions only when they were "narrowly tailored to further a substantial governmental interest, such as ensuring adequate and balanced coverage of public issues."[21] Under this liberal conception of media freedom and responsibility, broadcasters were to provide balanced coverage, and if they did not fulfill that obligation, the F.C.C. had the Supreme Court's blessing to require them to do so, at least in a limited fashion. In this particular case, however, the government restriction on broadcasters' freedom was not substantial enough, so the Court overturned it.

Justice Rehnquist disagreed. The government's interest in this situation was substantial, he argued, for broadcasters had willingly accepted funding from the federal government and were therefore obligated to play by the government's rules. He wrote:

In the Court's scenario the Big Bad Wolf cruelly forbids Little Red Riding Hood to take to her grandmother some of the food that she is carrying in her basket. . . . [I]t appears [however,] that some of the food in the basket was given to Little Red Riding Hood by the Big Bad Wolf himself, and that the Big Bad Wolf had told Little Red Riding Hood in advance that if she accepted his food she would have to abide by his conditions.[22]

By accepting public funding the public broadcasters had agreed to certain obligations, which, according to Rehnquist, they could be required to uphold. In his view, their first amendment rights were not in question, so this requirement of responsibility posed no conflict with the Constitution.

Justice—soon-to-be Chief Justice—Rehnquist's opinions appeared with increasing frequency during the early 1980s. Consistently conservative since his arrival on the Court in 1971, the themes of his jurisprudence became clearer over time. Rehnquist accepted government intervention with the media, as long as its purpose was to promote "the good." For example, he often voted against free expression in obscenity and libel cases in which the media, in his opinion, had acted unreasonably. In *Keeton v. Hustler Magazine*, for instance, he led all of his colleagues in condemning *Hustler*'s journalistic practices. A woman sued *Hustler* for libel in New Hampshire courts because the statute of limitations for libel had run out in every other state. She had minimal connection with New Hampshire (she lived in New York), as did *Hustler*. Despite this, Rehnquist wrote, "Where . . . *Hustler Magazine* has continuously and deliberately exploited the New Hampshire market [through circulating there], it must reasonably anticipate being haled into court there in a libel action based on the contents of the magazine."[23] For Rehnquist, the key was *Hustler*'s conduct, which in his opinion was reprehensible. States, including New Hampshire, thus had every right to "employ [their] libel laws to discourage the deception of [their] citizens."[24] To promote the good, state intervention was acceptable.

Justice Rehnquist's views on other topics were equally apparent. In an appeal the Court refused to hear, he argued that the issue presented in the case was vital to finding the balance between protected opinion and defamation. While Rehnquist's views in this case had no legal ramifications, they are important as they provide an early indication of his perspective on what kinds of opinion are protected by the first amendment. In *Ollman v. Evans*, a 1985 libel case, a lower federal court had concluded that two nationally syndicated columnists were within their first amendment rights to quote an anonymous source claiming that a particular political science professor had "no status within [his] profession." The professor appealed, but only Rehnquist and Chief Justice Burger voted to hear the appeal.[25] Rehnquist was appalled that *Gertz v. Welch* had been used to justify what he saw as an unacceptable attack on the professor's character and academic standing. In *Gertz* Justice Powell had written for the Court that "there is no such thing as a false idea," and in ensuing years lower courts had used that phrase to provide protection for opinion statements. Though he had joined Powell's opinion, Rehnquist argued that its meaning had been altered. Lower courts had used the phrase to undermine the common law of libel, he complained. In the common law before *New York Times v. Sullivan*, he explained, some statements were considered slander or libel *per se*, hence plaintiffs did not need to prove harm to win civil suits. Included in this type of libel *per se* were "statements which defame the plaintiff in connection with his business or occupation."[26] In Rehnquist's opinion the columnists' statement clearly qualified as libel *per se*, and thus went beyond the boundaries of acceptable expression. "True" opinion, he agreed, should be protected, but this was not true opinion. In a foreshadowing of later opinions—in which he commanded a majority of the Court[27]—he argued that the first amendment protects only political opinion:

At the time I joined the opinion in *Gertz*, I regarded this statement [that there is no such thing as a false idea] as an exposition of the classical views of Thomas Jefferson and Oliver Wendell Holmes that there was no such thing as a false "idea" in the political sense, and that the test of truth for political ideas is indeed the marketplace and not the courtroom. I continue to believe that this is the correct meaning of the quoted passage. But it is apparent from the cases cited by petitioner that lower courts have seized upon the word "opinion" . . . to solve with a meat axe a very subtle and difficult question, totally oblivious "of the rich and complex history of the struggle of the common law to deal with this problem."[28]

He believed the media should be protected in their exposition of political opinion. However, as shall be seen, Rehnquist's definition of opinion is fairly narrow whereas his expectations of media responsibility are broad.

Justice Rehnquist's conception of media responsibility in *Ollman v. Evans* is not surprising when examined as a part of his overall philosophy of free expression. He saw political expression as the only type of expression granted absolute protection by the first amendment. Further, protection of political expression is based on principle, whereas all other expression is protected only as policy. All individuals have, in his view, the right to believe and espouse their own political views. Any other kind of expression, from nonpolitical opinion statements to advertisements to pornography, does not have first amendment protection and may be regulated. The media and individuals are free to state their political beliefs, but they are accountable to society's needs in their nonpolitical expressions.

Rehnquist's views are clear, for example, in his 1986 dissent in *Pacific Gas and Electric v. Public Utilities Commission of California*, in which he favored granting an organization affirmative rights to promote its political perspective, even though this conflicted with traditional conservative views. Pacific Gas and Electric included in its billing envelope a newsletter containing editorials, stories on issues of public interest, suggestions for energy conservation, and so on. The group Toward Utility Rate Normalization (TURN) wanted to rebut some of the views in that newsletter. The utilities commission ruled that space in the billing envelope belonged to the utility's customers and allowed TURN to include its own publication in the billing envelope four times a year. Pacific Gas argued that this coerced speech violated the first amendment. Five justices favored the utility. Justice Lewis Powell, writing for the five and relying on *Miami Herald v. Tornillo*, argued that forcing a private corporation to "speak" against its will did indeed harm the corporation's expression rights. In a clear rejection of the affirmative interpretation of the first amendment, Powell wrote, "[Pacific Gas] does have the right to be free from government restrictions that abridge its own rights in order to 'enhance the relative voice' of its opponents."[29]

Though normally, as a conservative, Rehnquist might be expected to vote against an affirmative interpretation of the first amendment, the situation in this case led him to the opposite decision. First, he considered this a speech case, not a media case. Second, he noted, under California state property law the space in the billing envelope belonged to the utility's customers and not to the utility itself, a situation distinguishing this case from *Miami Herald v. Tornillo* (in which the sole property right belonged to the newspaper). Third, he thought that requiring a right of access to envelope space would have no "deterrent effect" on the speech of the utility. Fourth, the right not to speak, "applicable to individuals and perhaps the print media,"[30] should not be extended to nonmedia corporations. Finally, though the Court had previously held that the first amendment prohibited the government from "directly suppressing" the speech of corporations,[31] the justices had not ruled that it prohibited "government action that only *indirectly* and *remotely* affects a speaker's contribution to the overall mix of information available to society."[32] And this government action, in the form of the utilities commission requirement, was only an indirect and remote suppression of the corporation's speech. Thus, in this situation Rehnquist accepted a affirmative reading of the first amendment, for "the right of access here constitutes an effort to facilitate and enlarge public discussion; it therefore furthers rather than abridges First Amendment values."[33]

Despite his apparent approval of access rights to a public forum, Rehnquist was not willing to extend his views past the present situation. Corporations could be made to grant speech rights to others for the purpose of political speech, but individuals and the media could not. Nonmedia corporations differ from media corporations, he explained; thus, their first amendment rights, and responsibilities, are different. "Corporations generally have not played the historic role of newspapers as conveyors of individual ideas and opinion. . . . Pacific Gas and Electric is not an individual or a newspaper publisher; it is a regulated utility."[34] So nonmedia corporations should be held to different standards than media corporations and could be compelled to offer themselves as a public forum on political issues. Yet, Rehnquist seemed to imply something more; he seemed to imply that corporations—including the media—all have responsibilities where expression is concerned. He wrote, "[This Court has] recognized that corporate free speech rights do not arise because corporations, like individuals, have any interest in self-expression. . . . It held instead that such rights are recognized as an instrumental means of furthering the First

Amendment purpose of fostering a broad forum of information to facilitate self-government."[35] So perhaps the media, like other corporations, may be held accountable for this purpose: In Rehnquist's view, they do indeed have some responsibilities.

The years of Warren Burger's chief justiceship—1969 to 1986—can be seen as a time of transition from liberal to conservative power on the Supreme Court. The early years saw the diminishing dominance of the Warren Court liberals with their jurisprudential emphasis on equality of opportunity and protection of diverse viewpoints. During this period the justices continued to wrestle with the media's responsibility in the area of defamation and special press rights, discarding the "reasonable care" standard in libel and debating affirmative and libertarian interpretations of the first amendment. By 1975, the retirement of Douglas and the appointment of Stevens in his place gave the moderates a majority on the Court, thus ushering in a period of pragmatic, but not principled, decisions. The final years of Burger's tenure saw the increasing power of the Court conservatives, demonstrated in opinions demanding more responsibility of the media. However, the task of further defining the media's roles and responsibilities fell to the Rehnquist Court.

THE REHNQUIST COURT FIRST DECADE, 1986–1996

The final decade of Warren Burger's tenure had seen little change in Court personnel. Between John Paul Stevens' appointment in 1975 and William Rehnquist's elevation to chief justice in 1986, only one position on the Court changed hands. Beginning with Rehnquist's appointment as chief justice, however, the Court's makeup rapidly changed, and within eight years six new justices had joined the bench. Antonin Scalia took Rehnquist's place as associate justice in 1986. Anthony Kennedy, David Souter, and Clarence Thomas, all appointed by Republicans, replaced Lewis Powell, William Brennan, and Thurgood Marshall, respectively. Finally, Bill Clinton became the first Democrat in twenty-six years to appoint a justice when he nominated Ruth Bader Ginsburg to fill Byron White's seat. The following year Clinton again put his mark on the Court when Stephen Breyer replaced Harry Blackmun.

Ronald Reagan gained several more chances to influence the Court's makeup in 1986 and 1987. His appointment of Rehnquist as chief justice[36] and Scalia as associate justice sent a message both to the legal community at large and to the Court specifically that the White House expected a conservative interpretation of legal issues. It was, in the words of Court observer Benno Schmidt, "plainly designed to produce seismic change in the content of our constitutional law and in the role of the Supreme Court in our legal system."[37] Reagan continued his attempt to mold the Court in his own philosophy (as have all presidents) when he nominated Judge Robert Bork to replace Powell in 1987. Though Bork's nomination was defeated in the Senate partly because Bork was seen, fairly or not, as *too* conservative, Congress got the message and confirmed Anthony Kennedy with little complaint.[38]

Scalia, who had been a judge on the Court of Appeals for the District of Columbia and a colleague of Robert Bork, has become the "right-wing maverick" of the Court. He dissents when the decision is liberal, and he concurs in separate opinions when it is conservative. A positivist who uses a textualist approach, "under which the statutory text itself [is] virtually the only definitive source of meaning,"[39] Scalia represents much of what constitutes twentieth century conservative beliefs. He believes for the most part in leaving the executive and legislative branches of government alone, and does not believe judges should interfere with public policy. He also is a strong proponent of the market system, believing "that the market is not morally corrupting, its anti-egalitarianism results are natural, and markets teach people the virtues of labor, thrift, and fair dealing. . . . Markets are to be trusted, and economic liberty is to be protected against arbitrary government action."[40] He also upholds conservative beliefs concerning morality. Brisbin explains that Scalia believes "that the government should support the majority consensus on what constitutes the good life. He believes the community, through the legislative and administrative processes, can best define rights."[41]

Kennedy, also a conservative, is much more likely than Scalia to compromise. Even in his first term he received a number of assignments to write for the Court. His opinions tend to be "careful, narrow decisions that secure the support of conservatives and some liberal justices."[42] Giuffra called his appointment "the single most critical change in the Court's composition"[43] in the recent past, because it finally gave the conservatives a five-vote majority. At first his conservative leanings were obvious. In his first term (1987–1988) he voted with Scalia in just over 90 percent of nonunanimous cases; Kennedy and Scalia joined with the chief justice in nearly 87 percent of nonunanimous cases. Kennedy helped create a solid conservative majority, for he, Scalia, Rehnquist, O'Connor, and White voted together almost 85 percent of the time.[44]

Still, over the next few years Kennedy began a move toward the center of the Court. For example, in early first amendment cases he tended to value a collectivist approach, "defer[ing] individual speakers' interests to the accumulated normative vision of the community."[45] But within a few years of his appointment, he began to value individual speech rights more highly, as evidenced in his vote and concurring opinion in *Texas v. Johnson*,[46] in which the majority upheld the right to burn the American flag in political protest. By the early 1990s, Kennedy had staked out a position in the center of the Court, and by the mid-1990s his often became the deciding vote when the Court was deeply split.[47]

The Court's shift toward conservatism continued with George Bush's two appointments, David Souter and Clarence Thomas, who replaced William Brennan and Thurgood Marshall in 1990 and 1991, respectively. Souter, a former New Hampshire attorney general and state supreme court justice, had an immediate impact on the Court in his first term, casting "the decisive vote" in a number of

5–4 decisions that would likely have gone the other had his predecessor Brennan been on the bench.[48] But like Kennedy, in successive terms Souter moved toward the middle, until during the 1993 term he "became a reliable ally of Justices Stevens and Blackmun in key cases."[49] Thomas, however, joined the Court as and remained conservative, allying himself frequently with Scalia. The two had the highest level of agreement in nonunanimous votes of any two justices in Thomas' first term: They voted together nearly 79 percent of the time.[50] Their agreement, which "appears based on a shared judicial philosophy,"[51] continued over the next several terms. For example, during the 1994–1995 term they again had the highest level of agreement of any two justices, at just over 85 percent.[52]

By the 1992 presidential election, then, the Court had moved decidedly to the right. None of the Warren Court liberals remained, and the Court's two most liberal justices, Harry Blackmun and John Paul Stevens, had both been appointed by Republicans and at one point had themselves been considered at least moderately conservative. Of the other seven justices, three—Rehnquist, Scalia, and Thomas—were conservative by every measure and four—White, O'Connor, Kennedy, and Souter—were conservative or moderate, depending on the issue at hand. These four, however, formed a centrist bloc much like the one of the 1970s. And like their moderate predecessors, these justices held the power on the Court. They did not necessarily vote together, but both the conservative and liberal wings needed at least two of their votes to command a majority. As such, during the early 1990s "they controlled the outcomes of most cases by creating ad hoc, shifting majorities as they individually joined the consistent conservatives or liberals, depending on the issue presented in each case."[53]

A second woman, Ruth Bader Ginsburg, joined the Court in 1993. Then a member of the U.S. Court of Appeals for the District of Columbia, Ginsburg had been the founding director of the ACLU's Women's Rights Project and was known to some as "the Thurgood Marshall" of gender equity issues. Not surprisingly, she was expected to shore up the liberal side of the Court. Instead, she most often joined the moderate justices, adding to the power of the middle. In her first term she voted with each colleague at least 71 percent of the time; her lowest percentages of agreement were with the liberal Blackmun, at 73 percent, and conservatives Rehnquist and Thomas, at 73 percent and 71 percent.[54]

Ginsburg continued her moderate voting behavior the next term, when she and the others were joined by Stephen Breyer, replacing Harry Blackmun. Breyer, chief judge of the U.S. Court of Appeals for the First Circuit, was "an experienced judge of moderate leanings, a self-described pragmatist more interested in solutions than theories."[55] In the 1994–1995 term Breyer staked out a moderate-to-liberal position, allying himself most frequently with Ginsburg (nearly 79 percent of nonunanimous cases). The two joined with Souter in just under 75 percent of nonunanimous cases, and the three joined Justice Stevens 70 percent of the time. This compared to the conservative group of Scalia, Thomas, and Rehnquist, who voted together in just over 80 percent of nonunanimous cases.[56] In cases clearly dividing liberals and conservatives the Court split evenly, with

Rehnquist, O'Connor, Scalia, and Thomas on one side, Stevens, Ginsburg, Breyer, and Souter on the other, and Kennedy in the middle.[57]

After 1994, therefore, the Court had returned to an era of moderate power, with a strong conservative wing, a weaker liberal bloc, and a large group in the middle, casting more pragmatist, and less ideological, votes. Though this kind of alignment prevents any one political belief or philosophy from dominating the Court, it also leads to overall inconsistency in rulings, and in expectations of media roles and responsibilities.

Despite the growing conservative dominance, conformity on the issue of media responsibility was rare. In most media cases the tension between protecting media freedom and requiring responsibility was clear, and cases from this period provide some of the most interesting discussion on media responsibility of any cases examined. For example, the Court argued at one point that requiring responsible behavior of the media helped the first amendment; in another, it ruled that deliberately avoiding the truth was unacceptable; and in a third, the justices outlined a very narrow definition of what "opinion" is protected by the first amendment. "Media protection" cases are discussed first, followed by "media responsibility" cases.

In six of the ten cases examined here, the Supreme Court confronted situations in which the media had published information that perhaps should not have been published. In two of the six, the Court held that the publication was acceptable; that the media could not be held responsible for the consequences of those publications. In 1988 in *Hustler Magazine v. Falwell*, the justices ruled that a satirical cartoon, though reprehensible, was permissible expression, and in *Florida Star v. B.J.F.* in 1989 they decided that a newspaper could publish the name of a rape victim found in police records. In both situations the publication of the material was questionable, if not actually unethical. And in each case the justices struggled with the line between responsible behavior and protected speech.

Hustler Magazine v. Falwell, decided in February 1988, marked the first time the Supreme Court considered the tort of "intentional infliction of emotional distress." The Court concluded that even intentional harm by the media must meet the *New York Times* actual malice standard. *Hustler* had published a cartoon implying that conservative minister Jerry Falwell's first sexual experience was with his mother in an outhouse. *Hustler* editors labeled the cartoon as both a parody and fiction, but Falwell argued that the magazine nevertheless should be punished. Chief Justice Rehnquist wrote the opinion for a unanimous Court and, in a surprising move for a conservative, refused Falwell's request to bring into law a specific conception of the good. *Hustler*'s ad, he wrote, had been "gross and repugnant in the eyes of most" people; nevertheless, in some small way, it contributed to "the free flow of ideas and opinions on matters of public interest and concern."[58] Crucial to Rehnquist's analysis was the nature of the work. It was political satire, a form of opinion that "from the early cartoon portraying George Washington as an ass down to the present day . . . [has] played a prominent role in public and political debate."[59] It may have been reprehensible and inappropriate, but to Rehnquist it was protected. As in his dissent from the denial of writ of certiorari in *Ollman v. Evans*, Rehnquist argued for protection of political opinion. In addition, the element of intent, which Falwell had maintained was crucial to *Hustler*'s irresponsible behavior, was irrelevant, according to Rehnquist and the Court. Although intent to inflict emotional injury was appalling, it was not enough to justify a ruling against the press. If public figures like Falwell wish successfully to sue the media for intentional infliction of emotional distress, decided the Court, they must prove, as in libel, that publications are false and made with actual malice. The media, therefore, could intend to inflict emotional harm as long as they did so through use of satire or opinion—not through provably false statements. In this case, anyway, the Court did not require responsible behavior of the media.

In the next case concerning media responsibility, *Florida Star v. B.J.F.*, decided in June 1989, the Court again allowed publication of factual, though harmful, information. A Jacksonville, Florida, newspaper had violated Florida law and its own internal policy by naming a rape victim, information it had obtained from police records. Justice Thurgood Marshall, writing for the six-justice majority, noted that B.J.F. had asked the Court to punish the newspaper for publishing true, though extremely private, information, which he and the Court refused to do. However, they also declined to rule that publication of true information would always be protected. Previous Court cases, he noted, "have eschewed reaching this ultimate question, mindful that the future may bring scenarios which prudence counsels our not resolving anticipatorily."[60] Publication of true information, therefore, might possibly be punishable in rare instances, for example, publication of true information obtained unlawfully and private information obtained by means other than from public records. This situation did not meet that standard, of course, because the police department had included, though mistakenly, B.J.F.'s name in its records. To punish the newspaper for the mistake of the police department would not be fair, argued Marshall, even though newspaper personnel admitted they knew they were violating the law. Still, Marshall carefully couched the Court's ruling on where the government's role in guarding media responsibility lay:

We do not hold that truthful publication is automatically constitutionally protected, or that there is no zone of personal privacy within which the State may protect the individual from intrusion by the press, or even that a State may never punish publication of the name of a victim of a sexual offense. We hold only that where a newspaper publishes truthful information which it has lawfully obtained, punishment may lawfully be imposed, if at all, only when narrowly tailored to a state interest of the highest order.[61]

Three justices did not agree with the majority and argued for a conception of the good. White, joined by O'Connor and Rehnquist, maintained that the state had done everything it could to avoid the situation that occurred, and that protection of B.J.F.'s privacy rights was, in fact, an example of "state interest of the highest order." The majority's ruling gave *carte blanche* to the media to publish any private information, and thus took away any requirements of responsibility. "If the First Amendment prohibits entirely private persons (such as B.J.F.) from recovering for the publication of the fact that she was raped," wrote White, "I doubt that there remain any 'private facts' which persons may assume will not be published in the newspapers or broadcast on television."[62] The newspaper should not have invaded B.J.F.'s privacy, the three justices argued. Therefore, it should be punished. In drawing this line between acceptable and unacceptable publications, White, O'Connor, and Rehnquist put forth a conception of the good, a minimum moral standard for action.

The Court issued a limited ruling for the media again in 1994, when all nine justices agreed in *Campbell v. Acuff-Rose* that the rap group 2 Live Crew did not violate copyright law in its parody of the song "Pretty Woman." When "Pretty Woman" copyright holder Acuff-Rose denied permission to use parts of the original song, 2 Live Crew used them anyway. 2 Live Crew's misogynist version, filled with vulgar lyrics, was a clear, if tasteless, parody. Writing for all his colleagues, Justice Souter argued that this example, whose quality he refused to comment upon, must be protected to preserve artistic creativity: "[Parody] can provide social benefit, by shedding light on an earlier work, and, in the process, creating a new one,"[63] he wrote. But Souter refused to allow other forms of artistic borrowing. A parody, he explained, must offer some commentary on the original work. If the parody borrows only to "avoid the drudgery in working up something fresh," its first amendment protection is limited, if not nonexistent. Thus, the Court implied, responsible borrowing involves some kind of comment upon the work borrowed. Mere copying is not acceptable.

Hustler, B.J.F., and *Campbell* mark the only cases during the first ten years of the Rehnquist Court in which the justices voted for the media in cases involving significant questions of press responsibility. Much more common were votes at least partially against the media, which happened seven times in those ten years. In these seven cases, as in *Hustler, B.J.F.*, and *Campbell*, the justices struggled to find the dividing line between acceptable and irresponsible behavior, and these seven cases provide the largest group of decisions requiring media responsibility found at any time from 1931 to 1996. In *Carpenter v. United States* in 1987, the justices ruled in an unusual case that a newspaper's confidential prepublication information was its property, and that a reporter working for the paper could not use information for his own gain. *Hazelwood School District v. Kuhlmeier* in 1988 involved a high school paper, which the Court found could be held to a high standard of responsibility by school officials. In 1989 in *Harte-Hanks Communications Inc. v. Connaughton*, the justices concluded that though "unreasonable conduct" departing from the standards typical of responsible publishers did not alone prove actual malice in a libel case, "deliberate avoidance of the truth" did. In a 1990 libel case, *Milkovich v. Lorain Journal*, a majority upheld Chief Justice Rehnquist's ideas on protected opinion, when the Court ruled that a columnist's accusation that a coach had lied in court was not protected opinion. In 1991 in *Masson v. New Yorker* the justices concluded that attributing fabricated statements that changed the "material meaning" of a source's words was irresponsible. In *Cohen v. Cowles Media,* also decided in 1991, they ruled that newspapers could be held accountable for breaking a promise of confidentiality to a source. Finally, in *Turner Broadcasting System v. F.C.C.* in 1994 they concluded that the government could possibly require cable operators to reserve channels for local broadcast stations.

The majority opinion in *Carpenter v. United States,* like two others in this group of cases, was written by Justice White. White, though appointed by John Kennedy, had by the mid-1980s become a solid member of the Court's conservative wing. Here, however, he was joined by all of his colleagues in concluding that a *Wall Street Journal* reporter had acted irresponsibly in using insider information to buy and sell stocks. The reporter, Foster Winans, wrote a daily column giving stock tips, which influenced stock prices. He arranged to tell two brokers ahead of publication which stocks he would discuss, so they could buy and sell stocks accordingly. The three split the profits from these tips. Winans and one of the brokers were convicted of securities, wire, and mail fraud. The *Wall Street Journal* argued that its "property" had been stolen. Winans, who had been a trusted employee of the *Journal,* knew of a *Journal* policy forbidding release of information prior to publication, yet he "continued in the employ of the *Journal,* appropriating its confidential business information for his own use, all the while pretending to perform his duty of safeguarding it."[64] Winans, in the view of both the Court and the *Journal,* had failed to uphold his responsibility and was justifiably punished.

Justice White wrote the Court opinion in the next media responsibility case as well. *Hazelwood School District v. Kuhlmeier,* the only case considered here involving children and media responsibility, concerned articles by high school journalists on teen pregnancy and divorce. The student reporters had changed the names of their subjects, but at least one was recognizable by her situation. The principal, concerned that individuals could be identified, removed the two articles as well as other articles on two pages in the newspaper. There was not time, he explained, to rewrite the offending articles before publication, and delaying publication meant the paper would not have been published at all. The newspaper was part of a journalism class at the school, and as such was designed to teach students the standard practices of journalism. School board policy, noted White, declared that school publications would not "restrict free expression or diverse viewpoints within the rules of responsible journalism,"[65] implying that school officials apparently were the ones to define responsibility. That situation appealed to White, who wrote, "A school must be able to set up high standards for the student speech that is disseminated under its auspices—standards that may be higher than those demanded by some newspaper publishers . . . in the 'real' world—and may refuse to disseminate some students' speech that does not meet those standards."[66] School officials could direct, change, even censor student work, according to the majority, as long as changes were "reasonably related to legitimate pedagogical concerns."[67] Student journalists could, therefore, be held to greater standards of responsibility than professional journalists.

Three justices dissented. Brennan, joined by Marshall and Blackmun, argued that school officials had violated the students' first amendment rights. The articles in question "neither disrupt[ed] class work nor invade[d] the rights of others"; thus the principal's censorship was not "narrowly tailored to serve its purpose."[68] Teachers and administrators do have the right to refuse to sponsor some types of student publications, including those that are "ungrammatical, poorly written, inadequately researched, biased, or prejudiced,"[69] for the purpose of high school journalism classes is to teach the skills associated with quality journalism. But student work "convey[ing] a moral position at odds with the school's official stance"[70] should be protected, argued Brennan. In effect, then, according to the Court liberals, student journalists should be held responsible for the quality, but not the content, of their work.

The nine justices voted together to require responsibility in the next case examined. The libel case *Harte-Hanks Communications Inc. v. Connaughton* arose from a local election. The newspaper in Hamilton, Ohio, neglected to interview a key source who could have refuted charges the newspaper eventually published. The Court agreed that in this case the media had indeed acted irresponsibly. In refusing to cover the entire story, the newspaper went beyond "failure to investigate"—which an earlier Court had ruled did not constitute evidence of actual malice[71]—to a "deliberate decision not to acquire knowledge of the facts that might confirm the probable falsity of [the] charges."[72] Although the media could fail to investigate all sides of a story and not be held accountable, they could not "purposefully avoid the truth."[73] This action, agreed every justice, was indeed unacceptable behavior and evidence of actual malice. Though the idea of irresponsible behavior being applied was narrow, the Court did use this case to further define where the line between protection and responsibility would be drawn.

Chief Justice Rehnquist had outlined his views on the protection of opinion in his dissent from the denial of a writ of certiorari in 1985 in *Ollman v. Evans*. In *Milkovich v. Lorain Journal,* in 1990, he finally commanded a majority of the Court and authored a 7–2 opinion narrowly defining the types of opinion the first amendment protects, and expanding the Court's requirements of responsible behavior. In this case, an Ohio newspaper columnist had implied that a high school wrestling coach had lied under oath about a fight between his team and another. Specifically, the columnist wrote, "Anyone who attended the meet [and saw the fight] . . . knows in his heart that Milkovich and Scott [the school principal] lied at the hearing after each having given his solemn oath to tell the truth."[74] This, ruled the Court, was not protected opinion. Instead, it was libel.

The *Lorain Journal*, explained Rehnquist, wanted the Court to agree that the statement made was not a "fact" and, therefore, was protected by Justice Powell's dicta in *Gertz v. Welch*, which read, "Under the First Amendment there is no such thing as a false idea. However pernicious an opinion may seem, we depend for its correction not on the conscience of judges and juries but on the competition of other ideas."[75] Rehnquist disagreed. Powell's statement, he argued, had not created a special protection for opinion. Instead, it had merely rephrased Justice Oliver Wendell Holmes' concept of the marketplace of ideas. "Opinion" in Powell's second sentence meant, wrote Rehnquist, not "opinion" but "political idea." Political beliefs are indeed protected, but false, defamatory fact statements disguised as "opinions" are not. There is a difference, Rehnquist explained:

If a speaker says, "In my opinion John Jones is a liar," he implies a knowledge of facts which lead to the conclusion that Jones told an untruth. . . . Simply couching such statements in terms of opinion does not dispel these implications; and the statement, "In my opinion Jones is a liar," can cause as much damage to reputation as the statement, "Jones is a liar."[76]

But other statements could indeed be protected from liability. In order to win a libel suit, Rehnquist acknowledged, an individual must prove the statement in question false. Actual opinion statements cannot be proved false (or true), so they are not actionable. Therefore, opinion statements are automatically protected by existing first amendment doctrine:

[U]nlike the statement, "In my opinion Mayor Jones is a liar," the statement, "In my opinion Mayor Jones shows his abysmal ignorance by accepting the teachings of Marx and Lenin," would not be actionable. [*Philadelphia Newspapers v. Hepps*[77]] ensures that a statement of opinion relating to matters of public concern which does not contain a provably false factual connotation will receive full constitutional protection.[78]

Rehnquist, finally, had written his views on media responsibility and "opinion" into law: Opinion is protected by the first amendment, as long as it is indeed opinion, according to Rehnquist's definition. Only political opinion is accorded full first amendment protection, and the media are responsible and liable for statements including any potentially provable assertions. With Rehnquist able to command a majority of the justices, the Court's requirements of media responsibility had expanded.

In a rare instance of unanimous requirement of media responsibility, all nine justices agreed in *Masson v. New Yorker* that changing or making up quoted statements that significantly revise the meaning of a source's views is irresponsible and actually harms the first amendment.[79] Psychoanalyst Jeffrey Masson had been the subject of an article by Janet Malcolm in *New Yorker* magazine. She conducted extensive interviews with Masson, audiotaping most of them. Malcolm quoted in her article several startling and self-serving statements from Masson, including references to himself as an "intellectual gigolo" and "the greatest analyst who ever lived" after Sigmund Freud. Masson sued for libel, claiming that he had not made these statements and that they defamed him.

Malcolm argued that the questioned statements were not on her tapes but were in her written notes, the originals of which she had thrown away. Lower courts concluded that Malcolm had made up the statements, and found that action to constitute actual malice. The Supreme Court agreed that fabrication of source statements could be evidence of actual malice, and returned the case to a lower court for further action.

Quotation marks, wrote Justice Kennedy for the Court, provide a sign to the reader that the individual being quoted indeed made those statements. Quotation marks, he wrote, "add authority to the statement and credibility to the author's work. [They] allow the reader to form his or her own conclusions . . . instead of relying entirely upon the author's characterization of her subject."[80] The *New Yorker*, Kennedy noted, is a trustworthy magazine whose readers would likely believe statements in quotation marks were indeed made by the person quoted. Thus, he implied, both Malcolm and the *New Yorker* had broken the readers' trust. Changes in a source's statements beyond correction of grammar and syntax that "result in a material change in the meaning conveyed by the statement,"[81] ruled the Court, constitute knowledge of falsity, and thus actual malice under the *New York Times v. Sullivan* rule.

The Court, including liberals Marshall and Blackmun as well as the moderates, had broken new ground in the area of media responsibility: The media now were expected to be sure that statements quoted were exact and did not change the source's meaning. The Court's rationale for this requirement was, oddly enough, protection of the media's first amendment freedoms. As Kennedy explained, allowing the media to put quotation marks around paraphrases or fabrications would lower the public's trust in the media and would lead sources to avoid being quoted at all:

Were we to assess quotations under a rational interpretation standard [the Court of Appeals had held that quotations were protected if they were a "rational interpretation" of the source's statements], we would give journalists the freedom to place statements in their subjects' mouths without fear of liability. By eliminating any method of distinguishing between the statements of the subject and the interpretation of the author, we would diminish to a great degree the trustworthiness of the printed word, and eliminate the real meaning of quotations. Not only public figures but the press doubtless would suffer under such a rule. Newsworthy figures might become more wary of journalists, knowing that any comment could be transmuted and attributed to the subject, so long as some bounds of rational interpretation were not exceeded. We would ill serve the values of the First Amendment if we were to grant near absolute, constitutional protection for such a practice.[82]

This is a remarkable conclusion by the Court and significant for its views of the roles and responsibilities of the media. The values of the first amendment—presumably including the political and educational functions—are best served, concluded the Court, not by media *freedom* but by media *responsibility*.

Just four days after the *Masson* decision, a five-justice majority held that two Minnesota newspapers could be held accountable for failure to keep a verbal promise to a source. The Court opinion in *Cohen v. Cowles Media*, like so many others written by Justice White during this period, explained that the media, like any other institution or individual, must obey laws generally applicable to all. However, four dissenters argued that allowing irresponsible behavior in this case would actually aid the public.

Cohen arose during a gubernatorial campaign. Dan Cohen served as an adviser to the Republican challenger to the Democratic governor. A few days before the general election, Cohen contacted four media organizations, offering information about the current lieutenant governor, who was running for reelection on the Democratic ticket. In return for the information, Cohen wanted promises that his name would not be revealed as the source of it. Reporters for both the *Minneapolis Star and Tribune* and the *St. Paul Pioneer Press Dispatch* agreed to the conditions, and Cohen told them that the lieutenant governor had been arrested for shoplifting a number of years before. Both newspapers used the information, but editors at both overruled their reporters' promises of confidentiality, arguing that Cohen's ties to the Republican campaign and his attempt to smear the Democrats was a major story as well. After Cohen's name was published in both newspapers, he was fired from his job. He sued for breach of contract and eventually a jury awarded him $700,000. The Minnesota Court of Appeals overturned the punitive portion of that award—$500,000—but let the verdict stand. The Minnesota Supreme Court overturned the verdict altogether. The U.S. Supreme Court, in turn, reinstated the verdict.

Lawyers for the newspapers argued that Supreme Court precedent held that the media should not be punished for publishing lawfully obtained, truthful information, and that this case was similar in circumstances. The Court majority, however, dismissed this argument and chose instead to focus on other previous cases, stating that "generally applicable laws do not offend the First Amendment simply because their enforcement against the press has incidental effects on its ability to gather and report the news."[83] The press, Justice White noted, is not immune from general criminal laws: It "may not with impunity break and enter an office or dwelling to gather news";[84] reporters may not refuse to answer grand jury subpoenas; media cannot break copyright laws, and they must obey labor and antitrust laws. In short, though they are protected by the first amendment from unnecessary government intervention, media are responsible for obeying laws necessary to the functioning of society. And one law necessary to the functioning of society, according to the Court, is Minnesota's law "requir[ing] those making promises to keep them."[85] The first amendment, while protecting the media, does not insulate them from requirements of responsibility or accountability to their community. Clearly, here the Court articulated a collectivist theory of media freedom or what Dworkin calls a policy—a social goal subject to balancing against individual rights and other social goals.

Five justices—White, Rehnquist, Scalia, Kennedy, and Stevens—voted to hold the St. Paul and Minneapolis newspapers responsible for their actions. Four—Souter, Marshall, Blackmun, and O'Connor—saw a larger issue at stake. Holding the newspapers accountable, they argued, harmed the free flow of information, particularly information necessary for citizens to make competent decisions about their elected leaders. Justice Souter, who had joined the Court at the beginning of the term, wrote the dissent, maintaining that the information provided by the newspapers "expanded the universe of information" needed by Minnesota voters and thus was "of the sort quintessentially subject to strict First Amendment protection."[86] To Souter and the other three, the goal of treating people and institutions equally should be subordinated to that of providing society with as much political information as possible. The public good, as Souter termed it, would be better served by allowing irresponsible media behavior in this situation.

In the final major media responsibility case analyzed, the Court held in *Turner Broadcasting System v. F.C.C.* that the government might be able to require cable operators to reserve a certain number of channels for transmission of local broadcast stations. In an attempt to prevent local stations from being shut out of local cable systems, in 1992 Congress passed the Cable Television Consumer Protection and Competition Act. In passing the legislation Congress emphasized broadcasters' role as a source of political and educational information, Justice Kennedy explained in the Court opinion. Congress feared cable operators would refuse to transmit broadcast stations, thus harming the stations' economic viability and ultimately the marketplace of ideas. Cable operators, Kennedy wrote, "can thus silence the voice of competing speakers with a mere flick of the switch." And, using an affirmative view of the first amendment reminiscent of Justice Black's words in *Associated Press v. United States*, Kennedy continued: "The First Amendment's command that government not impede the freedom of speech does not disable the government from taking steps to ensure that private interests not restrict, through physical control of a critical pathway of communication, the free flow of information and ideas."[87]

Not all the justices agreed with this affirmative view. Justice O'Connor, joined by Justices Scalia, Ginsburg, and Thomas, concurred in part and dissented in part. In particular, she dissented from the majority view that the government could intervene to make cable operators behave responsibly. In a classic statement of the negative, libertarian interpretation of the first amendment, she argued that government could not require responsibility, even if that were an admirable goal: "But the First Amendment as we understand it today rests on the premise that it is government power, rather than private power, that is the main threat to free expression; and as a consequence, the Amendment imposes substantial limitations on the Government even when it is trying to serve concededly praiseworthy goals."[88]

The last major media responsibility case decided during the sixty-five years examined, *Turner* provides an appropriate ending point for the discussion, for it encapsulates many of the themes found throughout the analysis. Like so many cases before, *Turner* pitted classical libertarian views of the first amendment against views requiring some responsibility from the media. Unlike most cases, however, in *Turner* the Court majority agreed the government could potentially hold the media responsible. It seems appropriate that Justices Kennedy and O'Connor wrote the key opinions in the case, for it is they and their fellow moderates throughout the years who most often held the deciding votes in important cases involving media responsibility. And finally, while *Turner* marks the end of the Court's first sixty-five years of dealing with media responsibility, in many ways it heralds the beginning of new issues for the Court. For it is in *Turner* and cases yet to come that the justices must confront new technology and media of mass communication that will challenge old assumptions about the roles and responsibilities of American mass media.

NOTES

1. Of the 29 media cases considered during this time, O'Connor voted with both Burger and Rehnquist in 21. She sided against both conservative colleagues in four cases, with Burger against Rehnquist in three cases, and with Rehnquist against Burger in only one.

2. 104 S.Ct. 2199 (1984).

3. 105 S.Ct. 2218 (1985).

4. *Harper and Row v. Nation Enterprises*, 105 S.Ct. 2218, 2221–22 (1985), Justice O'Connor, Court opinion.

5. Publication of copyrighted material for noncommercial purposes, she pointed out, is more likely to be accepted as fair use.

6. *Harper and Row v. Nation Enterprises*, 105 S.Ct. 2218, 2231–32 (1985), Justice O'Connor, Court opinion.

7. *Harper and Row v. Nation Enterprises*, 105 S.Ct. 2218, 2231 (1985), Justice O'Connor, Court opinion.

8. This actually is an extension of the principle outlined in *Gertz v. Welch* in 1974. In *Gertz* the Court ruled that private persons libeled in the context of their involvement with public issues could not receive presumed and punitive damages from the media unless they (the plaintiffs) could prove actual malice. In *Dun & Bradstreet*, however, the public/private issue distinction was key—with statements based on private issues being held to a higher standard than those based on public issues.

9. *Dun & Bradstreet* was not a press case *per se*. The case arose from an erroneous report sent out by a credit reporting agency about a building contractor. Dun & Bradstreet, the reporting agency, wrongly reported to a number of Greenmoss Builders' creditors that the contractor had filed for bankruptcy. No media organizations were involved.

10. *Dun & Bradstreet v. Greenmoss Builders*, 105 S.Ct. 2939, 2948 (1985), Chief Justice Burger, concurring.

11. *Dun & Bradstreet v. Greenmoss Builders*, 105 S.Ct. 2939, 2948 (1985), Chief Justice Burger, concurring.

12. *Dun & Bradstreet v. Greenmoss Builders*, 105 S.Ct. 2939, 2949 (1985), Justice White, concurring.

13. *Dun & Bradstreet v. Greenmoss Builders*, 105 S.Ct. 2939, 2951 (1985), Justice White, concurring.

14. *Dun & Bradstreet v. Greenmoss Builders*, 105 S.Ct. 2939, 2952 (1985), Justice White, concurring.

15. *Globe Newspaper Co. v. Superior Court for Norfolk County*, 102 S.Ct. 2613, 2618–19 (1982), Justice Brennan, Court opinion.

16. *Harper and Row v. Nation Enterprises*, 105 S.Ct. 2218, 2240 (1985), Justice Brennan, dissenting.

17. *Harper and Row v. Nation Enterprises*, 105 S.Ct. 2218, 2247 (1985), Justice Brennan, dissenting.

18. *F.C.C. v. League of Women Voters of California*, 104 S.Ct. 3106 (1984), quote taken from synopsis of opinion provided by West Publishing.

19. *F.C.C. v. League of Women Voters of California*, 104 S.Ct. 3106, 3115 (1984), Justice Brennan, Court opinion.

20. *F.C.C. v. League of Women Voters of California*, 104 S.Ct. 3106, 3116 (1984), Justice Brennan, Court opinion.

21. *F.C.C. v. League of Women Voters of California*, 104 S.Ct. 3106, 3117–18 (1984), Justice Brennan, Court opinion.

22. *F.C.C. v. League of Women Voters of California*, 104 S.Ct. 3106, 3129 (1984), Justice Rehnquist, dissenting.

23. *Keeton v. Hustler Magazine*, 104 S.Ct. 1473, 1481 (1984), Justice Rehnquist, Court opinion.

24. *Keeton v. Hustler Magazine*, 104 S.Ct. 1473, 1479 (1984), Justice Rehnquist, Court opinion.

25. Four justices must vote to hear an appeal for it to be placed on the Court's docket. Rehnquist here was writing a dissent in response to the Court's vote to deny the case a hearing.

26. *Ollman v. Evans*, 105 S.Ct. 2664 (1985), Justice Rehnquist dissenting from denial of writ of certiorari.

27. *Hustler Magazine v. Falwell*, 108 S.Ct. 876 (1988), and *Milkovich v. Lorain Journal*, 110 S.Ct. 2695 (1990).

28. *Ollman v. Evans*, 105 S.Ct. 2664 (1985), Justice Rehnquist dissenting from denial of writ of certiorari.

29. *Pacific Gas and Electric Co. v. Public Utilities Commission of California*, 106 S.Ct. 903, 910 (1986), Justice Powell, Court opinion.

30. *Pacific Gas and Electric Co. v. Public Utilities Commission of California*, 106 S.Ct. 903, 917 (1986), Justice Rehnquist, dissenting.

31. In *First National Bank of Boston v. Bellotti*, 98 S.Ct. 1407, 1418 (1978).

32. *Pacific Gas and Electric Co. v. Public Utilities Commission of California*, 106 S.Ct. 903, 917 (1986), Justice Rehnquist, dissenting.

33. *Pacific Gas and Electric Co. v. Public Utilities Commission of California*, 106 S.Ct. 903, 921 (1986), Justice Rehnquist, dissenting.

34. *Pacific Gas and Electric v. Public Utilities Commission of California*, 106 S.Ct. 903, 921–22 (1986), Justice Rehnquist, dissenting.

35. *Pacific Gas and Electric Co. v. Public Utilities Commission of California*, 106 S.Ct. 903, 921 (1986), Justice Rehnquist, dissenting.

36. Some argue that Rehnquist was given his new position to keep him and his conservative philosophy on the bench. He apparently had been considering resigning before the promotion.

37. Benno C. Schmidt Jr., "The Rehnquist Court: A Watershed," *The Los Angeles Daily Journal*, 25 June 1986: 4.

38. Kennedy was actually the third nominee put forth by Reagan for that seat. Judge Douglas Ginsburg withdrew his name after admitting to smoking marijuana as a law school professor.

39. William S. Jordan III, "Justice David Souter and Statutory Interpretation," *University of Toledo Law Review* 23 (1992): 493.

40. Richard A. Brisbin, Jr., "The Conservatism of Antonin Scalia," *Political Science Quarterly* 105 (1990): 15.

41. Brisbin, 16.

42. Stephen Wermeil, "Chief Justice Rehnquist Emerges as a Skillful Leader of the Court's New Majority," *Chicago Daily Law Bulletin* (29 June 1989), 4.

43. Robert J. Giuffra, Jr., "The Rehnquist Court after Five Terms," *New York Law Journal* (30 July 1991), 4.

44. Brisbin, 3.

45. Lawrence Friedman, "The Limitations of Labeling: Justice Anthony M. Kennedy and the First Amendment," *Ohio Northern Law Review* 20.2 (1993): 230.

46. 491 U.S. 397 (1989).

47. See Christopher E. Smith, Joyce Ann Baugh, Thomas R. Hensley, and Scott Patrick Johnson, "The First-Term Performance of Justice Ruth Bader Ginsburg," *Judicature* 78.2(1994): 74–80; and Christopher E. Smith, Joyce Ann Baugh, and Thomas R. Hensley, "The First-Term Performance of Justice Stephen Breyer," *Judicature* 79.2 (1995): 74–79.

48. Christopher E. Smith and Scott Patrick Johnson, "The First-Term Performance of Justice Clarence Thomas," *Judicature* 76.4 (1993): 175.

49. Smith, Baugh, Hensley, and Johnson, "Justice Ruth Bader Ginsburg," 77.

50. Smith and Johnson, "Justice Clarence Thomas," 175.

51. Smith and Johnson, "Justice Clarence Thomas," 175.

52. Smith, Baugh, and Hensley, "Justice Stephen Breyer," 75.

53. Smith and Johnson, "Justice Clarence Thomas," 174.

54. Joyce Ann Baugh, Christopher E. Smith, Thomas R. Hensley, and Scott Patrick Johnson, "Justice Ruth Bader Ginsburg: A Preliminary Assessment," *University of Toledo Law Review* 26 (1994): 32. This figure includes all formally decided cases. If only nonunanimous cases are considered, Ginsburg's lowest percentage of agreement with another justice is 51 percent with Justice Thomas. See Smith, Baugh, Hensley, and Johnson, "Justice Ruth Bader Ginsburg," 75.

55. Christopher E. Smith, Joyce A. Baugh, and Thomas R. Hensley, "The First-Term Performance of Justice Stephen Breyer," *Judicature* 79.2 (1995): 74.

56. Smith, Baugh, and Hensley, "Justice Stephen Breyer," 75.

57. Smith, Baugh, and Hensley, "Justice Stephen Breyer," 77.

58. *Hustler Magazine v. Falwell*, 108 S.Ct. 876, 879 (1988), Chief Justice Rehnquist, Court opinion.

59. *Hustler Magazine v. Falwell*, 108 S.Ct. 876, 881 (1988), Chief Justice Rehnquist, Court opinion.

60. *Florida Star v. B.J.F.*, 109 S.Ct. 2603, 2608 (1989), Justice Marshall, Court opinion.

61. *Florida Star v. B.J.F.*, 109 S.Ct. 2603, 2613 (1989), Justice Marshall, Court opinion.

62. *Florida Star v. B.J.F.*, 109 S.Ct. 2603, 2618 (1989), Justice White, dissenting.

63. *Campbell v. Acuff-Rose*, 510 U.S. 569, Justice Souter, Court opinion.

64. *Carpenter v. United States*, 108 S.Ct. 316, 322 (1987), Justice White, Court opinion.

65. *Hazelwood School District v. Kuhlmeier*, 108 S.Ct. 562, 570 (1988), Justice White, Court opinion.

66. *Hazelwood School District v. Kuhlmeier*, 108 S.Ct. 562, 569 (1988), Justice White, Court opinion.

67. *Hazelwood School District v. Kuhlmeier*, 108 S.Ct. 562, 571 (1988), Justice White, Court opinion.

68. *Hazelwood School District v. Kuhlmeier*, 108 S.Ct. 562, 576 (1988), Justice Brennan, dissenting.

69. *Hazelwood School District v. Kuhlmeier*, 108 S.Ct. 562, 573 (1988), Justice Brennan, dissenting.

70. *Hazelwood School District v. Kuhlmeier*, 108 S.Ct. 562, 574 (1988), Justice Brennan, dissenting.

71. *Beckley Newspapers v. Hanks*, 88 S.Ct. 197 (1967).

72. *Harte-Hanks Communications, Inc., v. Connaughton*, 109 S.Ct. 2678, 2698 (1989), Justice Stevens, Court opinion.

73. *Harte-Hanks Communications, Inc., v. Connaughton*, 109 S.Ct. 2678, 2698 (1989), Justice Stevens, Court opinion.

74. *Milkovich v. Lorain Journal*, 110 S.Ct. 2695, 2698 (1990), Chief Justice Rehnquist, Court opinion.

75. *Milkovich v. Lorain Journal*, 110 S.Ct. 2695, 2705 (1990), Chief Justice Rehnquist, Court opinion, quoting 94 S.Ct. 2997, 3007 (1974).

76. *Milkovich v. Lorain Journal*, 110 S.Ct. 2695, 2705–06 (1990), Chief Justice Rehnquist, Court opinion.

77. 106 S.Ct. 1558 (1986).

78. *Milkovich v. Lorain Journal*, 110 S.Ct. 2695, 2706 (1990), Chief Justice Rehnquist, Court opinion.

79. Justices White and Scalia dissented in part, arguing that *any* change in a quotation is irresponsible.

80. *Masson v. New Yorker Magazine, Inc.*, 110 S.Ct. 2419, 2430 (1991), Justice Kennedy, Court opinion.

81. *Masson v. New Yorker Magazine, Inc.*, 110 S.Ct. 2419, 2433 (1991), Justice Kennedy, Court opinion.

82. *Masson v. New Yorker Magazine, Inc.*, 110 S.Ct. 2419, 2434 (1991), Justice Kennedy, Court opinion.

83. *Cohen v. Cowles Media*, 110 S.Ct. 2513, 2518 (1991), Justice White, Court opinion.

84. *Cohen v. Cowles Media*, 110 S.Ct. 2513, 2518 (1991), Justice White, Court opinion.

85. *Cohen v. Cowles Media,* 110 S.Ct. 2513, 2519 (1991), Justice White, Court opinion.

86. *Cohen v. Cowles Media,* 110 S.Ct. 2513, 2523 (1991), Justice Souter, dissenting.

87. *Turner Broadcasting System v. Federal Communications Commission,* 22 Med.L.Rptr. 1865, 1880 (1994), Justice Kennedy, Court opinion.

88. *Turner Broadcasting System v. Federal Communications Commission,* 22 Med.L.Rptr. 1865, 1890 (1994), Justice O'Connor, concurring in part and dissenting in part.

Chapter Six

Positivism and Policy

In the process of deciding well over three hundred cases involving the media, the forty-three justices sitting on the Court from 1931 to 1996 presented many conceptions of media responsibility. The justices grounded their discussions of the topic in several different philosophies, which they seldom explained explicitly or carefully. In addition, each time they determined whether to require that the media be responsible, they ran directly into a conflict over how to both protect media freedom guaranteed by the Constitution and acknowledge the media as only one of many institutions operating in society, institutions that cannot have complete freedom if society is to function. As part of society, the media necessarily must have limits on their behavior, and the justices had to admit that no one, no group, no institution, operating in a social context—including a press guaranteed freedom by the Constitution—can do whatever it wants. This conflict and the Court's attempts at its resolution underlay examination of media responsibility. With this conflict as a background, this final chapter offers both general conclusions and a return to the philosophical debate between collectivist and individualist theories, which summarizes the discussion of Supreme Court conceptions of media responsibility.

Several general conclusions emerged from this analysis of media cases the Court decided between 1931 and 1996. First, many factors play an important role in the Court's conceptions of media responsibility. The philosophies of the individual justices are crucial, but many factors influence those philosophies. Whether the justices are liberal or conservative in their politics and views of the Constitution, how they view their role as judges, whether they value all individual rights equally or some more than others, what role they see for government, whether they lean toward libertarianism or social responsibility, and whether they view media freedom as a social need or a right—each of these ultimately influences what justices see as the roles and responsibilities of the media. Also important, though not directly dealt with here, is the general political direction of the country, which affects presidential and congressional elections and thus who nominates and confirms Supreme Court justices. Clearly, no one factor or philosophy dominates conceptions of press responsibility; instead, the Court's views are influenced by many issues and factors.

Second, the distinction between responsibility and accountability and their relation to freedom was important to the discussion of theories of media responsibility articulated by the Supreme Court, for both appeared in the justices' opinions—concurring, dissenting, and those for the Court—across the sixty-five years of cases studied. In deciding individual cases, the Court often refused to hold the media legally accountable, while at the same time individual justices defined what they thought was appropriate, responsible behavior. Thus, the legal holdings of the Court, which involved the power of government to hold the media accountable, were sometimes quite different from the individual justices' conceptions of media responsibility.

Third, though the foundation of U.S. media freedom remains in libertarian philosophy, the concept of social responsibility has gained strength over time, particularly since 1969. Social responsibility, rather than being a derivative of libertarianism, appears to be evolving into an independent theory of media freedom and responsibility. While the Court never referred to the Hutchins Commission—originator of the social responsibility theory of the press—by name, some justices adopted its conclusions, particularly that with freedom come obligations and that the media had at times "engaged in practices which the society condemns."[1] The media, suggested both the Hutchins Commission and some justices, have responsibilities to the larger community; they are not free to act completely as they choose. This emphasis on the social responsibility of the media parallels, and is likely caused by, a shift toward conservatism on the Court overall since the late 1960s. Throughout the cases analyzed, the more conservative justices were more willing to articulate standards of acceptable media behavior. This had significance for the media as the conservative power on the Court grew. It seems likely that the overall political philosophy dominant on the Court at a given time directly affects how much responsible behavior is expected of the media.

In addition, the adoption of social responsibility theory by conservative justices in the 1980s and 1990s led to an important shift in the definition of the media's responsibilities to society. In earlier years, particularly during the Warren Court era, social responsibility was equated with liberal goals, primarily providing equal opportunity. However, toward the end of the time period studied, the media's social responsibility came to mean acting morally: keeping promises, not fabricating information, searching out the "truth," and so on. In both definitions, the media had responsibilities, but the character of those responsibilities changed significantly.

Fourth, during the period studied, the Court arrived at no conclusive, coherent definition or theory of media responsibility. In addition, because of the many judicial philosophies represented on the Court, the underlying conflict between collectivist and individualist political philosophies, the continual debate over the appropriateness of government intervention with the media, changing social definitions of acceptable behavior by the media, and even changes in the nature of media and media organizations, it seems unlikely that any Court in the near future will be able to agree upon a general definition of the responsibilities of the media in U.S. society.

CONCEPTIONS OF RESPONSIBILITY OVER TIME

The Supreme Court's conceptions of media responsibility changed significantly over the sixty-five years analyzed. The earliest years of Court interpretation of the press clause included clear distinctions between groups wanting to hold the media accountable for violations of ethical behavior and those favoring media freedom. A transition period was followed by a time when media responsibility was defined primarily as providing equal opportunity for many voices. Another transition period led to a more conservative era, in which the Court defined media responsibility as behaving morally—telling the truth and upholding promises.

The earliest period examined included the end of a long era of conservative dominance of the Court. By 1931, when the Court began its substantive adjudication of the first amendment's press clause, the conservative laissez-faire period was in decline. Still, four conservatives and three liberals debated within the 1930s media cases, with conservatives both holding media accountable to moral standards and defeating government attempts at media regulation. Liberals took the opposite stances.

A dramatic change in first amendment interpretation took place in 1937 and 1938, first with a shift in the balance of power to the liberals and their views on media roles and responsibilities, and second with a statement from the majority that the rights granted by the Bill of Rights—including freedom of the press—would be accorded a "preferred" position when rights and social goals were weighed against each other. These changes came about, apparently, because of the Court's recognition of President Franklin Roosevelt's political strength after the 1936 elections and a general change in the country's views of the purposes of government.

The changes of the late 1930s led to a long transition period on the Court. The 1940s and early 1950s were marked by conflict between collectivists—valuing social needs over individual rights—and individualists, who took the opposite point of view. This conflict was exemplified in the ongoing discussion within the opinions of Justices Felix Frankfurter and Hugo Black. In addition, Court opinions and expectations of the media were directly influenced by the world outside, in which the Cold War and McCarthyism created fear of dissident and nonmainstream political views.

The mid-1950s saw the rise of the "Warren Court," dominated by liberals who valued equal opportunity as well as individual freedom. Earl Warren, William Brennan, William O. Douglas, and Hugo Black were joined at various times by Tom Clark, Arthur Goldberg, Abe Fortas, and Thurgood Marshall to create a powerful liberal bloc. The highlight of this period was the unanimous ruling in *New York Times v. Sullivan*, which resulted in an entirely new definition of media responsibility, one the Court spent the next three decades explaining and refining. Throughout the 1960s the Court sometimes reflected, sometimes led the dramatic changes taking place in the social fabric of the country, as in the *New York Times* decision, which so strongly protected a constitutional right. At the same time, the Court struggled with questions of morality as it continually refined its definition of obscenity. Often during this period, the Court defined media responsibility in terms of equal opportunity, reflecting the politics of the times.

Some seeds of the movement toward conservatism were planted in decisions like *New York Times* and the obscenity cases, however. The dramatic protection given the media allowed them tremendous freedom, which led inevitably to some questionable behavior. The post-Warren years of the 1970s were, therefore, another transition period, this time to a more conservative era both on the Court and in the country, although at this point Court moderates held the power and the votes. During these years the Court continued to define media responsibility in the areas of libel, privacy, and commercial speech. Because of moderate dominance on the Court, no overall conceptions of media responsibility arose during this time.

The latest conservative period began, both symbolically and in earnest, with the election of Ronald Reagan and his appointment of Sandra Day O'Connor to the Court. Reagan symbolized the new conservatism in the United States, and including O'Connor he appointed three associate justices and one chief justice during his two terms in the White House. This, along with his successor George Bush's two appointments, meant that the political mood of the country was reflected in Court decisions, including those concerning media responsibility. As discussion in the 1990s political arena turned toward individual morality and responsibility, the Court has required significant responsibility from the media, defined in terms of morality, and has dramatically narrowed its protection of the media. It is too early to determine if President Bill Clinton's appointments will have a significant impact on the Court's views of media responsibility.

Over time, therefore, the Court has often followed—and occasionally led—the country in its views on responsibility. For example, in the 1950s the Court led the way in protecting nonmainstream opinions in and out of the media. As the political mood became more liberal in the 1960s, so did the Court's interpretation of the first amendment. Similarly, as the United States overall moved toward conservatism in the 1970s and 1980s, the Court followed. And in the 1990s as politicians have emphasized personal responsibility, the Court has emphasized media responsibility. Generally, then, the Court's conceptions of media responsibility have changed as the country's overall political climate has changed, moving from the traditional conservatism of the early 1930s through the influence of the New Deal, the Cold War, and the 1960s to the Reagan era and conservatism that followed in the 1990s.

COLLECTIVISM AND INDIVIDUALISM

Within American political philosophy a debate continues that influences key discussions on individual rights and responsibilities, the purposes of government, the role of society and the place of morals within public life. This debate, between collectivist and individualist political philosophies, appears in a number of forms throughout the cases analyzed. The legal positivism/natural law, social responsibility/libertarian models of the media, liberal/conservative, and affirmative/negative conceptions of freedom debates demonstrated the justices' differing views of media roles and responsibilities.

Libertarian political philosophy, which arose out of the liberal tradition, places great emphasis on individual rights and a limited government. It shares with natural law a belief in natural rights; with conservatism an opposition to government intervention in the affairs of business (including the media); and with liberalism a belief in not advocating a conception of the good or a common understanding of how society or the media "ought" to be. Thus, justices from many political philosophies may articulate libertarian views of media responsibility. All, however, support a negative interpretation of the first amendment—that is, that the media are seen as free from government intervention rather than free so that they may fulfill some obligation or role.

Several justices put forth libertarian or negative conceptions of press freedom and responsibility across the cases examined here. Douglas and Black (in his later years) epitomized libertarianism, with their stances against government intervention of any kind in the media. Liberals Brennan and Marshall, too, often upheld the libertarian model as they argued for media freedom and minimal demands of media responsibility.

But the conservatives also used libertarian arguments on occasion. For example, in *CBS v. Democratic National Committee,* Rehnquist and Burger disagreed with the liberals' call for equality of opportunity and access to broadcast. Though broadcasters have some special responsibilities, Rehnquist and Burger admitted, they also have wide discretion over what to air, and the government should not require them to sell advertising time if they do not wish to sell it.

While libertarian arguments came from both conservative and liberal justices in the cases studied, the assumptions of libertarianism informed all of the justices' discussions of media roles and responsibilities. When the justices used the libertarian model, they required no, or only minimum, responsibility of the media. In addition, media freedom was articulated as a right possessed by the media—or anyone acting as the media. And as the justices argued against government interference with this right, they tended to justify the right, usually by using the educational and political functions of the media. They fell, therefore, into the difficulty outlined by Hutchins Commission member William Hocking, who maintained that a right cannot be inalienable if reasons are given for its existence. That is, he explained, it cannot be a natural right, existing in spite of government. If a rationale is given to justify the right, it can only be the kind of right granted by the people through government. If this is the case, it can also be taken away by the people if they see the right as no longer necessary. So, by using the political and educational functions to justify media freedom under the libertarian model, the Court theoretically, according to Hocking's argument, actually lessened the media's protection by giving the public the opportunity to remove the media's freedom. Freedom of the press, in these instances, was seen not as a "right"—despite the language used—but as a social goal or means to an end. It was conceptualized by the Court as a policy, not a principle, and in collectivist, rather than individualist, terms.

The social responsibility model and the affirmative interpretation of the first amendment are not quite as synonymous as are libertarianism and the negative interpretation. Nevertheless, justices espousing the social responsibility model on occasion used affirmative interpretations. Both conceptions were sometimes identified with Court liberals, particularly in broadcast cases involving demands that broadcasters present diverse viewpoints (though in *Red Lion* the conservatives joined the Court opinion as well). Brennan, for example, argued strenuously for this interpretation in broadcast cases; but only then. He was not willing to apply the social responsibility model to the print media. Black, on the other hand, applied an affirmative interpretation to media freedom in his early years, in *Associated Press v. United States*. The liberal—not yet libertarian—Black argued that the Associated Press could not use its significant power to silence voices, and that government, through the Sherman Antitrust Act, could intervene to make sure it did not.

At other times conservatives adopted the social responsibility model and affirmative interpretation. In *Red Lion*, as mentioned, all nine justices joined to uphold the constitutionality of the F.C.C.'s Fairness Doctrine, requiring broadcasters to open their microphones to individuals criticized on the air. And many years later, in *Dun & Bradstreet v. Greenmoss Builders*, White and Burger used a social responsibility argument to call for the overturn of *Gertz v. Welch*, the libel case requiring public figures, but not private individuals, to prove actual malice.

While justices from both ends of the political spectrum used the social responsibility model and affirmative interpretation of the media at times, they always referred to those interpretations in relation to libertarianism. Each time a justice used the social responsibility argument, in other words, he or she seemed to feel compelled to explain precisely why libertarian assumptions would not satisfy the issue at hand and why social responsibility or affirmative arguments were used. It was clear that the justices saw libertarianism and the negative interpretation as the norm, with social responsibility and the affirmative interpretation as the deviation. In some sense, they saw media freedom as a right on one level, for they justified interference with it. However, they still did not see it as a natural right, but as a right granted in the Constitution, by the people. Any interference with that right, they seemed to believe, must be to advance another goal of the people. Again, as in cases using a libertarian perspective, the Court treated media freedom as a policy rather than a principle, as a social goal rather than a right.

The justices did not use perspectives from the natural law/legal positivism debate in the same way they used those from the social responsibility/ libertarianism or negative/affirmative freedom debates. The latter and their assumptions provided actual discussion on how to resolve the conflict between requirements of media freedom and of responsibility. However, the legal philosophical debate over the origin of rights simply was not a part of discussion by the Supreme Court in the media cases studied. In fact, the only time any justice confronted natural law directly was in *Curtis v. Butts*, when Justice Harlan suggested that media freedom may also belong to individuals needing to voice their opinions. But he did not use the term natural rights. Nevertheless, the assumptions underlying natural law and legal positivism played an important role in the Court's conceptions of media responsibility, which will be explained shortly.

THE DOMINANT VIEW OF MEDIA RESPONSIBILITY

A single definition of media responsibility, in cases over the sixty-five years analyzed, was not found. Many specific definitions were manifested, and these were clearest in the Court's views on the media's responsibilities regarding truth telling and stewardship. Nevertheless, over time a dominant view of the place media freedom and responsibility hold in U.S. society became clear.

Apparent in nearly every case, that view is that media freedom is very important to the functioning of U.S. democracy. Rationales for this freedom were usually couched in terms of the political and educational functions of the media. Media freedom is protected not because of its own intrinsic value, but because it has a larger purpose. The media were granted freedom so that they could provide citizens with needed information. The opinions studied showed that, despite the apparently absolute language of the first amendment, media freedom is a means, not an end. And because of that, the media can be, and often are, held accountable for their actions and to their purposes.

This dominant view appeared not as a definition of how the media should act; instead, it appeared in the ways the Court conceptualized media freedom. With a few exceptions, the justices saw the "right" of media freedom as a policy—a strong social need that could be overridden if necessary—rather than a principle. It seems likely that the Court's propensity to view media freedom as a policy, and thus to require accountability from the media, is a result of its reliance on legal positivism, rather than natural law.

The justices did not treat the legal positivism/natural law distinction as they did the others. The social responsibility/libertarianism, conservative/liberal, and affirmative/negative interpretations of freedom appeared in Court cases as various justices used them as the basis for arguments. The legal positivism/ natural law debate, however, did not *overtly* affect the justices' decisions. Instead, the assumptions underlying both legal philosophies are so fundamental in the justices' thinking that they never needed to discuss them. For example, legal positivists believe, like adherents of social responsibility and most collectivists, that rights are granted only through law: through constitutions, statutes, or judicial interpretation. There are no inherent rights or principles beyond the law to look to in making decisions. Laws themselves exist because they are created by individuals or bodies given that authority, and there is no necessary connection between laws and morality. Social morals may be enacted into law, but they do not have to be.

Natural law's basic assumptions, on the other hand, are similar to those of libertarianism and most individualist theories. Some laws and rights exist independently of legal systems, and there are separate rules or principles of morality that should be followed. According to Dworkin, legal decisions are, or at least should be, governed by principles, which are "a requirement of justice or fairness or some other dimension of morality"[2] that can be weighed, challenged, or subordinated to other principles without diminishing in value. Principles differ from policies, Dworkin has explained, because whereas principles establish rights, policies establish collective goals. Although laws make use of both policies and principles, policies are far weaker, for they must give way to principles.

Though the justices never directly discussed the issue of natural law versus legal positivism, they used a combination of the two in media cases. As mentioned above, only Harlan made a natural law argument, when he explained media freedom as an individual right. Even then, he was not really discussing the freedom of the press, but individual freedom of expression. The rest of the justices certainly discussed the meaning of media freedom and what they believed to be the media's functions, but they did not articulate their views on the origin or basis of media freedom as a right. While it is impossible to know exactly what their beliefs were, there seem to be two possibilities. First, the justices (or some of them, at least) may have assumed media freedom is an inalienable right and therefore saw no need to discuss its origins. This seems unlikely, however, for if the justices believed this, either they would not have set limits on the exercise of media freedom; or if they felt they had to set limits, they would have used the language of natural rights to explain the necessity of those limits. Second, and more likely, the justices might have believed media freedom is not an inalienable right, but is granted by the people through the Constitution for the purpose of securing a free and just society. If this was their belief, the justices would have on occasion limited media freedom but still would have felt compelled to give strong justifications for doing so.

If, in fact, the justices did see media freedom as granted by the people through the Constitution, then media freedom is indeed viewed as a collectivist goal or policy, not a principle or right. It is not a right existing beyond the bounds of organized society, but is a means to an end, albeit a noble end. The first amendment protects the communications industry, as Brennan described, "to the extent the press makes [the existence of democracy] possible,"[3] but no further. If the media, in this conception of freedom, do not uphold their responsibility and functions, they could lose their freedom. In this conception, media freedom is not a right of individuals but a collective obligation. The people, through their representatives and the Constitution, have given freedom to the media to pursue the goals of a free society. This view of media freedom reflects, then, a legal positivistic conception of rights, and is ultimately collectivist and policy based.

A major conclusion of this examination of Supreme Court conceptions of media responsibility, therefore, is that while there exists in Court media cases much discussion about media freedom and responsibility, discussion that uses both absolutist language and the rhetoric of rights, the Court has actually viewed media freedom not as a right protected in and of itself, but as a means to a free and just society. The Court consistently uses collectivist, rather than individualist, interpretations of the first amendment in its media cases. The media are protected because of their role in attaining and maintaining that society, and therefore have responsibilities to attempt to achieve that goal. This is an admirable reason for protecting media freedom. But in giving that—or any—reason for protecting the media, the Court makes media freedom into a social policy rather than a right or principle. And in so doing, it opens the way for requirements of responsibility, whatever those may be.

IMPLICATIONS FOR THE FUTURE

Though one cannot predict the future by looking to the past, some general conclusions may suggest future directions in the Court's views on media responsibility. First, it seems clear that the general political philosophies of the individual justices significantly affect their beliefs about the media's responsibilities. Conservatives tend more willingly to require responsible behavior, while liberals are more likely to value freedom. Libertarians, who can be either conservative or liberal, use the language of the first amendment to protect the media, while social responsibility arguments can be used by conservatives to demand general accountability, and by liberals to require presentation of diverse viewpoints. These political philosophies likely will continue to affect individual justices' views.

Second, justices who are strongly committed to their perspectives can have a powerful impact on the Court, either through their ability to muster a majority or through their concurring and dissenting opinions. Frankfurter and Brennan, for example, often were able to convince their colleagues to join them. Thus, they influenced legal requirements of press responsibility. Black and Douglas were less able to command majorities, but through their opinions they also greatly affected overall views of the media's roles and responsibilities. Both "team players" and "ideologues," therefore, had, and will continue to have, a role in defining media responsibility.

Third, no view of media responsibility—except perhaps for the view of media freedom as policy—is static. As the Court and the issues before it change, so do requirements of how the media should act. Since the 1970s, the Court has become more conservative, in the present-day meaning of that term, a change that in the late 1980s and early 1990s directly influenced legal requirements of media responsibility. As of the late 1990s, the Court appears to be at a crossroads: Either it will continue on its conservative path, or it will slightly reverse course and become more moderate. The second path seems more likely, for the Court may once again enter a moderate period, with the conservative wing represented by Rehnquist, Scalia, and Thomas, and the "liberal" wing represented by Stevens, Ginsburg, and Breyer. This leaves O'Connor, Kennedy, and Souter as the moderate swing votes. This even balance may lead to another period like the early 1970s, when both conservatives and liberals had to temper their views to gain a majority, and when the media could not count on any principled, consistent views coming from Court rulings. What seems most likely, however, is that, while the various Court definitions of media responsibility will continue to change, the justices' overall view of media freedom as policy will remain, ensuring that the media will always be held accountable as a means to a free, just society.

NOTES

1. Commission on Freedom of the Press, *A Free and Responsible Press* (Chicago: University of Chicago Press, 1947), 1.

2. Ronald Dworkin, *Taking Rights Seriously* (Cambridge: Harvard University Press, 1977),   23.

3. William J. Brennan, Jr., "Newhouse Dedication Lecture," *Media Law Reporter* 5 (1979): 1839.

Appendix

Chronological List of Media Cases

Case Name	Supreme Court Reporter	United States Reports
Near v. Minnesota (1931)	51 S.Ct. 625	283 U.S. 697
Federal Radio Commission v. Nelson Brothers Bond and Mortgage (1933)	53 S.Ct. 627	289 U.S. 266
Grosjean v. American Press Co. (1936)	56. S.Ct. 444	297 U.S. 233
Associated Press v. National Labor Relations Board (1937)	57 S.Ct. 650	301 U.S. 103
Lovell v. Griffin (1938)	58 S.Ct. 666	303 U.S. 444
Nichols v. Massachusetts (1939) *Schneider v. New Jersey *Snyder v. Milwaukee *Young v. California	60 S.Ct. 146	308 U.S. 147
F.C.C. v. Pottsville Broadcasting Co. (1939)	60 S.Ct. 437	309 U.S. 134
Weiss v. United States (1940)	60 S.Ct. 269	308 U.S. 321
Fly v. Heitmeyer (1940)	60 S.Ct. 443	309 U.S. 146
F.C.C. v. Sanders Brothers Radio Station (1940)	60 S.Ct. 693	309 U.S. 470

* Asterisks designate cases decided jointly by the Court.

Case Name	Supreme Court Reporter	United States Reports
Bridges v. California (1941) *Times-Mirror v. Superior Court of California, Los Angeles County	62 S.Ct. 190	314 U.S. 252
Scripps-Howard Radio v. F.C.C. (1942)	62 S.Ct. 875	316 U.S. 4
Valentine v. Chrestensen (1942)	62 S.Ct. 920	316 U.S. 52
Goldman v. United States (1942)	62 S.Ct. 993	316 U.S. 129
Columbia Broadcasting System v. United States (1942)	62 S.Ct. 1194	316 U.S. 407
National Broadcasting Co. v. United States (1942)	62 S.Ct. 1214	316 U.S. 447
Bowden v. Fort Smith (1942) *Jobin v. Arizona *Jones v. City of Opelika	62 S.Ct. 1231	316 U.S. 584
Jamison v. Texas (1943)	63 S.Ct. 669	318 U.S. 413
Murdock v. Pennsylvania (1943)	63 S.Ct. 870	319 U.S. 105
Martin v. Struthers, Ohio (1943)	63 S.Ct. 862	319 U.S. 141
National Broadcasting Co. v. United States (1943)	63 S.Ct. 997	319 U.S. 190
F.C.C. v. National Broadcasting Co. (1943)	63 S.Ct. 1035	319 U.S. 239
Benoit v. Mississippi (1943) *Cummings v. Mississippi *Taylor v. Mississippi	63 S.Ct. 1200	319 U.S. 583
Associated Press v. United States (1945)	65 S.Ct. 1416	326 U.S. 1
Radio Station WOW v. Johnson (1945)	65 S.Ct. 1475	326 U.S. 120
Ashbacker Radio Corp. v. F.C.C. (1945)	66 S.Ct. 148	326 U.S. 327
Marsh v. Alabama (1946)	66 S.Ct. 276	326 U.S. 501
Hannegan v. Esquire (1946)	66 S.Ct. 456	327 U.S. 146

Case Name	Supreme Court Reporter	United States Reports
Mabee v. White Plains Publishing Co. (1946)	66 S.Ct. 511	327 U.S. 178
Oklahoma Press Publishing Co. v. Walling (1946)	66 S.Ct. 494	327 U.S. 186
Pennekamp v. Florida (1946)	66 S.Ct. 1029	328 U.S. 331
F.C.C. v. WOKO, Inc. (1947)	67 S.Ct. 213	329 U.S. 223
Craig v. Harney (1947)	67 S.Ct. 1249	331 U.S. 367
United States v. Petrillo (1947)	67 S.Ct. 1538	332 U.S. 1
Donaldson v. Read Magazine (1948)	68 S.Ct. 591	333 U.S. 178
Winters v. New York (1948)	68 S.Ct. 664	333 U.S. 507
United States v. Paramount Pictures (1948)	68 S.Ct. 915	334 U.S. 131
F.C.C. v. WJR, The Goodwill Station (1949)	69 S.Ct. 1097	337 U.S. 265
Regents of the University System of Georgia v. Carroll (1950)	70 S.Ct. 370	338 U.S. 586
United States v. Alpers (1950)	70 S.Ct. 352	338 U.S. 680
Radio Corporation of America v. United States (1951)	71 S.Ct. 806	341 U.S. 412
Breard v. Alexandria (1951)	71 S.Ct. 920	341 U.S. 622
Lorain County Journal v. United States (1951)	72 S.Ct. 181	342 U.S. 143
Stroble v. California (1952)	72 S.Ct. 599	343 U.S. 181
Beauharnais v. Illinois (1952)	72 S.Ct. 725	343 U.S. 250
Public Utilities Commission of the District of Columbia v. Pollack (1952)	72 S.Ct. 813	343 U.S. 451
Burstyn v. Wilson (1952)	72 S.Ct. 777	343 U.S. 495
F.C.C. v. RCA Communications (1953)	73 S.Ct. 998	345 U.S. 86
Times-Picayune v. United States (1953)	73 S.Ct. 872	345 U.S. 594

Case Name	Supreme Court Reporter	United States Reports
Theatre Enterprises v. Paramount Film Distributing (1954)	74 S.Ct. 257	346 U.S. 537
F.C.C. v. American Broadcasting System (1954)	74 S.Ct. 593	347 U.S. 284
F.C.C. v. Allentown Broadcasting Co. (1955)	75 S.Ct. 855	349 U.S. 358
United States v. Storer Broadcasting Co. (1956)	76 S.Ct. 763	351 U.S. 192
Butler v. Michigan (1957)	77 S.Ct. 524	352 U.S. 380
Kingsley Books v. Brown (1957)	77 S.Ct. 1325	354 U.S. 436
Alberts v. California (1957) *Roth v. United States	77 S.Ct. 1304	354 U.S. 476
United States v. Radio Corporation of America (1959)	79 S.Ct. 457	358 U.S. 334
Marshall v. United States (1959)	79 S.Ct. 1171	360 U.S. 310
Farmers Educational and Co-op Union of America v. WDAY (1959)	79 S.Ct. 1302	360 U.S. 525
Barr v. Mateo (1959)	79 S.Ct. 1335	360 U.S. 564
Kingsley International Pictures Corp. v. Regents of the University of the State of New York (1959)	79 S.Ct. 1362	360 U.S. 684
Smith v. California (1960)	80 S.Ct. 215	361 U.S. 147
Talley v. California (1960)	80 S.Ct. 536	362 U.S. 60
Times Film Corp. v. City of Chicago (1961)	81 S.Ct. 391	365 U.S. 43
Irvin v. Dowd (1961)	81 S.Ct. 1639	366 U.S. 717
Communist Party of United States v. Subversive Activities Control Board (1961)	81 S.Ct. 1357	367 U.S. 1
Wood v. Georgia (1962)	82 S.Ct. 1364	370 U.S. 375
Bantam Books v. Sullivan (1963)	83 S.Ct. 631	372 U.S. 58

Case Name	Supreme Court Reporter	United States Reports
Rideau v. Louisiana (1963)	83 S.Ct. 1417	373 U.S. 723
New York Times v. Sullivan (1964)	84 S.Ct. 710	376 U.S. 254
Jacobellis v. Ohio (1964)	84 S.Ct. 1676	378 U.S. 184
Quantity of Copies of Books v. Kansas (1964)	84 S.Ct. 1723	378 U.S. 205
Garrison v. Louisiana (1964)	85 S.Ct. 209	379 U.S. 64
Freedman v. Maryland (1965)	85 S.Ct. 734	380 U.S. 51
Henry v. Collins (1965)	85 S.Ct. 992	380 U.S. 356
F.C.C. v. Schreiber (1965)	85 S.Ct. 1459	381 U.S. 279
Lamont v. Postmaster General (1965)	85 S.Ct. 1403	381 U.S. 301
Estes v. Texas (1965)	85 S.Ct. 1628	381 U.S. 532
Linn v. United Plant Guard Workers of America (1966)	86 S.Ct. 657	383 U.S. 53
Rosenblatt v. Baer (1966)	86 S.Ct. 669	383 U.S. 75
A Book Named 'John Cleland's Memoirs of a Woman of Pleasure' v. Attorney General of the Commonwealth of Massachusetts (1966)	86 S.Ct. 975	383 U.S. 413
Ginzburg v. United States (1966)	86 S.Ct. 942	383 U.S. 463
Mishkin v. New York (1966)	86 S.Ct. 958	383 U.S. 502
Ashton v. Kentucky (1966)	86 S.Ct. 1407	384 U.S. 195
Mills v. Alabama (1966)	86 S.Ct. 1434	384 U.S. 214
Sheppard v. Maxwell (1966)	86 S.Ct. 1507	384 U.S. 333
Time v. Hill (1967)	87 S.Ct. 534	385 U.S. 374
Associated Press (1967) v. Walker *Curtis Publishing Co. v. Butts	87 S.Ct. 1975	388 U.S. 130
Austin v. Kentucky (1967) *Gent v. Arkansas *Redrup v. New York	87 S.Ct. 1414	386 U.S. 767

Case Name	Supreme Court Reporter	United States Reports
Blankenship v. Holding (1967)	87 S.Ct. 1419	387 U.S. 95
Beckley Newspapers v. Hanks (1967)	88 S.Ct. 197	389 U.S. 81
Ginsberg v. New York (1968)	88 S.Ct. 1274	390 U.S. 629
Interstate Circuit, Inc. v. City of Dallas (1968)	88 S.Ct. 1298	390 U.S. 676
St. Amant v. Thompson (1968)	88 S.Ct. 1323	390 U.S. 727
Teitel Film Corp. v. Cusack (1968)	88 S.Ct. 754	390 U.S. 139
United States v. Southwestern Cable (1968)	88 S.Ct. 1994	392 U.S. 157
Citizen Publishing Co. v. United States (1969)	89 S.Ct. 927	394 U.S. 131
Stanley v. Georgia (1969)	89 S.Ct. 1243	394 U.S. 557
Red Lion Broadcasting Co. v. F.C.C. (1969) *United States v. Radio Television News Directors Association	89 S.Ct. 1794	395 U.S. 367
Rowan v. United States Post Office (1970)	90 S.Ct. 1484	397 U.S. 728
Greenbelt Cooperative Publishing Ass'n v. Bresler (1970)	90 S.Ct. 1537	398 U.S. 6
Blount v. Rizzi (1971)	91 S.Ct. 423	400 U.S. 410
Monitor Patriot v. Roy (1971)	91 S.Ct. 621	401 U.S. 265
Time v. Pape (1971)	91 S.Ct. 633	401 U.S. 279
Ocala Star-Banner v. Damron (1971)	91 S.Ct. 628	401 U.S. 295
United States v. 37 Photographs (1971) *United States v. Reidel	91 S.Ct. 1400	402 U.S. 363
Organization for a Better Austin v. Keefe (1971)	91 S.Ct. 1575	402 U.S. 415
United States v. Greater Buffalo Press (1971)	91 S.Ct. 1692	402 U.S. 549

Case Name	Supreme Court Reporter	United States Reports
Rosenbloom v. Metromedia (1971)	91 S.Ct. 1811	403 U.S. 29
New York Times v. United States (1971) *United States v. Washington Post	91 S.Ct. 2140	403 U.S. 713
United States v. Midwest Video (1972)	92 S.Ct. 1860	406 U.S. 649
Lloyd Corp. v. Tanner (1972)	92 S.Ct. 2219	407 U.S. 551
Kois v. Wisconsin (1972)	92 S.Ct. 2245	408 U.S. 229
Branzburg v. Hayes (1972) *In re Pappas *United States v. Caldwell	92 S.Ct. 2646	408 U.S. 665
Papish v. Board of Curators of the University of Missouri (1973)	93 S.Ct. 1197	410 U.S. 667
Columbia Broadcasting System v. Democratic National Committee (1973)	93 S.Ct. 2080	412 U.S. 94
Doe v. McMillan (1973)	93 S.Ct. 2018	412 U.S. 306
Miller v. California (1973)	93 S.Ct. 2607	413 U.S. 15
Paris Adult Theater v. Slaton (1973)	93 S.Ct. 2628	413 U.S. 49
Kaplan v. California (1973)	93 S.Ct. 2680	413 U.S. 115
United States v. 12 200-Foot Reels of Super 8mm. Film (1973)	93 S.Ct. 2665	413 U.S. 123
Pittsburgh Press Co. v. Pittsburgh Commission on Human Relations (1973)	93 S.Ct. 2553	413 U.S. 376
Heller v. New York (1973)	93 S.Ct. 2789	413 U.S. 483
National Cable Television Ass'n v. United States (1974)	94 S.Ct. 1155	415 U.S. 352
Teleprompter v. Columbia Broadcasting System (1974)	94 S.Ct. 1129	415 U.S. 394
Pell v. Procunier (1974) *Saxbe v. Washington Post	94 S.Ct. 2800	417 U.S. 817

Case Name	Supreme Court Reporter	United States Reports
Hamling v. United States (1974)	94 S.Ct. 2887	418 U.S. 87
Jenkins v. Georgia (1974)	94 S.Ct. 2750	418 U.S. 153
Miami Herald v. Tornillo (1974)	94 S.Ct. 2831	418 U.S. 241
National Association of Letter Carriers v. Austin (1974)	94 S.Ct. 2770	418 U.S. 264
Lehman v. City of Shaker Heights (1974)	94 S.Ct. 2714	418 U.S. 298
Gertz v. Welch (1974)	94 S.Ct. 2997	418 U.S. 323
Cantrell v. Forest City Publishing Co. (1974)	95 S.Ct. 465	419 U.S. 245
Times-Picayune Publishing Corp. v. Schulingkamp (1974)	95 S.Ct. 1	419 U.S. 1301
Cox Broadcasting Corp. v. Cohn (1975)	95 S.Ct. 1029	420 U.S. 469
Southeastern Promotions v. Conrad (1975)	95 S.Ct. 1239	420 U.S. 546
Murphy v. Florida (1975)	95 S.Ct. 2031	421 U.S. 794
Bigelow v. Virginia (1975)	95 S.Ct. 2222	421 U.S. 809
Erznoznik v. City of Jacksonville (1975)	95 S.Ct 2268	422 U.S. 205
Time v. Firestone (1976)	96 S.Ct. 958	424 U.S. 448
McKinney v. Alabama (1976)	96 S.Ct. 1189	424 U.S. 669
Virginia State Board of Pharmacy v. Virginia Citizens Consumer Council (1976)	96 S.Ct. 1817	425 U.S. 748
Young v. American Mini Theaters, Inc. (1976)	96 S.Ct. 2440	427 U.S. 50
Nebraska Press Association v. Stuart (1976)	96 S.Ct. 2791	427 U.S. 539
Gruner v. Superior Court of California (1976)	97 S.Ct. 7	429 U.S. 1314
Marks v. United States (1977)	97 S.Ct. 990	430 U.S. 188

Case Name	Supreme Court Reporter	United States Reports
Oklahoma Publishing Co. v. District Court for Oklahoma County (1977)	97 S.Ct. 1045	430 U.S. 308
Smith v. United States (1977)	97 S.Ct. 1756	431 U.S. 291
Splawn v. California (1977)	97 S.Ct. 1987	431 U.S. 595
Carey v. Population Services (1977)	97 S.Ct. 2010	431 U.S. 678
Ward v. Illinois (1977)	97 S.Ct. 2085	431 U.S. 767
Dobbert v. Florida (1977)	97 S.Ct. 2290	432 U.S. 282
Jones v. North Carolina Prisoners' Labor Union (1977)	97 S.Ct. 2532	433 U.S. 119
Bates v. State Bar of Arizona (1977)	97 S.Ct. 2691	433 U.S. 350
Zacchini v. Scripps-Howard Broadcasting (1977)	97 S.Ct. 2849	433 U.S. 562
Philadelphia Newspapers v. Jerome (1978)	98 S.Ct. 546	434 U.S. 241
Nixon v. Warner Communications (1978)	98 S.Ct. 1306	435 U.S. 589
First National Bank of Boston v. Bellotti (1978)	98 S.Ct. 1407	435 U.S. 765
Landmark Communications v. Virginia (1978)	98 S.Ct. 1535	435 U.S. 829
Pinkus v. United States (1978)	98 S.Ct. 1808	436 U.S. 293
Zurcher v. Stanford Daily (1978)	98 S.Ct. 1970	436 U.S. 547
F.C.C. v. National Citizens Committee for Broadcasting (1978)	98 S.Ct. 2096	436 U.S. 775
Houchins v. KQED (1978)	98 S.Ct. 2588	438 U.S. 1
F.C.C. v. Pacifica Foundation (1978)	98 S.Ct. 3026	438 U.S. 726
New York Times v. Jascalevich (1978)	98 S.Ct. 3058	439 U.S. 1301

Case Name	Supreme Court Reporter	United States Reports
New York Times v. Jascalevich (1978)	99 S.Ct. 11	439 U.S. 1331
Friedman v. Rogers (1979)	99 S.Ct. 887	440 U.S. 1
F.C.C. v. Midwest Video Corporation (1979)	99 S.Ct. 1435	440 U.S. 689
Broadcast Music v. Columbia Broadcasting System (1979)	99 S.Ct. 1551	441 U.S. 1
Herbert v. Lando (1979)	99 S.Ct. 1635	441 U.S. 153
Lo-Ji Sales v. New York (1979)	99 S.Ct. 2319	442 U.S. 319
Smith v. Daily Mail Publishing Co. (1979)	99 S.Ct. 2667	443 U.S. 97
Hutchinson v. Proxmire (1979)	99 S.Ct. 2675	443 U.S. 111
Wolston v. Reader's Digest (1979)	99 S.Ct. 2701	443 U.S. 157
Gannett v. DePasquale (1979)	99 S.Ct. 2898	443 U.S. 361
Morland v. Sprecher (1979)	99 S.Ct. 3086	443 U.S. 709
Snepp v. United States (1980)	100 S.Ct. 763	444 U.S. 507
Kissinger v. Reporters Committee on Freedom of the Press (1980)	100 S.Ct. 960	445 U.S. 136
Vance v. Universal Amusement Co., Inc. (1980)	100 S.Ct. 1156	445 U.S. 308
Consolidated Edison Co. of New York v. Public Service Commission of New York (1980)	100 S.Ct. 2326	447 U.S. 530
Central Hudson Gas and Electric Corp. v. Public Service Commission of New York (1980)	100 S.Ct. 2343	447 U.S. 557
Richmond Newspapers v. Virginia (1980)	100 S.Ct. 2814	448 U.S. 555
Chandler v. Florida (1981)	101 S.Ct. 802	449 U.S. 560
F.C.C. v. WNCN Listeners Guild (1981)	101 S.Ct. 1266	450 U.S. 582

Case Name	Supreme Court Reporter	United States Reports
United States Postal Service v. Council of Greenburgh Civic Associations (1981)	101 S.Ct. 2676	453 U.S. 114
Columbia Broadcasting System v. F.C.C. (1981)	101 S.Ct. 2813	453 U.S. 367
California ex rel Cooper v. Mitchell Brothers Santa Ana Theater (1981)	101 S.Ct. 172	454 U.S. 90
In re R.M.J. (1982)	102 S.Ct. 929	455 U.S. 191
State Department v. Washington Post (1982)	102 S.Ct. 1957	456 U.S. 595
Globe Newspaper Co. v. Superior Court for Norfolk County (1982)	102 S.Ct. 2613	457 U.S. 596
Loretto v. Teleprompter Manhattan (1982)	102 S.Ct. 3164	458 U.S. 419
New York v. Ferber (1982)	102 S.Ct. 3348	458 U.S. 747
Avenue Bookstore v. Tallmadge (1982)	103 S.Ct. 356	459 U.S. 997
Lawrence v. Bauer Publishing (1982)	103 S.Ct. 358	459 U.S. 999
KPNX Broadcasting v. Arizona Superior Court (1982)	103 S.Ct. 584	459 U.S. 1302
Community Television of Southern California v. Gottfried (1983)	103 S.Ct. 885	459 U.S. 498
Minneapolis Star and Tribune Co. v. Minnesota Commissioner of Revenue (1983)	103 S.Ct. 1365	460 U.S. 575
Bolger v. Youngs Drug Products Corp. (1983)	103 S.Ct. 2875	463 U.S. 60
Press-Enterprise Co. v. Superior Court of California for Riverside County (I) (1984)	104 S.Ct. 819	464 U.S. 501
Keeton v. Hustler Magazine (1984)	104 S.Ct. 1473	465 U.S. 770
Calder v. Jones (1984)	103 S.Ct. 1482	465 U.S. 783

Case Name	Supreme Court Reporter	United States Reports
F.C.C. v. ITT World Communications (1984)	104 S.Ct. 1936	466 U.S. 463
Bose Corp. v. Consumers Union (1984)	104 S.Ct. 1949	466 U.S. 485
Seattle Times v. Rhinehart (1984)	104 S.Ct. 2199	467 U.S. 20
Waller v. Georgia (1984)	104 S.Ct. 2210	467 U.S. 39
Capital Cities Cable v. Crisp (1984)	104 S.Ct. 2694	467 U.S. 691
Regan v. Time (1984)	104 S.Ct. 3262	468 U.S. 82
F.C.C. v. League of Women Voters of California (1984)	104 S.Ct. 3106	468 U.S. 364
Harper and Row v. Nation Enterprises (1985)	105 S.Ct. 2218	471 U.S. 539
Zauderer v. Office of Disciplinary Counsel of Supreme Court of Ohio (1985)	105 S.Ct. 2265	471 U.S. 626
Ollman v. Evans (1985)	105 S.Ct. 2662	471 U.S. 1127
McDonald v. Smith (1985)	105 S.Ct. 2787	472 U.S. 479
Brackett v. Spokane Arcades (1985)	105 S.Ct. 2794	472 U.S. 491
Dun & Bradstreet v. Greenmoss Builders (1985)	105 S.Ct. 2939	472 U.S. 749
Lorain Journal v. Milkovich (1985)	106 S.Ct. 322	474 U.S. 953
Pacific Gas and Electric Co. v. Public Utilities Commission of California (1986)	106 S.Ct. 903	475 U.S. 1
Renton v. Playtime Theatres (1986)	106 S.Ct. 925	475 U.S. 41
Philadelphia Newspapers v. Hepps (1986)	106 S.Ct. 1558	475 U.S. 767
City of Los Angeles v. Preferred Communication (1986)	106 S.Ct. 2034	476 U.S. 488

Case Name	Supreme Court Reporter	United States Reports
Coughlin v. Westinghouse Broadcasting (1986)	106 S.Ct. 2927	476 U.S. 1187
Anderson v. Liberty Lobby (1986)	106 S.Ct. 2505	477 U.S. 242
Press-Enterprise Co. v. Superior Court of California for Riverside County (II) (1986)	106 S.Ct. 2735	478 U.S. 1
Posadas de Puerto Rico Associates v. Tourism Co. of Puerto Rico (1986)	106 S.Ct. 2968	478 U.S. 328
Arcara v. Cloud Books (1986)	106 S.Ct. 3172	478 U.S. 697
Federal Election Commission v. Massachusetts Citizens for Life (1986)	107 S.Ct. 616	479 U.S. 238
F.C.C. v. Florida Power (1987)	107 S.Ct. 1107	480 U.S. 245
Arkansas Writers' Project, Inc. v. Ragland (1987)	107 S.Ct. 1722	481 U.S. 221
Meese v. Keene (1987)	107 S.Ct. 1862	481 U.S. 465
Pope v. Illinois (1987)	107 S.Ct. 1918	481 U.S. 497
San Francisco Arts and Athletics, Inc. v. U.S. Olympic Committee (1987)	107 S.Ct. 2971	483 U.S. 522
Carpenter v. United States (1987)	108 S.Ct. 316	484 U.S. 19
Hazelwood School District v. Kuhlmeier (1988)	108 S.Ct. 562	484 U.S. 260
Virginia v. American Booksellers (1988)	108 S.Ct. 636	484 U.S. 383
Hustler Magazine v. Falwell (1988)	108 S.Ct. 876	485 U.S. 46
United States v. Providence Journal (1988)	108 S.Ct. 1502	485 U.S. 693
City of New York v. F.C.C. (1988)	108 S.Ct. 1637	486 U.S. 57

Case Name	Supreme Court Reporter	United States Reports
City of Lakewood v. Plain Dealer Publishing Co. (1988)	108 S.Ct. 2138	486 U.S. 750
Dow Jones and Co. v. Simon (1988)	109 S.Ct. 377	488 U.S. 946
Texas Monthly v. Bullock (1989)	109 S.Ct. 890	489 U.S. 1
Fort Wayne Books v. Indiana (1989)	109 S.Ct. 916	489 U.S. 46
Justice Department v. Reporters Committee on Freedom of the Press (1989)	109 S.Ct. 1468	489 U.S. 749
Frank v. Minnesota News Association (1989)	109 S.Ct. 1734	490 U.S. 225
Florida Star v. B.J.F. (1989)	109 S.Ct. 2603	491 U.S. 524
Harte-Hanks Communications Inc. v. Connaughton (1989)	109 S.Ct. 2678	491 U.S. 657
Justice Department v. Tax Analysts (1989)	109 S.Ct. 2841	492 U.S. 136
Sable Communications v. F.C.C. (1989)	109 S.Ct. 2829	492 U.S. 115
Michigan Citizens for an Independent Press v. Thornburgh (1990)	110 S.Ct. 398	493 U.S. 38
Butterworth v. Smith (1990)	110 S.Ct. 1376	494 U.S. 624
United States v. Kokinda (1990)	110 S.Ct. 3115	497 U.S. 720
Milkovich v. Lorain Journal (1990)	110 S.Ct. 2695	497 U.S. 1
Cable News Network v. Noriega (1990)	111 S.Ct. 451	498 U.S. 976
Feist Publication, Inc. v. Rural Telephone Service, Inc. (1991)	111 S.Ct. 1282	499 U.S. 340
Leathers v. Medlock (1991)	111 S.Ct. 1438	499 U.S. 439
Mu'Min v. Virginia (1991)	111 S.Ct. 1899	500 U.S. 415
Chambers v. Nasco (1991)	111 S.Ct. 2123	501 U.S. 33

Case Name	Supreme Court Reporter	United States Reports
Masson v. New Yorker Magazine, Inc. (1991)	111 S.Ct. 2419	501 U.S. 496
Cohen v. Cowles Media (1991)	111 S.Ct. 2513	501 U.S. 663
Burson v. Freeman (1992)	112 S.Ct. 1846	504 U.S. 191
International Society for Krishna Consciousness v. Lee (1992)	112 S.Ct. 2701	505 U.S. 672
City of Cincinnati v. Discovery Network (1993)	113 S.Ct. 1505	507 U.S. 410
Newark Morning Ledger v. United States (1993)	113 S.Ct. 1670	507 U.S. 546
F.C.C. v. Beach Communications (1993)	113 S.Ct. 2096	508 U.S. 307
United States v. Edge Broadcasting (1993)	113 S.Ct. 2696	509 U.S. 418
Alexander v. United States (1993)	113 S.Ct. 2766	509 U.S. 544
Campbell v. Acuff-Rose (1994)	114 S.Ct. 1164	510 U.S. 569
Ibanez v. Florida Department of Business and Professional Regulation (1994)	114 S.Ct. 2084	510 U.S. 1067
Turner Broadcasting System v. F.C.C. (1994)	114 S.Ct. 2445	509 U.S. 952
United States v. X-Citement Video (1994)	115 S.Ct. 464	510 U.S. 1163
Lebron v. National Railroad Passenger Corporation (1995)	115 S.Ct. 961	510 U.S. 1105
McIntyre v. Ohio Elections Commission (1995)	115 S.Ct. 1511	+
Rubin v. Coors (1995)	115 S.Ct. 1585	
Rosenberger v. Rector and Visitors of University of Virginia (1995)	115 S.Ct. 2510	
Liquormart v. Rhode Island (1996)	116 S.Ct. 1495	

+ For this and following cases, the United States Reports citations were not available at press time.

Case Name	Supreme Court Reporter	United States Reports
Denver Area Educational Telecommunications Consortium v. F.C.C. (1996)	116 S.Ct. 2374	

Bibliography

Ahlstrom, Sydney E. *A Religious History of the American People*. Vol. 2. Garden City, N.Y.: Image Books, 1975.

Barron, Jerome. *Freedom of the Press for Whom? The Right of Access to Mass Media*. Bloomington: Indiana University Press, 1973.

———. "Access to the Press: A New First Amendment Right." *Harvard Law Review* 80 (1967): 1641–78.

Baugh, Joyce Ann, Christopher E. Smith, Thomas R. Hensley, and Scott Patrick Johnson. "Justice Ruth Bader Ginsburg: A Preliminary Assessment." *University of Toledo Law Review* 26 (1994): 1–34.

Berns, Walter. *The First Amendment and the Future of American Democracy*. New York: Basic Books, 1976.

Black, Virginia. "Natural Law, Constitutional Adjudication and Clarence Thomas." *University of California–Davis Law Review* 26 (1993): 769–89.

Blanchard, Margaret A. *Revolutionary Sparks: Freedom of Expression in Modern America*. New York: Oxford University Press, 1991.

———. "The Hutchins Commission, The Press and the Responsibility Concept." *Journalism Monographs* 49 (1977).

Blasi, Vincent, ed. *The Burger Court: The Counter-Revolution that Wasn't*. New Haven: Yale University Press, 1983.

Bollinger, Lee C. *Images of a Free Press*. Chicago: University of Chicago Press, 1991.

———. "Freedom of the Press and Government Power to Structure the Press." *University of Miami Law Review* 34 (1980): 819–89.

Bork, Robert H. *Tradition and Morality in Constitutional Law*. Washington, D.C.: American Enterprise Institute, 1984.

Brennan, William J., Jr. "Newhouse Dedication Lecture." *Media Law Reporter* 5 (1979): 1837–42.

Brisbin, Richard A., Jr. "The Conservatism of Antonin Scalia." *Political Science Quarterly* 105 (1990): 1–29.

Brock, Beau James. "Mr. Justice Antonin Scalia: A Renaissance of Positivism and Predictability in Constitutional Adjudication." *Louisiana Law Review* 51 (1991): 623–50.

Carter, T. Barton, Marc A. Franklin, and Jay B. Wright. *The First Amendment and the Fourth Estate*, 5th ed. Mineola, N.Y.: The Foundation Press, 1991.

Commission on Freedom of the Press. *A Free and Responsible Press*. Ed. Robert D. Leigh. Chicago: University of Chicago Press, 1947.

Corwin, Edward S. *Constitutional Revolution, Ltd*. Claremont, Calif.: Claremont Colleges, 1941.

Davis, Sue. *Justice Rehnquist and the Constitution*. Princeton: Princeton University Press, 1989.

Dennis, Everette E., Donald M. Gillmor, and Theodore L. Glasser, eds. *Media Freedom and Accountability*. Westport, Conn.: Greenwood Press, 1989.

Dennis, Everette E., Donald M. Gillmor, and David L. Grey, eds. *Justice Hugo Black and the First Amendment*. Ames: Iowa State University Press, 1978.

Dreschel, Robert E. "Media Ethics and Media Law: The Transformation of Moral Obligation into Legal Principle." *Notre Dame Journal of Law, Ethics and Public Policy* 6.1 (1992): 5–32.

Dworkin, Ronald. *A Matter of Principle*. Cambridge, Mass.: Harvard University Press, 1985.

———. "'Natural' Law Revisited." *University of Florida Law Review* 34 (1982): 165–88.

———. "Liberalism." In *Public and Private Morality*. Ed. Stuart Hampshire, 113–43. Cambridge: Cambridge University Press, 1978.

———. *Taking Rights Seriously*. Cambridge, Mass.: Harvard University Press, 1977.

———. "The Elusive Morality of Law." *Villanova Law Review* 10 (1965): 631–39.

Elfenbein, Donald. "The Myth of Conservatism as a Constitutional Philosophy." *Iowa Law Review* 71 (1986): 401–88.

Elliott, Deni. "Foundations for News Media Responsibility." In *Responsible Journalism*. Ed. Deni Elliott, 32–44. Beverly Hills: Sage Publications, Inc., 1986.

Ely, John Hart. "Foreword: On Discovering Fundamental Values." *Harvard Law Review* 92 (1978): 5–55.

Emerson, Thomas I. "Freedom of the Press Under the Burger Court." In *The Burger Court: The Counter-Revolution that Wasn't*. Ed. Vincent Blasi, 1–27. New Haven: Yale University Press, 1983.

———. "The Affirmative Side of the First Amendment." *Georgia Law Review* 15 (1981): 795–849.

———. *The System of Freedom of Expression*. New York: Vintage Books, 1970.

———. *Toward a General Theory of the First Amendment*. New York: Random House, 1963.

Etzioni, Amitai. *Rights and the Common Good: The Communitarian Perspective*. New York: St. Martin's Press, 1995.

Ferre, John P. "Grounding an Ethics of Journalism." *Journal of Mass Media Ethics* 3.1 (1988): 18–27.

Franklin, Marc A., and David A. Anderson. *Mass Media Law: Cases and Materials*, 4th ed. Westbury, N.Y.: Foundation Press, Inc., 1990.

Friedman, Lawrence M. "The Limitations of Labeling: Justice Anthony M. Kennedy and the First Amendment." *Ohio Northern University Law Review* 20.2 (1993): 225–62.

———. *A History of American Law*. New York: Simon and Schuster, 1985.

Fuller, Lon. *The Morality of Law*. Rev. ed. New Haven: Yale University Press, 1969.

———. "A Reply to Professors Cohen and Dworkin." *Villanova Law Review* 10 (1965): 655–66.

———. "Positivism and Fidelity to Law—A Reply to Professor Hart." *Harvard Law Review* 71 (1958): 630–72.

———. *The Law in Quest of Itself*. Chicago: The Foundation Press, Inc., 1940.

Galloway, Russell. *The Rich and the Poor in Supreme Court History, 1790–1982*. Greenbrae, Calif.: Paradigm Press, 1982.

Gerald, J. Edward. *The Social Responsibility of the Press*. Minneapolis: University of Minnesota Press, 1963.

Gillmor, Donald M. "The Terrible Burden of Free and Accountable Media." In *Media Freedom and Accountability*. Ed. Everette E. Dennis, Donald M. Gillmor, and Theodore L. Glasser, 1–10. Westport, Conn.: Greenwood Press, 1989.

Gillmor, Donald M., Jerome A. Barron, Todd F. Simon, and Herbert A. Terry. *Mass Communication Law: Cases and Comment*, 5th ed. St. Paul: West Publishing, 1990.

Giuffra, Robert J., Jr. "The Rehnquist Court after Five Terms." *New York Law Journal* 30 July 1991: 1ff.

Glasser, Theodore L. "Three Views on Accountability." In *Media Freedom and Accountability*. Ed. Everette E. Dennis, Donald M. Gillmor, and Theodore L. Glasser, 179–88. Westport, Conn.: Greenwood Press, 1989.

———. "Press Responsibility and First Amendment Values." In *Responsible Journalism*. Ed. Deni Elliott, 81–98. Beverly Hills: Sage Publications, Inc., 1986.

Glendon, Mary Ann. *Rights Talk: The Impoverishment of Political Discourse*. New York: The Free Press, 1991.

Hale, F. Dennis. "Free Expression: The First Five Years of the Rehnquist Court." *Journalism Quarterly* 69 (1992): 89–104.

Hall, Kermit L., ed. in chief. *The Oxford Companion to the Supreme Court of the United States*. New York: Oxford University Press, 1992.

———. *The Magic Mirror: Law in American History*. New York: Oxford University Press, 1989.

Hart, H.L.A. *The Concept of Law*. Oxford: Clarendon Press, 1961.

———. "Positivism and the Separation of Law and Morals." *Harvard Law Review* 71 (1958): 593–629.

Hartung, Barbara W. "Attitudes Toward the Applicability of the Hutchins Report on Press Responsibility." *Journalism Quarterly* 58 (1981): 428–33.

Higdon, Philip R. "The Burger Court and the Media: A Ten-Year Perspective." *Western New England Law Review* 2 (1980): 593–680.

Hindman, Elizabeth Blanks. "First Amendment Theories and Press Responsibility: The Work of Zechariah Chafee, Thomas Emerson, Vincent Blasi and Edwin Baker." *Journalism Quarterly* 69 (1992): 48–64.

Hocking, William Ernest. *Freedom of the Press: A Framework of Principle*. Chicago: University of Chicago Press, 1947.

Hodges, Louis W. "Defining Press Responsibility: A Functional Approach." In *Responsible Journalism*. Ed. Deni Elliott, 13–31. Beverly Hills: Sage Publications, Inc., 1986.

Hofstadter, Richard. *The Age of Reform*. New York: Knopf, 1955.

Holmes, Oliver Wendell. "The Path of the Law." *Harvard Law Review* 10 (1897): 457–78.

Hunsaker, David M. "Freedom and Responsibility in First Amendment Theory: Defamation Law and Media Credibility." *Quarterly Journal of Speech* 65 (1979): 25–35.

Jaffe, Louis, L. "The Editorial Responsibility of the Broadcaster: Reflections on Fairness and Access." *Harvard Law Review* 85 (1972): 768–92.

Jordan, William S., III. "Justice David Souter and Statutory Interpretation." *University of Toledo Law Review* 23 (1992): 491–530.

Kalven, Harry, Jr. *A Worthy Tradition: Freedom of Speech in the United States*. Ed. Jamie Kalven. New York: Harper and Row, 1988.

————. "Uninhibited, Robust, and Wide-Open—A Note on Free Speech and the Warren Court." *Michigan Law Review* 67 (1968): 289–302.

————. "The New York Times Case: A Note on 'The Central Meaning of the First Amendment.'" *Supreme Court Review* (1964): 191–221.

Kammen, Michael. *Sovereignty and Liberty: Constitutional Discourse in American Culture*. Madison: University of Wisconsin Press, 1988.

Kannar, George. "Strenuous Virtues, Virtuous Lives: The Social Vision of Antonin Scalia." *Cardozo Law Review* 12 (1991): 1845–67.

Kelley, David, and Roger Donway, "Liberalism and Free Speech." In *Democracy and the Mass Media*. Ed. Judith Lichtenberg, 66–101. Cambridge: Cambridge University Press, 1990.

Lambeth, Edmund B. *Committed Journalism: An Ethic for the Profession*. Bloomington: Indiana University Press, 1992.

Lange, David. "The Speech and Press Clauses." *U.C.L.A. Law Review* 77 (1975): 77–119.

Levy, Leonard W. *Constitutional Opinions: Aspects of the Bill of Rights*. New York: Oxford University Press, 1986.

Lewis, Anthony. *Make No Law: The Sullivan Case and the First Amendment*. New York: Random House, 1991.

Lichtenberg, Judith. "Foundations and Limits of Freedom of the Press." In *Democracy and the Mass Media*. Ed. Judith Lichtenberg, 102–35. Cambridge: Cambridge University Press, 1990.

Mason, Alpheus Thomas. *The Supreme Court from Taft to Burger* (originally published as *The Supreme Court from Taft to Warren*). Baton Rouge: Louisiana State University Press, 1979.

Mayer, Robert. *The Court and the American Crises: 1930–1952*. Millwood, N.Y.: Associated Faculty Press, Inc., 1987.

McCloskey, Robert G. *The Modern Supreme Court*. Cambridge: Harvard University Press, 1972.

McIntyre, Jerilyn S. "Repositioning a Landmark: The Hutchins Commission and Freedom of the Press." *Critical Studies in Mass Communication* 4 (1987): 136–60.

————. "The Hutchins Commission's Search for a Moral Framework." *Journalism History* 6 (1979): 54–57, 63.

Merrill, John C. "Three Theories of Press Responsibility and the Advantages of Pluralistic Individualism." In *Responsible Journalism*. Ed. Deni Elliott, 47–59. Beverly Hills: Sage Publications, 1986.

Murphy, Jeffrie G., and Jules L. Coleman. *The Philosophy of Law: An Introduction to Jurisprudence*. Totowa, N.J.: Rowman and Allanheld, 1984.

Murphy, Paul L. *The Shaping of the First Amendment, 1791 to the Present*. New York: Oxford University Press, 1992.

———. "*Near v. Minnesota* in the Context of Historical Developments." *Minnesota Law Review* 66 (1981): 95–160.

———. *The Constitution in Crisis Times, 1918–1969*. New York: Harper and Row, 1972.

Murphy, Walter F., James E. Fleming, and William F. Harris, II. *American Constitutional Interpretation*. Mineola, N.Y.: The Foundation Press, Inc., 1986.

Nagel, Thomas. "The Supreme Court and Political Philosophy." *New York University Law Review* 56 (1987): 519–24.

Nelson, Harold L., ed. *Freedom of the Press from Hamilton to the Warren Court*. New York: Bobbs-Merrill, 1967.

Perry, Robert Christopher. *Patterns on the U.S. Supreme Court: Revised Description and Explanation*. Ph.D. diss. University of Minnesota, 1982. Ann Arbor: UMI, 1982, 8308109.

Peterson, Theodore. "Social Responsibility—Theory and Practice." In *The Responsibility of the Press*. Ed. Gerald Gross, 33–49. New York: Simon and Schuster, 1966.

Powe, Lucas A. *The Fourth Estate and the Constitution: Freedom of the Press in America*. Berkeley: University of California Press, 1991.

Presser, Stephen B., and Jamil S. Zainaldin. *Law and Jurisprudence in American History*, 2nd ed. St. Paul, Minn.: West Publishing, 1989.

Pritchett, C. Herman. *The Roosevelt Court: A Study in Judicial Politics and Values, 1937–1947*. New York: Macmillan, 1948.

Rabban, David M. "The Emergence of Modern First Amendment Doctrine." *University of Chicago Law Review* 50 (1984): 1205–1355.

Rehnquist, William H. "The Notion of a Living Constitution." *Texas Law Review* 54 (1976): 693–706.

———. "The First Amendment: Freedom, Philosophy and the Law." *Gonzaga Law Review* 18 (1976): 1–18.

Richards, David A. J. "Moral Philosophy and the Search for Fundamental Values in Constitutional Law." *Ohio State Law Journal* 42 (1981): 319–33.

———. *The Moral Criticism of Law*. Encino, Calif.: Dickenson Publishing Co., 1977.

———. "Free Speech and Obscenity Law: Toward a Moral Theory of the First Amendment." *University of Pennsylvania Law Review* 123 (1974): 45–91.

Rivers, William L., and Wilbur Schramm. *Responsibility in Mass Communication*, rev. ed. New York: Harper and Row, 1969.

Rohde, David W., and Harold J. Spaeth. "Ideology, Strategy and Supreme Court Decisions: William Rehnquist as Chief Justice." *Judicature* 72 (1989): 247–50.

———. *Supreme Court Decision Making*. San Francisco: W.H. Freeman, 1976.

Rosenberg, Norman L. *Protecting the Best Men: An Interpretive History of the Law of Libel*. Chapel Hill: University of North Carolina Press, 1986.

Rubin, Thea F., and Albert P. Melone. "Justice Antonin Scalia: A First-Year Freshman Effect?" *Judicature* 72.2 (1988): 98–102.

Schmidt, Benno C., Jr. "The Rehnquist Court: A Watershed." *The Los Angeles Daily Journal* 25 June 1986: 4.

———. *Freedom of the Press v. Public Access*. New York: Praeger Publishers, 1976.

Schwartz, Bernard. *The Ascent of Pragmatism: The Burger Court in Action*. Reading, Mass.: Addison-Wesley, 1990.

Siebert, Fred S., Theodore Peterson, and Wilbur Schramm. *Four Theories of the Press*. Urbana: University of Illinois Press, 1956.

Smith, Christopher E., Joyce Ann Baugh, and Thomas R. Hensley. "The First-Term Performance of Justice Stephen Breyer." *Judicature* 79.2 (1995): 74–79.

Smith, Christopher E., Joyce Ann Baugh, Thomas R. Hensley, and Scott Patrick Johnson. "The First-Term Performance of Justice Ruth Bader Ginsburg." *Judicature* 78.2 (1994): 74–80.

Smith, Christopher E., and Scott Patrick Johnson, "The First-Term Performance of Justice Clarence Thomas." *Judicature* 76.4 (1993): 172-78.

Smith, Rogers M. *Liberalism and American Constitutional Law*. Cambridge: Harvard University Press, 1990.

Stewart, Potter. "Or of the Press." *Hastings Law Journal* 26 (1975): 631–37.

Wermeil, Stephen. "Chief Justice Rehnquist Emerges as a Skillful Leader of the Court's New Majority." *Chicago Daily Law Bulletin* (29 June 1989): 1ff.

White, G. Edward. *The American Judicial Tradition: Profiles of Leading American Judges*. Expanded ed. New York: Oxford University Press, 1988.

Woodward, Bob, and Scott Armstrong. *The Brethren: Inside the Supreme Court*. New York: Avon, 1979.

Wuliger, Gregory T. "The Moral Universes of Libertarian Press Theory." *Critical Studies in Mass Communication* 8.2 (1991): 152–67.

Index

About the Author

ELIZABETH BLANKS HINDMAN is Assistant Professor of Communication at North Dakota State University.

ISBN 0-313-29922-6

90000>

9 780313 299223

HARDCOVER BAR CODE

DATE DUE

GAYLORD			PRINTED IN U.S.A.